CASANOVA'S MEMOIRS

CASANOVA'S MEMOIRS

EDITED BY

Joseph Monét

DRAWINGS BY

Vincente Minnelli

Fredonia Books
Amsterdam, The Netherlands

Casanova's Memoirs

Edited by
Joseph Monét

Drawings by
Vicente Minnelli

ISBN 1-58963-157-9

Copyright © 2001 by Fredonia Books

Reprinted from the 1930 edition

Fredonia Books
Amsterdam, The Netherlands
http://www.fredoniabooks.com

All rights reserved, including the right to reproduce this book, or portions thereof, in any form.

In order to make original editions of historical works available to scholars at an economical price, this facsimile of the original edition of 1930 is reproduced from the best available copy and has been digitally enhanced to improve legibility, but the text remains unaltered to retain historical authenticity.

INTRODUCTION

Since the first edition of Casanova's memoirs in the early thirties of the last century, an untold number of other editions have been published and translated into almost every European language.

These memoirs were so entertaining, so utterly frank, and apparently so incredible in the richness and variety of their adventures that for almost two score of years serious and intelligent authorities doubted their authenticity.

Ugo Foscolo the classic Italian poet expressed this doubt in the Westminster Review (1827). It was shared by a Mr. Querard, an expert on anonymous and pseudonymous manuscripts, also by Paul Lacroix, the scientific bibliophile Jacob, who recognized in the memoirs the style of Stendhal. Several French authors suspected that Henri Beyle had played a literary hoax on his contemporaries. Others simply dismissed the memoirs as a collection of silly lies. Another, Frederick Masson, the historian of François de Bernis, later Cardinal de Bernis, would not believe that the ex-protege of Cardinal de Fleury and of Madame de Pompadour would, while acting as Ambassador of France in Venice where Casanova then was, so derogate from his position as to share with the adventurer the experiences described in the memoirs.

Over fifty authors dedicated their time, energy and wits to the study of Casanova. The most prominent of these were Armand Baschet, O. Uzanne Aldo Rave, Charles Henry, Charles Samaran,

Doctor Gnède, Benedetto Croce, Gustave Kahn, Remy de Gourmont, Arthur Symons, Havelock Ellis, Joseph Le Gras.

Books, pamphlets, articles were published, some denying, some affirming the existence of such a versatile, efficient and lucky libertine.

Even the description of Casanova's imprisonment and escape from the prison called Piombi (Leads) in Venice, was viewed as a piece of interesting fiction.

But the indefatigable investigators searched high and low for letters and documents at the chateau Dux, in the Venetian and Parisian archives, in fact all over Europe, and the result was a remarkably complete rehabilitation of the truthfulness of Casanova's account. Strange as it may seem, some enthusiastic Casanovians accused their hero of not having related all of his adventures and love affairs in the twelve volumes of his memoirs out of delicacy and fastidiousness.

Havelock Ellis wrote a keen analysis of Casanova and remarked of his great gift as a raconteur, "He is a consummate master in the dignified narration of undignified experiences."

Thackeray and Oliver Wendell Holmes who was once bold enough to champion Casanova, both found him good enough to steal from.

The romantic George Sand wrote of him: "His amours, like his good fortunes, find me sometimes incredulous. A strange man who made himself valued everywhere and was everywhere worthless. Casanova will remain in history and in literature the most lively expression of the 18th century; which such a man seems to condense in himself; sceptical like Diderot without Diderot's talent and honesty; libertine like Crébillon the younger without his grace and charm; a rascally infidel and an obscene rake, Casanova lived as a philosopher and died as a Christian."

The last were Casanova's own dying words.

INTRODUCTION

Carducci, Italian poet and critic, had him in mind when speaking of: "Those Italian adventurers who paraded through the world the spectacle of Italian shame . . ."

Alfred de Musset penned a review of the memoirs for a Parisian paper in 1831. "Activity, energy, invention and courage were his elements. Not only did he never hesitate but he never imagined that he could hesitate. Unfortunately he was of lowly birth, his struggles with circumstance were of the sordid sort, and he was a man of small parts. A quality which was missing in his moral makeup was perhaps the reason for his failure. He lacked character.

"But in spite of all he was the first among adventurers. To analyze the book would be like trying to analyze his life. It evades the scalpel. There is never a grain of reason, there is little religion and less conscience.

"Cheating fools with delight; deceiving women in good faith; a little too lucky at the gaming table; a divine raconteur, promenading through the world his whims and his folly, but always returning to his dear Venice. There running after masked girls, here gravely walking in the gardens of the pope as a scented abbe, rhyming for a beautiful marquise, fighting for a dancer; a redoubtable brawler, (he was nearly six feet in height) a great generous lord and honest withal."

Those who love Cellini will certainly love this book. There is between them this similarity, that both tell incredible stories, but there is this difference, that Cellini lies three fourths of the time and that Casanova tells the truth even when it is damaging to himself.

All who have read him say the same thing, that he has left an indelible impression on them. Mr. Aubry de Vitry a short time ago gave us a sort of abridgment of the memoirs in which the ending of all the stories was decently cut. Several very technical names had disappeared.

> Le latin dans ses vers brave l'honnêteté;
> Mais le lecteur français veut être respecté.

Why? The wise lawmakers of Parnassus should explain. This great prudery of the eyes and of the ears demanding the hypocritical periphrase which nevertheless brings the naked thought to the mind, will one day be analyzed. This has not yet been done but obviously if the mind guesses the word, then it must be the organ that is afraid.

Volumes of Casanova's letters have been collected, and Arthur Symons on a trip to chateau Dux examined the voluminous portfolios containing letters addressed to the Venetian Don Giovanni from Paris, Rome, Venice, Prague, Bayreuth, The Hague, Genoa, Fiume, Trieste. The investigators tried to guess the real names and characters under the initials and pseudonyms as used in the memoirs. They discovered that C. C. was Caterina Colonda and Mlle. X. C. V. was Justinienne Wynne who married count Philippe Orsini Rosemberg.

In a letter to count d'Argenson Casanova explains the reason for writing his memoirs. "Convinced of the justice of his observation (count Carlo Grimani's objection to his writing a truthful account of his life) I owed that I would never commit such a folly. And yet I have committed it every day—during the past seven years. Nay, more, I have convinced myself that I have contracted a solemn obligation to continue to the end, heedless of whatever qualms of conscience I may suffer. Thus do I continue to write, but always with a secret hope that this narrative of my life may never see the light and that, in a fit of remorse, I shall burn all this scribble. If, however, no such *auto-da-fé* takes place, I implore the reader to forgive me. My hand has been forced by a crowd of profligates

INTRODUCTION

who frequent the chateau of count Waldstein at Dux, where I am now residing. 1797."

Prince de Ligne, who was a great admirer of Casanova, suggested to him the writing of his adventures, as did count Waldstein and the "crowd of profligates" who frequented the chateau Dux and listened among the wine cups to the old Don Juan's adventures. Besides, Prince de Ligne insinuated to Casanova that count Waldstein expected to reap a financial benefit from the sale of the memoirs.* But the book did not see the light until twenty years after the author's death.

SUMMARY OF MY LIFE

My mother brought me into the world in Venice the 2nd of April on Easter day of the year 1725. The night before, she felt a craving for shrimps. I am very fond of them. I was christened Jacques-Jerôme. I was an idiot up to the age of eight and a half. After a hemorrhage lasting three months, I was sent to Padua, where cured of idiocy, I studied diligently and at the age of sixteen I became a doctor and was given the priest's robes to make my fortune in Rome.

In Rome the daughter of my French teacher was the cause of my dismissal by my patron the cardinal Acquaviva.

At the age of eighteen I entered the service of my country and went to Constantinople. Two years later I returned to Venice. I abandoned the profession of honor and, throwing discretion to the winds, embraced the career of fiddler. This horrified my friends but did not last long.

When I was twenty-one, one of the foremost lords of Venice

---

* The first volume of the memoirs was in type a year before Casanova's death.

adopted me as his son, and being somewhat in funds I visited Italy, France, Germany and Vienna, where I met count Roggendorf. I returned to Venice, where two years later the Venetian inquisitors for wise and just reasons had me locked up in the Piombi.

It is a state's prison from which nobody had ever been able to escape, but I, with the help of God, escaped at the end of fifteen months and went to Paris.

In two years I did so well in business that I became a millionaire, but I was soon bankrupt. I went to Holland and made money, then I had some ill luck in Stuttgart, then some good luck in Switzerland, then I visited M. de Voltaire. After that I had some adventures in Genoa, in Marseilles, in Florence and in Rome, where Pope Rezzonico, a Venetian, created me knight of St. John Lateran and *pronotaire apostolique.* That was in 1760. In the same year I had some adventures in Naples, in Florence I eloped with a young girl and the following year I went to the Congress of Augsburg, empowered with a commission by the king of Portugal. That Congress did not meet and after the declaration of peace I went to England. A sad mishap made me run away the following year (1764). I avoided the gallows, which nevertheless would not have dishonored me but only hanged me.

In the same year I vainly sought my fortune in Berlin and Petersburgh, but I found it in Warsaw the following years. Nine months later I lost it for having fought a pistol duel with General Branicki. I wounded him in the belly, but he got well in eight months and I was glad of it.

Being forced to leave Poland I went to Paris in 1767. A *Lettre de Cachet* caused me to flee to Spain, where great ill luck befell me. My crime consisted in having paid nightly visits to the viceroy's mistress, a very infamous woman. On the Spanish border I escaped some paid assassins and went to Aix-en-Provence where I fell ill. I was at the point of death, after spitting blood during eighteen days.

In the year 1769 I published my *Defense of the Government of Venice*, in three thick volumes, against *Amelot de la Houssaye*.

The following year the English minister at the court of Turin sent me to Leghorn well recommended. I desired to go to Constantinople with the Russian fleet, but Admiral Orloff not having agreed to my conditions, I changed my itinerary and went to Rome under the pontificate of Ganganelli.

A happy love made me leave Rome to go to Naples and three months later another unhappy love made me return to Rome. For the third time I fought a sword duel with Count Medini, who died four years ago in London in prison for debt.

Possessing a good deal of money I went to Florence. On Christmas day three days after I arrived, the Archduke Leopold, who died emperor four or five years ago, exiled me from his states. I had a mistress who through my counsel became Marquise XXX in Bologna. Being tired of traipsing all over Europe, I decided to beg indulgence from the state inquisitors in Venice. For this purpose I settled down in Trieste, where after I had waited two years my petition was granted. That was on the 14th of September 1774. My return to Venice after nineteen years of absence was the most beautiful moment of my life.

In the year 1782 I quarrelled with the whole Venetian nobility. I voluntarily left my ungrateful country in the beginning of 1783 and went to Vienna. Six months later I went to Paris to live, but my brother, who had been there twenty-six years, made me forget my interests for his.

I freed him from his wife and took him to Vienna, where prince Kaunitz induced him to settle in the capitol. He is still there, younger than I by two years. I placed myself at the service of M. Foscarini, Venetian ambassador, to write his dispatches. Two years later he died in my arms of gout which had gone to his chest. Then I decided to go to Berlin hoping to get an appointment at the Academy, but when I was half way there, count Waldstein stopped me at Toeplitz and took me to Dux where I am still living and where in all probability I shall die.

This is the only summary of my life which I have written and I permit it to be used in any way desired.

Non erubesco Evangelium. This November the 17th, 1797.

JACQUES CASANOVA.

Why do we find Casanova's memoirs so fascinating? Assuredly not because of the erotica alone, for other amateurs and professionals writing on the subject have gone much more thoroughly into the technique of alcove manners and the purely physical aspect of love-making than our Don Giacomo.

No real working knowledge can be acquired, nor can any worth while proficiency be gained by secretly studying erotic or obscene literature and least of all Casanova. Any tyro of love will tell you that effective experience or training is to be gained solely through living Kama-Sutras.

Besides, this surreptitious admiration for the great Don Juans is but an unexpressed envy, an awe at anybody above the average, a wonder at the rare and precious gift of the genius lover, who is as rare as the genius poet, artist or musician.

Jean Jacques Rousseau, who was a genius in other ways, was negatively gifted in love-making. He tells rather pathetically in his "Confessions" how after an unsuccessful attempt to seduce him, a Venetian girl told him in utter contempt and disgust: "Giacomo, studia le matematiche e lascia l'amore."—Jacques, study mathematics and let love alone.

INTRODUCTION

The other Giacomo was a genius at love. His marvelous power as a raconteur stood him in good stead in that subtle art,—for the ear must be hypnotized as well as the eye. Casanova used this gift of story-telling all his life. Half of his personal fascination consisted in his clever prattle. His specialty was the narration of love adventures and more appropriately his own.

When he discovered that he could no longer be a "satyr in the forest," he whiled away his time, his long and dreary hours in the library at Dux, by reviewing through his imagination his long, voluptuous and hectic life.

The profound and lasting value of his memoirs lies in the vivid description of the customs of the people of his time. As Le Gras says: "Casanova never describes; his impressions come out naturally through his story in revealing lines. He is full of the places he visits, he has so perfectly observed the manners, known the life so intimately, that he almost unconsciously gives us the nuances which make local color real. He has left us the most animated and most illuminative of pictures of the Europe of the 18th century."

Casanova has become a classic and an immortal; a classic in the literature of adventure and an immortal in the annals of erotica.

Casanova's fame was created by a host of discriminating and intelligent readers and is merely increased by all who read him surreptitiously, the hypocrites, the envious impotents, the degenerates, the secret voluptuaries of the reform societies for the suppression of sex complexes.

We cannot vouch for all of the truth of Casanova's adventures, but as the Italians shrewdly remark when anybody tells an incredible story: "Se non è vero e ben trovato." If it isn't true it's based on truth.

CONTENTS

INTRODUCTION 7

I. BETTINE 23

II. POPE BENEDICT XIV..................... 36

III. PROSPER CREBILLON 43

IV. MME. DE POMPADOUR, LOUIS XV AND QUEEN OF FRANCE........................ 49

V. THE BEAUTIFUL O-MORPHI.............. 54

VI. MLLE. C. C. 60

VII. A NOVEL LOVE CURE..................... 89

VIII. FLIGHT FROM THE PIOMBI.............. 99

IX. M. DE CHOISEUL AND M. DE BERNIS...... 144

x. THERESE DE LA MEURE.................. 150

xi. MADEMOISELLE X. C. V. 173

xii. ABBE DE BERNIS AND JEAN JACQUES ROUSSEAU 205

xiii. VOLTAIRE 209

xiv. FREDERICK THE GREAT.................. 231

xv. CATHERINE OF RUSSIA.................... 239

xvi. NINA BERGONZI........................... 249

xvii. LIA OF TURIN............................. 256

xviii. LIA, DAUGHTER OF MORDECAI 268

CASANOVA'S MEMOIRS

Chapter I

BETTINE

FOR three or four months after our return to Padua my good master spoke only of my mother, every day and on all occasions. Bettine found five yards of glossy silk and twelve pairs of gloves in the package my mother had given her. At once she became quite fond of me and took such good care of my hair that within six months I no longer had to wear a wig. She came every morning to comb my hair, often before I was up, saying that she had no time to wait until I was dressed. She washed my face, neck, and breast, and petted me in a way which was innocent enough but which excited and mortified me.

As I was three years younger than she her endearments could not possibly mean anything, and this realization put me in a bad humor. When sitting on my bed she said that I was getting stout and when furthermore she used her hands to verify the statement, she caused me the keenest emotion, but I let her do as she liked for fear that she would notice my sensitiveness. When she remarked on the softness of my skin I had a tickling sensation which made me shrink. I was angry with myself for not daring to do to her what she was doing to me, but delighted that she could not guess how I felt.

When I was dressed she gave me the sweetest kisses, calling me her dear child, but no matter how much I desired to follow her example I did not yet have the hardihood. Later, however, I grew bolder, and as Bettine had ridiculed my shyness I returned her kisses ardently, stopping only when I felt like going too far. At such times I turned my head, making believe I was looking for something, and then she usually left. As soon as she had gone I was desperate at not having followed nature's inclination and astonished that Bettine untroubled could do all that she did to me, while I with the greatest effort could barely control myself. Every day I promised myself a different outcome.

At the beginning of the autumn the doctor received three new pupils. One of them, fifteen years old, appeared to me in less than a month to be on excellent terms with Bettine.

This observation created in me a feeling of which I had hitherto had no idea and which I analyzed only a few years later. It was neither jealousy nor indignation but a worthy disdain and I did not see fit to suppress it. I could not understand why Cordiani, ignorant, coarse, without breeding, son of a simple farmer, should be preferred to me just for being a little older. My budding conceit told me that I was clearly his superior, and I vented my spite on Bettine although, unconsciously, I was in love with her.

She guessed it by the way I received her when she came to comb my hair in bed. I pushed her hands away and did not return her kisses. One day she asked me the reason for my behavior. I answered that there was none. She said pityingly that I was jealous of Cordiani. I protested vehemently, telling her that I thought Cordiani was worthy of her and she of him. She left smiling but with the intention of revenging herself by showing me what jealousy was. First, however, she must make me realize that I was in love with her and she went about it in this manner.

One morning when the doctor had gone to mass she came to my bed bringing me a pair of white stockings which she had been knitting for me. She combed my hair, then said that she must try the stockings on me so if they did not fit she could get them right next time. I attempted to take certain liberties and we quarrelled. Then Bettine left me alone with my thoughts.

They were painful. I imagined that I had dishonored her, that I had abused the confidence of her family, broken the sacred laws of hospitality, that, finally, I had committed a horrible crime which I could expiate only by marrying her, if Bettine could be induced to marry a man so unworthy.

Following these reflections there came a deep gloom which grew darker day by day as Bettine ceased altogether to come to my bed. During the first week I thought she was doing the right thing by staying away, and my sadness would have turned to ideal love if her behavior toward Cordiani had not put the poison of jealousy into my soul—not, however, that I believed her guilty toward him of the crime she had committed on me. Then thinking it over I became convinced that what she had done to me had been intentional and that a sort of repentance prevented her from returning. My conceit was flattered, as I imagined her in love, and I decided to write her a letter to set her mind at ease. I did not say much but I said enough to reassure her in case she felt remorseful or suspected me of feelings contrary to those which her vanity demanded.

I thought my letter a masterpiece. Now she would adore me and wonder how she could have wavered a single instant between myself and Cordiani. Half an hour after she had received my letter she told me that next morning she would return to my room as before our scene.

I waited in vain. I was indignant, but at table she appeased me by asking if I wanted her to help me dress as a girl, for a ball which Dr. Olivo, one of our neighbors, was giving in five or six days. Everybody applauded the decision and I agreed. I saw in this circumstance an opportunity to have an explanation and come to an intimate mutual understanding without any more surprises due to the weakness of the senses.

A real tragi-comedy interfered with this arrangement. Dr. Gozzi's wealthy old godfather who lived in the country had had a long illness, and thinking he was at the point of death he sent his carriage begging the doctor and old man Gozzi to come at once to his bedside and cheer his dying moments. This gave me my chance. I was too impatient to wait till the night of the ball, so I told Bettine that I would leave my hall door open and wait for her after every body had gone to bed. She said that she would not fail me. She slept on the ground floor in an alcove which was separated from old man Gozzi's room by a partition. I slept alone in Dr. Gozzi's room while the doctor was away. The three boys were in another room apart. There was nothing to interfere with my plans, and in delighted expectancy I beheld my hour approaching.

As soon as I was in my room I locked up but left a corridor door unlatched so Bettine had only to push it to enter. Then I blew out the light without taking my clothes off.

Readers think a novelist is exaggerating when he writes of the feelings of a lover in that kind of situation, but I can certainly vouch for the verisimilitude of Ariosto's portrayal of Roger waiting for Alcine.

I waited until midnight without too many misgivings, but when two, three, four o'clock passed and she did not come, my blood began to boil and I became furious. The snow fell in large flakes, but I was dying of rage and did not notice the cold.

An hour before sunrise, unable to control my impatience, I decided to go downstairs without my shoes, so as not to wake the dog, and place myself at the bottom of the stairs a few steps from Bettine's door, which would have to open if she came out. I went up to the door and found it locked. As it could be locked only from the inside I supposed Bettine had gone to sleep. I wanted to knock but the dog would have heard me. Behind that door, a dozen steps away, was Bettine. I wavered, overcome by chagrin, shivering with cold, and fearing at any moment to be discovered by the servant who would think I was crazy. Finally I made up my mind to go back to bed. I turned, but at the same instant I heard a noise in Bettine's room. Certain that she was going to appear I felt my spirits revive. I approached the door, it opened, but instead of Bettine I saw Cordiani, who gave me a powerful kick in the belly that landed me far out in the snow. Without stopping Cordiani locked himself in the large room where he slept with the two Feltrini boys, his comrades.

I got up quickly with the intention of venting my fury on Bettine. I found the door closed and gave it a lusty kick, the dog started to bark, and I fled upstairs to my room, locked myself in and crawled between the covers to rest my body and soul, for I was half dead.

Deceived, humiliated, ill treated, an object of pity to the triumphant Cordiani, I passed three hours meditating the direst of vengeance. In that terrible moment I could have poisoned them both without a qualm. From this project I passed to another, no less extravagant than cowardly, to tell her brother at once. As I was only twelve years old and a novice in such affairs my mind had not acquired the cold faculty of reflecting on schemes of heroic revenge inspired by the so-called sense of honor.

While I was tossing in frenzy I suddenly heard the hoarse voice of Bettine's mother squawking out that her daughter was dying. Angry that Bettine should die before I could get even with her I hastily rose and went downstairs. Bettine was lying in her father's bed in horrible convulsions and the whole family stood around her. She was half dressed, and her body heaved up, turning from right to left as she kicked the air and struck out with her fists and violently wrested herself away from the grasp of those who were endeavoring to hold her down.

With the happenings of the night fresh in my innocent young mind I did not know what to think of this tableau. At the same time I was astonished to find myself an unmoved spectator capable of self control in the presence of two persons, one of whom I wanted to kill and the other to dishonor. At the end of an hour Bettine went to sleep. A midwife and Dr. Olivo entered at the same time. The former said the convulsions were due to hysteria. The doctor contradicted her and ordered rest and cold baths. For my part I laughed at both without saying a word, for I knew, or thought I knew, that the girl's illness was merely the result of her nightly labors or the fright caused by my meeting with Cordiani. Be that as it might, I decided to postpone my vengeance until the arrival of her brother. I had no idea that Bettine could have feigned these convulsions. It seemed impossible that she should have so much strength.

I had to pass Bettine's little alcove to enter my room. Seeing her pocketbook lying on the bed I yielded to the temptation to see what was in it. I found a piece of paper with what I recognized as Cordiani's handwriting on it and took it to my room to read at leisure.

I was astonished at the girl's imprudence, for her mother might have found the note, and not knowing how to read would have shown it to Dr. Gozzi. I thought then that Bettine had lost her mind, but consider what I felt when I read these words:

"While your father is away I suppose I can come in at any time and not have to watch out to see if you have left the door open for me. I'll be hiding in the little room right after dinner."

After a moment of astonishment I was moved to laughter, and finding myself a perfect dupe I thought I was cured of my love. I was ready to forgive Cordiani and despise Bettine. I congratulated myself on having received an excellent lesson that would last the rest of my life. I even went so far as to admit that Bettine had been right in preferring Cordiani, who was fifteen years old, while I was only a child. Then I remembered how Cordiani had kicked me and decided that I wouldn't forgive him after all.

BETTINE

At noon while we were sitting at a table in the kitchen because of the cold, Bettine's attack came on again. Everybody ran over to her, except myself. I quietly finished my dinner and went back to my studies.

At suppertime I noticed that they had moved Bettine's bed into the kitchen so as to have her near her mother who usually slept there. This fact left me indifferent, nor did I pay any attention to the noise which was made during the night and next day when the convulsions started again. That evening Dr. Gozzi returned. Cordiani was afraid of me and asked what I was going to do. I darted at him with my pen knife open and he decamped in haste. I no longer had any idea of relating the scandalous story now that my grand wrath was over.

Next morning mother Gozzi interrupted our lesson to tell Dr. Gozzi, after a long preamble, that she believed she had discovered the character of Bettine's ailment, that it was the result of a spell cast by a witch and that she knew who the witch was.

"That may be, my dear mother, but we must not make a mistake. Who is she?"

"Our old servant. I have proof."

"What kind of proof?"

"I barred the door to my room with two broom handles placed crosswise so that she would have to uncross them to enter, but when she saw them she drew back and went in at the other door. Now wouldn't she have uncrossed them if she weren't a sorceress?"

"Not necessarily. Tell the woman to come here."

As soon as the servant appeared the abbe asked her, "Why did you not enter the room this morning through the usual door?"

"I don't know what you mean."

"Didn't you see the cross of St. Andrew on the door?"

"What kind of a cross is that?"

"Don't try to plead ignorance," said the mother. "Where did you sleep last Thursday night?"

"At my niece's. She was having a baby."

"I know better. You went to the Sabbath, for you are a witch and you have bewitched my daughter."

The maligned woman spat in mother Gozzi's face. Mother Gozzi, infuriated, ran to get a stick. The abbe tried to restrain her, then hurried after the servant who as she ran down the stair was yelling in a way to bring out the neighbors. He caught her and succeeded in calming her by giving her some money.

After this scandalous and ridiculous scene he got his priestly garb to exorcise his sister and to see if she really was in the power of the devil. The novelty of these mysteries made quite an impression on me, though I was vastly amused at the idea of devils in Bettine's body. As we approached the bed her breath seemed to fail nor could I see that her brother's exorcisms served to bring it back. Dr. Olivo arrived in the meantime and asked if he was not wanted. The other inquired if he had the faith. Olivo went away saying that his faith was limited to the miracles of the Testament.

Soon afterward Dr. Gozzi returned to his room. Finding myself alone with Bettine I leaned over and whispered, "Be brave and get well. I'm going to keep my mouth shut tight." She turned her head away without answering, but that night she had no convulsions.

I thought I had cured her, but the next day the fit went to her head and in her delirium she pronounced a haphazard string of senseless Greek and Latin words. Nobody doubted then that she really was possessed. Her mother went out and returned an hour later with the most famous exorcist of Padua, a very ugly monk called Father Prospero da Vovolenta.

As soon as Bettine saw the exorcist she burst out laughing and heaped upon him the vilest insults. The onlookers felt that they were getting their money's worth, as none but the devil would dare treat a monk in such a manner. The monk, hearing himself called a stinking, meddling ignoramus, began to strike Bettine with his great crucifix, saying that he was beating the devil. He stopped only when he saw her ready to throw the chamber pot at his head.

"If the devil has shocked you with words," she said, "fight him with words, you donkey. As there is no devil in me, you ill bred boor, do try and respect me. Go away!"

I saw Gozzi blush. But the monk kept the field, and fully armed he began to read a terrible exorcism, after which he commanded the wicked spirit to give his name.

"My name is Bettine."

"No. That is the name of a baptized girl."

"Then the devil is a girl who hasn't been baptized? Know, ignorant monk, that the devil is an angel and as such has no sex. But as you believe that the devil is speaking through my mouth, promise to answer the truth and I will promise to give in to your exorcism."

"Very well. I promise."

"Tell me, do you believe you are wiser than I am?"

"No, but I believe myself more powerful in the name of the Holy Trinity and by right of my sacred cloth."

"If you are more powerful than I am then prevent me from telling the truth. You are vain of your beard, and you comb it ten times a day, and you wouldn't sacrifice a hair of it to make me come out of this body. Shave, and I swear to you that I will come out."

"Father of lies, I shall double your suffering."

"I defy you."

At these words Bettine burst into a fit of laughter that I could not help joining. Then the monk turned to Dr. Gozzi and told him that as I did not have faith I must leave the room. I did so, telling him that he was right about my lack of faith. I wasn't through the door when to my delight I saw Bettine spit on the monk's hand, which he had offered to her to kiss.

It was wonderful to see this clever girl confound the monk while the devil got the blame. I could not imagine what she was up to.

The monk dined with us and during the repast he talked a lot of foolishness. Afterwards he returned to Bettine's room to give her the blessing. As soon as she saw him she caught up a large glass containing some black mixture from the apothecary's and threw it at his head. Cordiani who was near him received a good share of it, and that caused me intense joy. Bettine did well to grasp the occasion, as everybody made the poor devil responsible. Father Prospero on leaving said to the doctor with some vexation that the girl was without doubt possessed, but that they had better find another exorcist as God evidently did not intend that he should be the one to deliver her.

After his departure Bettine passed six quiet hours and surprised us in the evening by coming to supper. She assured her father and mother that she felt quite well, spoke to her brother, then turned to me and said that she would comb my hair in the morning and dress me as a girl for the dance that was to take place that night. I thanked her, saying that she had been quite ill and must spare herself. She went to bed early and we sat awhile talking of her.

I went up to my room and while preparing for bed I found the following note in my night cap:

"Either you dress as a girl and come to the dance with me or I shall show you a sight that will bring tears to your eyes."

I waited for the doctor to go to sleep then wrote the following reply:

"I am not going to the dance. I don't ever want to be alone with you again. About the sad sight you threaten me with, I suppose you will keep your word, but I beg you to spare my feelings. I love you as if you were my sister. I have forgiven you, dear Bettine, and

I wish to forget everything. I am returning a note which you will be glad to have back again. You see what a chance you were taking by leaving the pocketbook on the bed with this in it. Now haven't I proved that I mean to be your friend?"

The evening of the dance Bettine fell dangerously ill. She had the small pox and high fever. The thirteenth day the crisis was over and she was assailed by an intolerable itching. No medicine could have had such potency to calm her as these words which I repeated over and over, "Bettine, remember that you are going to get well, but if you dare to scratch yourself you will be so ugly that nobody can love you."
She finally opened her beautiful eyes. She was well enough to return to her own room but she had to stay in bed till Easter. Three pimples with which she inoculated me have left their permanent mark on my face, but they honored me with her for they were a proof of my care for her, and she recognized my claim on her affection. As a result we loved each other frankly and tenderly and without the plucking of a flower which, if prejudice be regarded, is sacred to Hymen.

Chapter II

POPE BENEDICT XIV

CASANOVA is under the protection of Cardinal Acquaviva, who permits him to have love affairs on condition that he tell his patron all about them. One of these is a brief amour with Donna Lucrezia, wife of a lawyer. When she leaves Rome Casanova casts his longing eye on the Marchioness G., mistress of Cardinal Acquaviva. A promising affair comes to naught when Casanova, assisting the daughter of his French teacher in a romantic elopement and innocently giving her shelter in his room one night, is requested to leave the cardinal's house.

* * * * *

The next day I went to Monte Cavalli and straight to the room where the Pope was, as soon as I was told that I might enter. He was alone. I knelt and kissed the cross on his very holy slipper. His Holiness asked me who I was. I told him and he answered that he knew me, congratulating me on my connection with such an important cardinal. Then he asked me how I happened to be here. I told him the whole story, beginning with my arrival at Martorano. He laughed heartily at what I had to say about the good bishop and informed me that I might employ the Venetian idiom instead of Tuscan as he himself spoke the dialect of Bologna. Finding myself quite at ease with him I told him so many amusing things that he said he would be pleased if I would visit him often.

I asked his permission to read all the forbidden books. He

granted my request and promised to write me out a formal dispensation—then forgot to do so.

Benedict XIV was a man of culture, wit, and charm. He had a keen sense of humor. I met him another time at the Villa Medici, where, calling to me to come and walk with him, he entertained me with jocose conversation. We were accompanied by Cardinal Albani and the Venetian ambassador. A man of modest mien came up. The pontiff asked him what he wanted. The man replied in a low voice. The Pope, after listening to him politely, said, "You are right. You must look to God," and gave him a blessing.

The poor man went away sadly and the Holy Father continued his walk.

"That man," I said, "most Holy Father, is not satisfied with the answer your Holiness has given him."

"Why not?"

"Evidently he had already looked to God before speaking to you. When your Holiness bade him address his petition higher he found himself, as the proverb says, sent from Herod to Pilate."

The Pope burst out laughing and so did his two followers. I kept a straight face. "I cannot do anything," said the Pope, "without God's help."

"True, Holy Father, but your Holiness is Heaven's prime minister and the man knows it. Imagine, then, his confusion on being remanded to the Master. Now there is none to serve him as intermediary but the beggars of Rome, who if given an alms will all be ready to pray for him, thus preserving their credit. I, however, will be content with no less influential an intercessor than your Holiness. I beg you to deliver me of an inflammation of the eyes by giving me a dispensation permitting me to eat more meat."

"Eat more meat, my son."

"Most Holy Father, may I have your blessing?"

He gave it to me but said this did not exempt me from observing the fast days.

The next day at the appointed time I went to Monte Cavalli, which takes its name from the two marble horses in the square in front of the Holy Father's palace. I did not need to be announced, as any Christian may present himself to the Pope as soon as the doors are opened, moreover I had known his Holiness at Padua when he occupied the episcopal seat in that city, but I was glad to have the honor of being announced by a cardinal.

After I had saluted the Commander of the Faithful and kissed the holy cross embroidered on his holy slipper the Pope placed his hand on my shoulder and told me he remembered that in Padua I always took my departure as soon as he began the rosary.

"Most Holy Father, I now have greater sins to reproach myself with, and that is why I have come to kneel at your sainted feet to receive absolution." He absolved me, which is a matter of routine in Rome, and asked me graciously what favor he could grant me.

"Your holy intercession to return in safety to Venice."

"We must speak to the ambassador before giving you an answer. Do you often go to see Cardinal Passionei?"

"I have been to see him three times. He presented me with his 'Funeral Oration for Prince Eugene' and to show my gratitude I have sent him a volume of my Pandects."

"Has he received it?"

"I believe so, most Holy Father."

"If he has he will send you Winckelmann to repay you."

"That would be treating me as a bookseller. I refuse to be paid back."

"In that case he will return the Pandects. That is his way."

"If his Eminence returns the Pandects I shall send him back his oration."

At this retort the Pope held his sides for laughter.

"It will be agreeable to us to know the sequel of this story, without permitting the world to be a party to our innocent curiosity."

After these words a solemn benediction announced that the audience was at an end.

The following day I went again to see the Pope. As soon as he perceived me he said, "The Venetian ambassador has informed us that if you wish to return to your country you must present yourself to the secretary of the tribunal."

"Most Holy Father, I am quite ready to take this step if your Holiness will give me a letter in your own writing. Without this protection I will not expose myself to the danger of being locked up in a place from which the visible hand of God extricated me by a miracle."

"You are in gallant attire, which you certainly did not put on to do penance."

"No, most Holy Father, nor to wear to any ball."

"We know the whole story of the return of the presents. Admit that you were merely indulging your egotism."

"Yes, at the expense of a greater."

Seeing that the Pope was amused at my answer I knelt and begged permission to present my Pandects to the library of the Vatican. For answer I received a blessing which in papal language signifies, "Get up, the favor is granted."

"You will receive," he said, "a mark of our particular esteem, without having to pay the cost of registration at the Chamber."

A second benediction was the signal for me to withdraw. I have often wished that his language could be used by everybody to send away the bores one is obsessed with and to whom one dare not say, "Get out!"

I was curious to know the nature of the mark of particular esteem the Pope had spoken of. I was afraid it would be a consecrated rosary bead, for which I had no use.

I was sitting at dinner in the home of M. Mengs when a cameriere of our lord the most Holy Father was announced. On entering he asked M. Mengs if I lived there and when I was pointed out to him he gave me from his most holy master the cross of the Order of the Holy Spur with a diploma and patent bearing the great pontifical seal and declaring me in my quality of doctor of laws, *pronotarius apostolicus extra urbem.*

When I presented myself to the Pope to thank him I placed the cross modestly in my button hole. Five years later in Warsaw, Czartoryski, the Russian Prince Palatinate, made me take it off, saying, "What do you wear that bauble for? It makes you look like a charlatan."

In the evening after a drive in my landau I went to the Theater Aliberti, where the *castrato* who had the rôle of the prima donna was the talk of the town.

He was the favorite and minion of Cardinal Borghese and supped every evening tête-à-tête with his Eminence. The eunuch had a marvelous voice, but his chief merit was his beauty. I had seen him in masculine garb on the promenade and his countenance had made no impression on me, as one could at once observe that he was a mutilated man, but on the stage the illusion was perfect: he excited passion.

Laced in a skillfully made corset he had the figure of a nymph, and incredible as it may seem his bust was not inferior in beauty nor dissimilar in shape to that of a well proportioned woman. It was on that particular point that this monster created mischief. Although you were aware of his ambiguous nature, if curiosity made you glance at his breast an inexpressible charm acted on you and made you fall madly in love against your will. To resist the attraction or to remain insensible to it one would have had to be as phlegmatic as a German.

As he crossed the stage awaiting his turn to sing, his walk was at once majestic and voluptuous and when he favored the boxes with a glance the tender and demure expression in his black eyes brought delight to the heart. It was obvious that he desired to foster the passion of those who loved him as a woman and who very likely would have paid no attention to him had he been a woman in fact.

Saintly Rome does everything in her power to force all men to become pederasts but does not like to admit what are the effects of an illusion which she has done her best to create.

As I was reflecting aloud on this subject a gentleman with wristbands who was sitting near me clinched my point by saying, "You are right. Why allow a *castrato* to expose a breast which would be the pride of the most beautiful of Roman girls and then insist on having everybody know that he is a man and not a woman? If the stage is closed to the fair sex for fear that their beauty may excite illicit desires, why open it to a class of monsters who excite desires which are much more criminal? Don't people know how common pederasty is? Do they really believe what they try to tell you, that the few who are attracted are disappointed when they have experimented? Many intelligent men practise this indulgence and end by finding it so sweet that far from renouncing it they prefer these creatures to the most beautiful women."

"The Pope would deserve a heavenly reward if he put an end to this abuse."

"Oh, I don't know. One cannot without scandal invite a beautiful cantatrice to supper tête-à-tête, but it's perfectly proper to sup with a eunuch. It is well known that the same pillow receives their heads afterward, but what everybody knows everybody ignores. One may sleep with a man, one may not with a woman."

"It's true, signor, appearances are saved, and 'hidden sin is half forgiven' as they say in Paris."

"In Rome we say that it is quite forgiven, 'Peccato nascosto non offende.'"

This Jesuitical conversation had interested me, as the speaker was well known for his avowed partiality to the forbidden fruit.

Chapter III

PROSPER CREBILLON

WHILE we were talking, M. Patu, my new acquaintance, had brought me to Silvia's door. He congratulated me on knowing her and we separated. This charming actress was entertaining distinguished guests. She introduced me to each in turn. The name of Crebillon arrested me.

"An unexpected pleasure, monsieur!" I said. "Your works have delighted me for the last eight years and I had hardly anticipated meeting you in the flesh. May I have your attention a moment?"

I then recited my translation into Italian blank verse of the best passage of his *Zenobie et Rhadamiste*. Silvia enjoyed seeing how gratifying it was to Crebillon at the age of eighty to hear his work recited in a language which he knew and loved almost as he did his own. He recited the same scene in French and pointed out passages which he politely said I had embellished. I thanked him without being deceived by the compliment. We sat down to dinner and as I was asked what I had seen to admire in Paris I related all the experiences of the day except my conversation with Patu.

After I had been talking a long time, Crebillon, who better than anyone else could appreciate at what pains I had been to register my good and bad impressions of his nation, said to me, "For a newcomer, monsieur—I think you said this was your first day in Paris—I find you very promising and I have no doubt you will progress rapidly. You have the gift of narrative and your speech is perfectly comprehensible though after all it is only Italian masquerading in a French garb. It has the double advantage of being novel and foreign, and since my countrymen make a cult of these two qualities you can readily command an audience. Nevertheless you must at once make an effort to learn how to speak our language correctly, or within two or three months the same persons who praise you now will have begun to mock you."

"So I fear, monsieur. My first thought on arriving was, how shall I set about polishing my French? My difficulty is in obtaining a teacher. I am a vexatious pupil, insatiable and always asking questions; and supposing I could find a master patient enough to put up with me, I am not in a position to pay him."

"For fifty years, monsieur, I have been looking for the kind of pupil you say you are. If you will come to my home, The Marais in the street of the Douze Portes, I will give you lessons and pay you besides. I have the best Italian poets and I want them translated into French—perhaps you will not prove so insatiable as you think."

I was at a loss for words to express my gratitude, but the frank eagerness with which I accepted the offer he may have counted no ill repayment to his bluff generosity.

Six feet in height, three inches taller than myself, Crebillon was a colossus of a man. He was a hearty eater, a pleasant speaker though not given to merriment, an excellent table companion, famous for his wit. However he went out rarely, preferring to remain at home, always with a pipe in his mouth, seeing almost nobody, forever surrounded by a score of cats and playing with them the greater part of the day. He had an old housekeeper, a cook, and a valet. His housekeeper looked after everything, supplied all his needs, kept his money for him, and never rendered him an account as he never asked for one.

Crebillon's physiognomy was much like that of a cat—or of the lion; it is the same thing.

PROSPER CREBILLON

He was royal censor and he told me he had a good deal of fun performing his duties. His housekeeper read him the works which were submitted for approval and when she thought a passage required censoring she paused and looked over at him expectantly. Sometimes their opinions differed and then their disputes were highly entertaining. I heard this housekeeper one day dismiss a hopeful genius with the words, "Come back next week. We haven't had time yet to examine your manuscript."

For a whole year I went to M. Crebillon's three times a week. From him I learned all the French I know, but it was impossible for me to get rid of a certain Italianate turn of phrasing. I notice this defect in the speech of another but when it occurs in my own writing I am not conscious of it, just as I never have been able to feel the vice of Latinity which is imputed to Livy.

I once composed a stanza of eight lines, on I don't know what subject, and submitted it to Crebillon for correction. After reading it attentively he said, "These eight verses are quite correct, the thought is poetical, the language perfect, and in spite of all this the poem is bad."

"How is that?"

"I don't know. There is something missing which I cannot explain. Imagine a man whom you consider handsome, virile, intellectual, amiable, and, in fine, perfect according to your severest judgment. A woman comes along, looks him over, and goes away saying she does not like the man. 'But what fault do you find in him, madame?' 'None. I just don't like him.' You go back to the man, you examine him again, and you discover that an angelic voice has taken away your favorable impression and you are forced to agree with the woman's spontaneous disapproval."

It was by such a comparison that Crebillon explained to me something almost inexpressible, the something which is beyond all rules and must be left to taste and feeling.

At this first dinner party Crebillon spoke a good deal about Louis XIV whom he had attended for fifteen consecutive years, and about whom he could recount some very curious anecdotes which had not been circulated. He assured us that the ambassadors from Spain were rogues in the pay of Mme. de Maintenon. He likewise informed us that he had left his tragedy of Cromwell incomplete because the king had once told him never to waste his pen on a knave. Crebillon spoke also of his *Catiline,* asserting that it was one of the weakest of his plays and that he had not been able to interest himself in the subject. To make Cæsar appear on the stage as a young man, he said, was as ridiculous as portraying Medea prior to the arrival of Jason. He frequently praised the talent of Voltaire but accused him of plagiarizing the senate scene. He added, in justice, that Voltaire was a born historian whose histories read like tragedies but were probably falsified, and certainly overloaded with the countless tales and anecdotes thrown in to retain the interest. According to Crebillon the Man in the Iron Mask was a fairy tale, Louis XIV had told him so.

That day the Italian theater was presenting *Cenia,* a play by Mme. de Graffigny. I went early to get a good seat in the orchestra. The bediamonded ladies entering the boxes interested me and I observed them minutely. I had on a beautiful coat but my ruffles were open and the buttons placed all the way down made me conspicuous as a foreigner, because this fashion did not then prevail in Paris. While I was looking about and seeing what was to be seen, a man richly dressed and three times as big as myself came up to me and asked if I was a stranger. When I answered in the affirmative he asked me how I liked Paris. I said I liked it very well. At the same moment an enormous lady covered with jewelry entered a box nearby. Her tremendous bulk impressed me, and like a fool I asked the gentleman, "Who is that fat sow?"

"She, monsieur, is the wife of this fat pig."

"O—a thousand pardons!"

But my fat man required no placation, for instead of being angry he was bursting with laughter. Only French good sense, which, keenly appreciative of the ludicrous wherever found, is often mistaken for levity, could thus have condoned so frightful an insult. I was frantic with confusion and this fat lord was fairly holding his sides. Finally he got up, left the orchestra, and a moment later I saw him enter the box and speak to his wife. Without openly staring I was looking at them from the corner of my eye. The lady partook of her husband's mirth and laughed with all her might. Their merriment increased my embarrassment and I decided to go out, when I heard him call me, "Monsieur! Monsieur!"

I could not leave without being rude so I went up to the loge. Changing his tone and becoming serious he nobly begged my pardon for having laughed so much, and cordially begged me to do him the honor of supping at his house the same night. I thanked him politely and excused myself, saying I was engaged. He urged me and his wife insisted most winningly. To convince them that I was not trying to evade the invitation I told them that I was expected at Silvia's.

"I am sure I can disengage you. If you do not find it inconvenient I will see about it at once."

There was no refusing. He got up, went out, and returned a moment later followed by my friend Balletti, who said his mother was delighted that I should know such fine people and that she expected me to dinner next day. My friend told me aside that this gentleman was M. de Beauchamp, comptroller general.

As soon as the curtain was lowered I offered madame my arm and all three climbing into a magnificent carriage we went to their hotel. I found there profuse abundance of all that is to be expected in Parisian houses of that class, brilliance, gayety, good cheer. The supper did not end till after one o'clock. This house was open to me all during my stay and I must not forget to add that I met there certain personages whose acquaintance proved decidedly advantageous.

They are right who say that strangers have a dull time the first fortnight they are in Paris. It usually takes at least that long to get any introductions, but as for myself I was fortunate enough to be made quite at home within the first twenty-four hours.

Chapter IV

MME. DE POMPADOUR, LOUIS XV AND QUEEN OF FRANCE

IN the month of August there was held at the Louvre a public exhibition of paintings by the artists of the royal Academy. Seeing no battle pictures I immediately thought of my brother Francesco in Venice who excelled in handling that type of subject. I wrote to my brother and to Signor Grimani, his patron, and succeeded in convincing them that as Paroselli, the only French historical painter, had died, a profitable field was open in Paris, but it was not until the beginning of the following year that Francesco was able to come.

Louis XV, who was passionately fond of hunting, passed six weeks of every year at Fontainebleau, returning to Versailles toward the middle of November. This trip cost him, or rather cost France, five millions. He took along everything which could contribute to the pleasure of the foreign ministers and of his own vast retinue. Specially selected troupes from the Comédie Française, the Comédie Italienne, and the Opera were transported to Fontainebleau which during these six weeks was more brilliant than Versailles at any time. Paris, meanwhile, was not without dramatic and operatic entertainment, as the personnel of the great companies was numerous enough to admit of this division. Balletti's father, who had quite recovered his health, was ordered to Fontainebleau as were Silvia and the rest of the family. They invited me to accompany them and to accept lodgings in a house they had taken. In addition to retaining the proximity of my friends I should have an opportunity, not to be lightly cast away, of observing at close range the manners of the court of Louis XV and of the foreign embassies.

I presented myself to M. de Morosini, today procurator of Saint Mark and at that time the republic's representative in Paris. He permitted me to escort him to the opening performance of the opera. One of Lulli's arrangements was being rendered. I sat in the orchestra directly under the loge of La Pompadour, whom I did not know. In the first act the famous Le Maur came on the stage emitting such a loud and unexpected cry that I thought her mad. I burst out laughing, in all innocence, not thinking that anybody would object. A knight of the Holy Ghost who was sitting near La Pompadour asked me dryly where I came from.

In the same tone I answered, "From Venice."

"I have been there and had many a laugh at Italian recitative."

"I do not doubt it, monsieur, and I am positive nobody thought of interfering with you."

My rather tart reply made Mme. Pompadour laugh. She asked me if I really came from down there.

"I beg your pardon, where?—'down there'—"

"Venice, monsieur."

"Venice, madame, is not 'down there,' it's 'up there'."

This reply they found stranger than the first and the whole loge was in conference to determine whether Venice was down there or up there. Evidently they decided that I was right, for they let me alone. ·

I refrained from laughing during the rest of the performance, but being afflicted with a cold I frequently had to blow my nose. The same knight, whom I did not know, and who was Marshal de Richelieu, addressed me again, inquiring if I lived in draughty quarters. I answered that he was mistaken, that all my windows were *calfoutrées,* then everybody burst out laughing and I was greatly embarrassed by the realization of having made a bad break.

I meant *calfeutrées,* but the distinction between *eu* and *ou* is the torture of most foreigners.

Half an hour later M. de Richelieu asked me which one of the actresses I preferred in point of beauty.

"That one, monsieur."

"I don't like her legs."

"Well, monsieur, legs apart, isn't she rather attractive?"

This unintentional witticism focused all eyes upon me and everybody in the box was eager to make my acquaintance. The Marshal asked M. de Morosini who I was and intimated that a visit from me would be most welcome. When I went to see him he accorded me a kind reception and my chance repartee became famous.

The day after my arrival at Fontainebleau I went alone to the court and saw the handsome King Louis XV and the entire royal family going to mass. The court ladies were as remarkable for lack of good looks as the court ladies of Turin for wealth of them. Among all these homely creatures I was astonished to see one real beauty. From a gentleman standing nearby I ascertained her name.

"She is Mme. de Brionne, as good as she is beautiful. There is not so much as a rumor about her. She has never even furnished the gossips an opporunity for inventing a slander."

"Perhaps she simply hasn't been found out."

"Ah, monsieur, at court everything is known."

Continuing my tour of the inner chambers I suddenly saw a dozen ugly women who seemed to be running instead of walking, and who were so poorly balanced that they appeared constantly in danger of falling forward. I asked someone where they came from and why they walked that way.

"They have just come from the presence of the queen who is now about to dine. They walk as they do because the heels of their slippers are six inches high and the effort to keep from falling on their noses makes them sway-backed."

"Why don't they wear lower heels?"
"High heels are the fashion."
What an absurd fashion!
Entering a gallery at random I saw the king pass by, leaning heavily on the shoulders of M. d'Argenson.

"How," I thought to myself, "can one man be so servile and another, in the pride of power, permit him?"

Louis XV had the most beautiful head imaginable and he carried it with as much grace as nobility. The expression on this superb countenance as the monarch turned around to favor someone with a glance was such as no artist has ever been able to reproduce. It was a countenance to compel instant admiration. Here, I thought, I had met ideal majesty, which I had found so shockingly wanting in the king of Sardinia. I did not doubt the story of Mme. de Pompadour falling in love with the king at first sight and demanding to be presented to him. It may not have been true, but to look at Louis XV was to give credence to the tale.

I entered a magnificent hall where I saw a dozen courtiers walking about and a table with service as if for many diners but prepared in fact for one alone.

"For whom is the table set?"
"For the queen. Here she comes."

The queen of France entered. She was simply dressed, and with her head covered by a large cap and with no rouge on her cheeks she looked like an elderly pietist. Two nuns placed a dish of fresh butter on the table and she thanked them graciously. She sat down and at once the dozen courtiers ranged themselves in a semi-circle ten paces from the table. I stood near them, maintaining, like them, respectful silence. Without looking up from the plate her majesty began to eat. Liking a dish which had been served to her, she asked for it again. Then she glanced at the circle in front of her, doubtless seeking one among the observers to whom she could communicate her appreciation of the tidbit.

She found him and said, "M. de Lowendal."

A fine looking man came forward and bowed his acknowledgment, "Madame."

"A most delicious chicken fricassee."

"Madame, I am of the same opinion."

After delivering this reply with sepulchral seriousness the Marshal retired, proceeding backward, to his place. The queen continued her repast without a word, and having finished, returned to her apartment.

I thought if the queen of France ate all her meals in that way I did not covet the honor of being her table companion. I was delighted to have seen the conqueror of Berg-op-Zoom, but I thought it a shame that a famous warrior should be reduced to passing judgment on a chicken fricassee in the tone of a judge pronouncing the sentence of death.

Chapter V

THE BEAUTIFUL O-MORPHI

I WAS at the fair of St. Laurent with my friend Patu, when he took the fancy to sup with a Flemish actress named Morphi and invited me to share his caprice. This girl did not tempt me, but what can we refuse to a friend? I went along. After having supped with the belle, Patu was ready to pass the night in a sweeter occupation. Not desiring to leave him, I asked if there was a couch where I could quietly sleep.

The Morphi woman had a sister, a little slattern thirteen years old, who told me that if I would give her a half ecu, she would let me share her bed. I agreed, and was led to a small room where I found a mattress on four planks.

"And you call this a bed, my child?"

"I have no other, monsieur."

"I don't want it, you shall not have your half ecu."

"Oh, were you going to undress?"

"Certainly."

"What an idea! We have no bed sheets."

"Then you sleep with your clothes on?"

"Of course not."

"Very well, lie down the way you always do, and I shall give you the half ecu."

"What for?"

"I want to see what you look like."

"Will you not do anything to me?"

"Not the slightest thing."

She lay on the poor mattress, covering herself with an old curtain. In that condition her rags were forgotten; I saw naught else but a perfect beauty. But I desired to see her in a state of nature. I attempted to satisfy my whims. She resisted; but an ecu of six francs rendered her complaisant. Finding nothing wrong in her but an absolute want of cleanliness, I washed her with my own hands.

You will permit me, my dear readers, to suppose in you a knowledge as simple as natural, to the effect that admiration of a character like the one under discussion is inseparable from another kind of approbation. Happily and quite naturally I found the little Morphi disposed to let me do everything, except one thing I did not care to do. She warned me that that would not be permitted, for in the opinion of her sister, that was worth twenty-five louis. I informed her that we would bargain another time on the main point, and for the moment we would leave it alone. This reservation being respected, everything else was at my disposal, and I discovered in her quite a well-perfected talent, although so precocious.

Little Helene faithfully handed over to her sister the six francs I had given her, and told her how she had earned them. Before we left Morphi came to tell me that she was in need of money, and if I desired it, she would lower the price somewhat. I answered laughingly that I would see her the next day.

I told Patu about it, and he taxed me with exaggeration. Desiring to uphold my reputation as a connoisseur in beauty, I demanded that he see Helene as I had seen her. He agreed that the chisel of Praxiteles never could have produced anything so perfect. White as a lily, Helene had every beauty that nature or the art of the painter can fashion. The perfection of her face had something so bland that it carried to the soul an ineffable sense of happiness, a delicious calm. She was fair; nevertheless, her beautiful blue eyes had all the sparkle of the deepest black ones.

I went to see her the next day. We could not agree upon the price, six hundred francs, so I stipulated with the sister that I would give her twelve francs every time I wished to pay Helene a friendly visit in the sister's room, until such time as I should make up my mind that complete possession was worth six hundred francs. This was stiff usury, but the Morphi belonged to a race of sharps which are above vain scruples. I had no intention of giving the sum, because I did not feel the desire to obtain all she had for sale. I got enough from her as it was.

The elder sister believed me a gull. In two months I spent three hundred francs without doing anything, and they attributed my self-control to avarice. Expensive avarice! I wanted a picture of the magnificent body and a German artist painted her most divinely for six louis. The pose was ravishing. She was lying on her stomach leaning her arms and breasts on a pillow, with her head turned three-quarters of the way. The artist, a man of skill and taste, had drawn the inferior part with such rare art and truth that nothing more beautiful could be desired. I was enchanted with the portrait; it was a speaking likeness, and I wrote underneath, "O-Morphi," a word which is not Homeric, but which nevertheless is Greek, and means beautiful.

But who can foretell the secret ways of destiny?

My friend Patu desired a copy of this portrait. One does not refuse a friend such a slight favor, so the same painter was asked to make a duplicate.

But this painter, having been called to Versailles, exhibited this charming picture among other portraits, and M. de Saint-Quentin found it so beautiful that he at once showed it to others. His very Christian Majesty, great connoisseur on the subject, wanted to assure himself with his own eyes if the painter had copied faithfully, and if the original was as beautiful as the copy. The descendant of St. Louis knew well to what uses it could be put.

M. de Saint-Quentin, this complaisant friend of the prince, was charged with the mission. He asked the painter if the original could be brought to Versailles; and the artist, believing the matter possible, promised to find out.

He came, in consequence, to communicate to me the proposition. It was agreeable to me. Without much ado I informed the sister, who trembled with pleasure. She put herself to the trouble of washing her young sister, and two or three days later, Helene being properly dressed, they departed with the painter to try the adventure.

The valet de chambre of the minister to the King's pleasure having received the word of order from his master, came to receive the two females, whom he locked up in a pavillion in the park, and the painter awaited at the hostelry the result of his negotiations. The king, half an hour later, entered the pavillion alone. He asked the young Morphi if she was a Greek, took the portrait out of his pocket, looked the little one over, from head to foot, and exclaimed, "I have never seen a better likeness!" Soon afterwards he sat down, took the little girl on his knees, caressed her, and gave her a kiss.

O-Morphi looked attentively at her master and smiled.

"What are you laughing about?"

"I am laughing because you look just like a six-franc ecu."

This naïveté provoked the king into a fit of laughter, and he asked her if she wished to stay at Versailles.

"It depends on my sister," said the little one. And the sister hastened to say to the king that nothing could make her happier.

The king locked them up again, and went away; but a quarter of an hour later, Saint-Quentin came to get them, placed the little one in an apartment, in the care of a duenna, and with the elder sister rejoined the German painter, to whom he gave fifty louis for the portrait, though he gave nothing to Morphi. He merely took her address, promising her that she should hear from him.

She received a thousand louis the next day.

The good German gave me twenty-five louis for my portrait, promising to copy with the greatest care the one in Patu's possession. Moreover, he offered to do gratis as many portraits of girls as I desired.

I had real pleasure in seeing the joy of the good Flemish woman while contemplating the five hundred double louis given her. Seeing herself rich, and considering me the author of her fortune, she was at a loss to express her gratitude.

The young and beautiful O-Morphi,—for the king always called her that,—pleased the monarch even more by her naïveté and her pretty ways than by her rare beauty, the most perfect I had ever seen.

He placed her in an apartment of his Deer Park, the harem of this voluptuous monarch, where nobody could go, except the ladies who had been presented at court. At the end of a year the little one gave birth to a son, who went the way of so many others—whither nobody knows; for as long as Queen Mary lived, the destinies of the natural sons of Louis XV were a dark mystery.

O-Morphi fell in disgrace after three years, but the king in sending her away ordered four hundred and fifty thousand francs to be given to her. This she brought as a dowry to a Breton officer.

In 1783, finding myself at Fontainebleau, I made the acquaintance of a charming young man, twenty years old, the fruit of that marriage, and a perfect likeness of his mother, of whose history he was completely ignorant. I did not see fit to enlighten him. I inscribed my name in his memorandum book, asking him to convey my compliments to his mother.

A piece of spite on the part of Madame de Valentinois, sister-in-law of the Prince of Monaco, was the cause of the disgrace of the beautiful O-Morphi. This lady, well-known in Paris, said one day to O-Morphi that to make the King laugh, she had only to ask him how he treated his old woman. Too simple to suspect the trap, the young girl asked the King that insolent question. Louis XV, indignant, looked at her furiously and said:

"Wretched girl! who taught you to ask me that?"

The poor O-Morphi, more dead than alive, threw herself at his knees and told him the truth.

The King left her, and never saw her again. The Countess of Valentinois reappeared at Court only two years later.

This prince, who was well aware of his laxity as a husband, was jealously observant of all that affected him as a King, and woe to anyone who showed disrespect towards the Queen!

Chapter VI

MLLE. C. C.

AT ORIAGO, a little distance out of Padua, I encountered a cabriolet drawn by two post horses, which came on a dead run. Inside were a pretty woman and a man in German uniform. A few paces from me the cabriolet overturned on the side, and the woman, falling over her escort, ran the greatest danger of rolling into the Brenta. I jumped out without stopping, and flew to the assistance of the lady, restoring with a chaste hand the disorder which the fall had occasioned to her attire.

Her companion picked himself up unhurt and ran over to us. The lady sat there dazed, and less confused by her fall than by the indiscretion of her skirts which had disclosed all that an honest woman never shows to a stranger. All the time her postillion and mine were righting the cabriolet, she was thanking me, calling me her savior, her guardian angel.

The damage was repaired: the lady continued her way towards Padua, I towards Venice, where I arrived in time to mask and go to the opera.

The next day I masked myself early to join the procession following the Bucentaure, which, the weather favoring, was to be brought over to the Lido for the great and ridiculous ceremony of marriage to the Adriatic. This function, not only rare but unique, depends upon the courage of the admiral of the Arsenal, who has to stake his head upon the constancy of the weather for the slightest wind could overturn the vessel and drown the Doge with all the highborn lords, the ambassadors, and the papal nuncio sponsoring this burlesque marriage which the Venetians revere to the point of superstition. A tragic accident, if ill luck should ordain it, could not fail to make all Europe laugh, and say that the Doge of Venice had finally gone to consummate his marriage.

I had my mask off and was taking coffee under the arcades of the square of St. Mark, when a masked beauty gave me a dexterous whack on the shoulder. Not knowing who she was, I did not pay much attention to the teasing, and after finishing my coffee, I put my mask on, and wandered towards the quay of the sepulchre, where one of M. de Bragadin's gondolas awaited me. Towards the bridge of La Paille I saw the same woman attentively looking at a freak which was exhibited for ten sous. I approached her, and asked her by what right she had struck me.

"I wanted to punish you for not knowing me, after having saved my life."

I guessed that she was the lady I had helped the day before on the shores of the Brenta; and after having complimented her, I asked her if she expected to follow the Bucentaure.

"I would willingly go, if I had a safe gondola."

I offered her mine, which was of the largest; and having consulted the man at her side, she accepted. As they were preparing to step in, I begged them to take their masks off, but they told me they had reasons for remaining unknown. Then I asked them to inform me if they belonged to some embassy, for in that case I should find myself forced to beg them to withdraw; but they assured me they were Venetians. The gondola being in the livery of a patrician, I might have been compromised with the State Inquisitors, and that I wished to avoid.

We followed the Bucentaure, and, sitting near the lady, I permitted myself some liberties, but she disconcerted me by moving away.

After the function we returned towards Venice, and the officer told me that if I would do them the honor of dining with them at the Sauvage, I should oblige them. I accepted, for I was curious to know that woman; what I had seen of her at the time of the fall rendered my curiosity quite natural. The officer left me alone with her and went ahead to order the dinner.

As soon as I was alone with the belle, and the more audacious as we were masked, I told her that I was in love with her, that I had a box at the opera which I offered her, and that if she gave me the hope of not losing my time I would serve her during the whole carnival.

"If your intention is to be cruel with me, I beg you to tell me frankly."

"I beg you likewise to tell me whom you think you are talking to."

"To a very amiable woman, whether you be a princess or of low estate. Thus I hope that, from today on, you will give me proofs of your kindness, or after dinner I shall have the honor to salute you farewell with reverence."

"You shall do what you please; but I hope that after dinner you will change your language, for the tone you take is not attractive. It seems to me that before coming to such an understanding, we ought to have become acquainted. Do you understand?"

"Yes, I understand; but I am afraid of being cheated."

"How singular! And it is this fear which makes you begin where one would naturally end?"

"Today, I ask only a word of encouragement. Offer it to me, and you shall see me modest, submissive, and discreet."

"Control yourself."

We found the officer at the door of the Sauvage, and we went upstairs. As soon as we were in the room, she unmasked, and I found her better than the day before. It remained for me to discover, for the sake of form and ceremony, if the officer was her husband, her lover, her kinsman, or simply her escort; for being experienced in adventures, I desired to know the nature of the one I had now begun.

We sat down to table, and the deportment of the gentleman and lady was such that I felt obliged to be cautious. I offered him the opera box, and he accepted; but as I did not have the tickets, after dinner I went to get them, under the pretext of business. I bought them at the opera Buffa, where Pertici and Lasqui were showing.

After the opera I treated to supper in a hostelry; then I took the pair home in a gondola, where, favored by the darkness, I obtained of the belle such favors as can be granted before a third party who must be managed discreetly. On our separation, the officer said to me:

"You will hear from me tomorrow."

"How and when?"

"Wait and see."

The next morning an officer was announced. It was the same person. After the usual compliments I thanked him for the honor he had done me the evening before and begged him to tell me with whom I had the pleasure of speaking. This is what he answered, speaking very easily and well, but without looking at me:

"My name is P. C. My father is rich and well considered at the Bourse; but we have quarreled. I live at the quay of St. Mark. The lady you have seen is a born O——. She is the wife of agent C——, and her sister is the wife of the patrician P. M.——. Madame C—— has quarreled with her husband, and I am the cause of it, as I have quarreled with my father for her sake. I wear this uniform by right of a brevet as captain in the Austrian army, but I have never served. I am charged with supplying cattle to the Venetian State, and I get the supply from Styria and Hungary. The profits of this enterprise net me ten thousand florins per annum; but an unexpected difficulty, which I must remedy,—a fraudulent bankruptcy and extraordinary expenses,—places me at this moment in great straits. Four years ago I heard of you, I conceived the desire of making your acquaintance, and I believe heaven brought this about the day before yesterday. I do not hesitate to ask you an essential favor, which will unite us in the closest friendship. Help me. You will run no risk. Accept these three letters of exchange, and do not fear having to pay them on maturity, for I turn over to you three others, the payment of which will be due before yours. And what is more, I give you the cattle deal for the whole year, so that if I should fail you, you could sequestrate all the cattle in Trieste, the only point of delivery."

Amazed that he should think I could be taken in by a proposition so preposterous on the face of it, which, furthermore, promised me nothing but tedious manipulation of a kind particularly irksome to me, I did not hesitate to tell him that I could never accept his offer.

His eloquence redoubled, but I embarrassed him by saying I felt surprised that he should have preferred me to all his acquaintances, when he had met me only two days before.

"Sir," he said, unperturbed, "having known you as a man of great intelligence, I persuaded myself that you would see at once the advantage of my offer, and that in consequence, you would make no bones about accepting."

"You must be undeceived by this time. You know you would think I was a fool if I did accept."

He left, begging my pardon, hoping that he would see me that evening in St. Mark's square, where he would be with Mme. C. He also left me his address, saying that he occupied the apartment unknown to his father. It was an indirect way of saying that he expected a return of his call, but if I had been wise I would not have gone.

Disgusted by the pretenses of this man, I lost all interest in my

adventure with his belle, as it seemed to me that that couple had resolved to make a dupe of me, and as I had no desire of becoming one, I avoided meeting them in the evening at St. Mark's. I should have let the matter rest there. But the next day, impelled by my evil genius and judging that a visit of politeness would have no consequences, I went to see them.

A servant having led me to his room, the officer received me with many kind attentions, and gently reproached me for not having made my appearance the evening before. Then he spoke again of his business, and showed me a bundle of papers, which annoyed me considerably.

"If you are willing to accept my three notes," he said, "I will associate you in my enterprise."

By the token of extraordinary friendship he would make me, according to him, richer by five thousand florins a year. But in reply I begged him not to mention it again.

I was taking my leave, when he told me that he desired to present me to his mother and sister. He went out, and two minutes later reentered with them. The mother was a woman of respectable and innocent air, but the daughter was a model of beauty. I was dazzled by her.

A quarter of an hour later, the too confiding mother asked my permission to retire, and her daughter remained. Only half an hour was necessary for her to captivate me. I was enchanted by her manifold perfections, her vivacious spirit, naïve and novel to me, her candor, her ingenuousness, her natural and lofty feelings, her gay and innocent vivacity,—that combination, in fine, which forms beauty, wit and innocence, a combination which always had over me an absolute sway, and which now made me the slave of the most perfect woman that one could imagine.

Mlle. C. C. never went out without her mother, who was devout but nevertheless indulgent. She had only the edifying books of her good father to read, and she was dying to peep into a novel. Likewise she had the greatest desire to know Venice. Nobody visited the house, and she had never yet been told that she was a real prodigy.

While the brother was writing, I was conversing with her,—or, better said, I was answering the numerous questions she asked me. I could not satisfy all her curiosity, save by adding to the ideas she already possessed, and which she was quite astonished to recognize, as her soul was still in a chaos. Nevertheless, I did not tell her that she was beautiful and that she interested me in a supreme degree; for having lied in that matter to so many others, I was afraid to make her suspect my veracity.

I left the house pensive, deeply impressed by the rare qualities I had discovered in this charming person, and I promised myself at first not to see her again, for I felt that I was not to sacrifice my liberty entirely by asking her to be my wife, although I judged her created to make my happiness.

Two days had passed since my visit to P. C., when I met him on the street. He told me that his sister spoke all the time of nothing but me, that she had remembered many things I had said to her, and that her mother was enchanted that she had made my acquaintance.

"She would be," he said, "a good match for you, for she will have ten thousand ducats for a dowry. If you come to see me tomorrow, we shall take coffee with my mother and sister."

I had made up my mind never again to set foot in his house; but I did not keep my word. In such a case a resolution is easily broken.

I passed three hours talking to this charming person, and I left exceedingly smitten with her. I told her before going away that I envied the fate of the person who would have her as wife; and this compliment, the first of the kind that she had received, covered her face with blushes of the most vivid pink.

As I retired, I examined the character of the feeling I felt for her, and I became afraid of it, for I could not flatter myself with the hope of obtaining her hand, and it seemed to me that I would have stabbed anyone who had advised me to seduce her. I needed distraction, so I gambled. Sometimes gambling is an excellent sedative for love.

The next day P. C. came to see me, and told me gaily that his mother had permitted his sister to go to the opera with him, that the girl was delighted because she had never been there, and that if it pleased me I could meet them somewhere.

"But does your sister expect me to be of the party?"

"Yes, and she is very much elated with the idea."

"And does your mother know of it?"

"No, but when she hears about it, she won't be angry, for you have inspired her with confidence."

"I shall try to get a box."

"Very well—you'll wait for us at a certain place."

The rogue did not speak to me any more about notes, and observing that I did not court his lady any longer, and that I was in love with his sister, he had conceived the amiable project of selling her to me. I was sorry for the mother and sister who confided in such a person, but I had not manhood enough to refuse the invitation. I even went so far as to persuade myself that, as I loved the girl, I must accept to protect her from other pitfalls, for had I refused, someone less scrupulous would have been found, and this idea was unbearable to me. It seemed that with me she would run no risk.

I bought a box at the Opera St. Samuel, and was waiting at the appointed place long before the hour. When they arrived I was delighted by the looks of my young friend. She was elegantly masked, and her brother was in uniform. In order not to expose this charming person to being recognized through her brother, I made them enter my gondola. He asked to be let out at the house of his mistress, who was sick, he told us, begging us to go on to our loge, where he would join us. I was surprised that C. C. did not show either surprise or distaste at remaining alone with me in the gondola; but as to the disappearance of the brother, it did not astonish me in the least, for it was obvious that he expected to profit by it.

I told C. C. that we would sail about until the time for the opera; and suggested that, the heat being great, she ought to unmask, which she did at once.

The duty that I had imposed upon myself to respect her, the noble assurance which illumined her features, as well as the trustfulness of her behavior, the innocent joy which she expressed, all served to increase my passion.

Not knowing what to say to her,—for naturally, I could speak of nothing but love, and the point was delicate,—I looked in silence at her charming face, not daring to glance towards two budding breasts, for fear of alarming her modesty.

"Say something," she said. "You just look at me without a single word. You have sacrificed yourself today, as my brother would have taken you to his lady, who, he says, is beautiful as an angel."

"I have seen that lady."

"She must be very clever."

"Perhaps she is, but I had not the opportunity of judging. I have never been in her house, and my intention is never to go there. You needn't think, my beautiful C., that I am making any sacrifice at all."

"I thought you were. And, as you did not speak, I supposed you were sad."

"If I do not speak, it is because I am too much moved by the happiness I feel in your angelic trustfulness."

"I am enchanted, but how could I lack confidence in you? I feel freer and much more secure with you than with my brother. My mother says that one cannot be mistaken in you, that you surely are an honorable man. Moreover, you are not married; that is the first thing I asked my mother. Do you remember that you told me you envied the fate of him who should have me to wife? And I said at the same time, that the one who shall have you as husband will be the happiest woman in Venice."

These words, pronounced with the most candid naïveté, and with that sweet tone which comes from the heart, made on me an impression hard to describe. I suffered, for I dared not imprint the tenderest of kisses on the vermilion lips which had just spoken, but at the same time I felt the most delicious pleasure at being loved by this angel.

"In this agreement of feelings," I said, "we could then, amiable C., find perfect love if we could be united inseparably. But I am old enough to be your father."

"You my father! What an idea! Do you know that I am fourteen?"

"Do you know that I am twenty-eight?"

"Well, then! Where is the man who, at your age, has a daughter of my age? I have to laugh at the thought of my father resembling you. Anyway I am never shy nor reserved with him."

At theatre time we stepped out of the gondola, and entered the opera box. The spectacle engrossed her completely. Her brother did not come till nearly the end, for this was part of his scheme.

I invited them to supper in a hostelry, where the pleasure of seeing this charming person eat heartily made me forget that I had not dined. I barely spoke during the whole dinner, for I was lovesick, and in such a state of irritation as was impossible to endure any longer. To excuse my taciturnity, I simulated a tooth-ache. They sympathized and left me to my silence.

After supper, P. said to his sister that I was in love with her, and that I should feel relieved if she allowed me to embrace her. Her only response was to turn toward me with laughing lips which invited kisses. I was burning, but I respected so much this innocent and naïve creature that I only kissed her on the cheek and that in an apparently cold manner.

"What a kiss!" exclaimed P. "Go on, give her a good loving kiss."

I did not budge. The impudent instigator annoyed me. But his sister, turning her head, said with emotion:

"Don't coax him, for I have not the happiness to please him."

This was an alarm to my love; I was no longer master of myself.

"What!" I exclaimed impetuously. "What! Beautiful C., you do not attribute my restraint to a sentiment that you inspire me with? You believe that I am not pleased with you? If a kiss is all that you need to prove my love, receive it with all the intensity that I feel."

Then taking her in my arms and pressing her tenderly to my breast, I imprinted on her mouth the long and ardent kiss which I was dying to give her. But in her heart, the shy dove felt that she had fallen into the claws of a vulture. She unloosened my arms, quite astonished to have discovered in that fashion how much I was in love. Her brother applauded me, while she replaced her mask to hide her embarrassment.

I asked her if she still believed that she did not please me.

"You have convinced me," she said. "But you should not punish me in undeceiving me." I found this answer very subtle, for it was dictated by sentiment; but her brother, who was not pleased by it, called it nonsense.

As soon as we had put on our masks, we departed, and after having taken them home, I retired very much enamored, and sad, although well satisfied.

The next day P. C. entered my room with an air of triumph, saying that his sister told her mother that we loved each other, and that if she had to get married she could be happy only with me.

"I adore your sister," I said, "but do you believe your father would give her to me?"

"I don't, but he is old. Meanwhile, love. My mother permits her to go to the opera with us this evening."

"Well, my friend, then we shall go——"

"I am forced to beg you to render me a slight service."

"Command me."

"There is some excellent Cyprian wine for sale, cheap; I can have a barrel on a note payable in six months. I am certain to be able to sell it at once profitably, but the merchant demands a guarantee, and he will accept yours if you will be so kind. Will you sign the note?"

"With pleasure."

I signed without demur, for where is the mortal lover who in such a case would have refused a service to one who to revenge himself for refusal could have made him unhappy? Then we made an appointment for the evening, and we separated satisfied with one another.

After having dressed, I went out and bought a dozen pairs of gloves, as many pairs of silk stockings, and a pair of embroidered garters with golden clasps, very much pleased to be able to make a present to my new friend.

I do not need to say that I was punctual at the rendezvous. Nevertheless, on arriving there I noticed that they were looking for me. If I had not suspected the intentions of P. C., I should have felt flattered by his attentions. As soon as I joined them, P. C. told me that as he had business on hand he would leave me with his sister, and that he would meet us at the theatre. When he had gone, I told C. C. that the only thing we could do was to ride about in a gondola up to the time of the opera.

"No," she said, "let us rather go to a garden in the Zucca."

"I am quite willing."

I took a public gondola, and we went to Saint Blaise, to a garden which I knew and which for a sequin I rented for the whole day so that nobody else could enter. It happened that neither of us had dined; so having ordered a good meal, we mounted to an apartment, whence after having unmasked we redescended into the garden. The amiable C. C. wore only a jacket made of taffeta and a small skirt of the same material; but she was ravishing in this light costume. My loving eyes pierced these veils, and my soul saw her naked; I sighed with desire, passion and restraint.

As soon as we came to the greensward, my young companion, as quick as a deer, seeing herself free on the lawn after having long been pent up indoors, started to run to the right and to the left, with all the signs of joy which animated her. Soon she stopped because out of breath, and she started to laugh at seeing me contemplate her in silence and in a sort of ecstasy of admiration. Soon, she dared me to race with her, I liked the idea; I accepted, but I wanted to interest her in a bet.

"The loser," said I, "will be obliged to do everything that the winner demands."

"I am willing."

We decided on the goal, and started. I was sure of winning, but I wanted to lose to see what she would condemn me to do. At first she ran with all her strength, while I was husbanding mine, so that she arrived at the winning post before me. While taking her breath, she thought of a good forfeit, then she hid behind a tree and asked me to find her ring. She had hidden it on her person, and in this way she placed me at liberty to search her. I found the idea charming, for I saw in it a clear intention. Nevertheless, I felt that I must not take undue advantage of her naïve confidence, as it needed coaxing.

We sat on the lawn, I searched her pockets, the folds of her jacket, those of her skirt, then her shoes, and finally up to the garters, which were clasped over the knees.

Having found nothing, I continued my investigation, as the ring was on her person, and I had to find it.

The reader guesses, without doubt, that I suspected the charming hiding-place where my belle had placed it; but before arriving at that point I intended to procure myself a lot of pleasure, which I enjoyed deliciously.

The ring was finally discovered between two of the most beautiful guardians that nature had ever fashioned; but I was so moved on taking my hand out that it trembled quite visibly.

"Why do you tremble?" she asked.

"I tremble with pleasure on having found the ring, for you have hidden it so well! But you owe me a return match. This time you shall not win."

"We shall see."

We started, and not seeing her running very fast, I thought that I could overtake her at will. But I was deceived. She had saved her strength, and when we were two-thirds from the goal, advancing at once, she passed me, and I found that I was losing. Then I conceived a stratagem which never fails, I pretended to fall down headlong, uttering a cry of pain. The poor little creature stopped and ran towards me, quite scared, and helped me to get up, comforting me the while. When I was up and ahead of her I began to laugh, and starting to run, reached the goal, leaving her quite distanced.

The charming runner, astounded, said:

"Then you are not hurt?"

"No, because I fell down purposely."

"Purposely? To deceive me? I would not have believed you capable of that. It is not fair to win by fraud, and I have not lost."

"Certainly! You have lost, for I have reached the goal ahead of you. And, cunning for cunning, admit that you tried to deceive me by taking a spurt."

"But that is allowed, and your trick, my dear friend, is of quite another sort."

"It has brought me victory:

> Vincasi per fortuna o per inganno
> Il vincer sempre fu laudabil cosa."

> Victory wrought of fortune or deceit,
> Is ever victory and ever sweet.

"That is what I have heard my brother say quite often, but never my father. Well, I admit having lost. Command me, I shall obey."

"Wait. Let us sit down, for I must have time to think. I command you to exchange garters with me."

"Garters? You have seen mine. They are ugly and worthless."

"Never mind. I shall think twice a day of the person I love, and about the same time you will be forced to think of me."

"It's quite a pretty idea, and it flatters me. I forgive you now for having cheated me. Here are my ugly garters."

"Here are mine."

"Ah, my dear deceiver, how beautiful they are! What a nice gift! How they will please my mother! Surely they were a present to you, as they are quite new?"

"No, they are not a present, I bought them for you, and I have been searching my mind for a means of making them acceptable to you. Love it was that suggested making them the prize of a race. Now you can imagine my disappointment when I saw you on the point of winning. My vexation inspired a deceit founded on a feeling which honors you; for you must confess that you would have shown a bad heart had you not run to my assistance."

"And I am sure that you would not have employed this ruse had you guessed the pain it caused me."

"You take such a deep interest in me?"

"I will do everything in the world to convince you of it. I am delighted with my pretty garters. I will not have any others, and I shall see to it that my brother does not steal them."

"Would he be capable of it?"

"Quite capable, especially if the clasps are of gold."

"They are of gold. But tell him they are of gold-plated copper."

"But you shall teach me how to hook the pretty clasps."

"Yes, most assuredly."

We went to dinner. After the repast, to which as I remember we did equal honors, she became merrier and I more enamored of her, but likewise more to be pitied for the reason that I had imposed upon myself a hard duty.

Impatient to put her garters on, she begged me to help her, with the best intention in the world, and without coquetry or ulterior motive.

A young, innocent girl, who in spite of her fifteen summers had not yet loved, and who had not lived with other girls or frequented society, did not know the violence of passion nor understand what causes it. She certainly had no idea of the danger of a tête-à-tête. When instinct made her fall in love for the first time, she imagined the object of her love worthy of all her confidence, and she thought to return her love by showing an undeserved trustfulness.

Finding that the stockings were too short to clasp the garter over her knee, she said that she would put on longer ones. At once dexterously taking out of my pocket those that I had bought, I begged her to accept them. Joyous and grateful, she sat in my lap, and in the effusion of her contentment, she gave me all the kisses she would have given to her own father if he had made her a similar gift. I returned her kisses, trying to control the violence of my desires, and saying only that a single kiss of hers was worth more than a kingdom.

My charming C. C. took her stockings off and put on a pair which came about halfway up her thigh. The more I discovered her innocence the less I dared make up my mind to seize this fascinating prey.

We went back to the garden, and after having walked about until evening, we attended the opera, taking care to keep our masks on, as the theatre was small, and we might have been recognized. My sweet friend was certain that her father would not allow her to go out any more if he discovered her enjoying this pleasure.

We were quite astonished not to find her brother. At our left we had the Marquis de Montalegre, the Spanish ambassador, with Mademoiselle Bola, his chief mistress; and to our right two masks, man and woman. These two masks kept their eyes constantly on us, but my young friend, who had her back turned to them, could not see them. During the ballet, C. C. having placed the program on the partition of the next box, the mask put his hand forward and took it. Judging by the action that we must be known to them, I informed my friend, who turned around and recognized her brother. The female mask could not be anybody else but his friend C. As P. C. knew the number of our box, he had engaged the next one, and as that could not have been done without intention, I foresaw that he was going to have his sister to supper with that woman.

I was angry, but I could not prevent it without breaking up the party; and I was in love.

After the second ballet he came into our box with his belle.

Following the usual amenities, the acquaintance was struck, and we had to go to supper at the casino.

As soon as the ladies had unmasked, they embraced each other, and the mistress of P. C. complimented and flattered my young friend. At the table she affected to treat her with extreme kindness, and C. C., not knowing the ways of the world, treated her with respect. Nevertheless, I saw that C., in spite of all her art, showed the spite caused her by viewing the superiority of the charms which I had preferred to hers.

P. C. almost beside himself with joy, wasted himself on silly pleasantries which only made his belle laugh; and his sister, who did not understand them, could not answer them.

In fine, our quadrille, being ill-assorted, was boresome. At the dessert P. C., somewhat heated by the wine, embraced his belle, and dared me to follow his example with his sister. I told him, that loving Mlle. C. C. truly, I would not take any liberties until I had acquired the right over her heart. P. C. started to joke on the subject, but C. made him shut up. Being grateful for this act of delicacy, I pulled out of my pocket, the dozen gloves which I had brought, and after having presented her with six pairs, I begged my friend to accept the other six.

P. C. got up from the table, snickering, dragging along his mistress, who was somewhat in the cups, and then threw himself with her on a sofa. The scene becoming embarrassing, I placed myself in such a manner as to hide them, then I gently led my friend into the recess of a window. I could not prevent C. C. from seeing in a mirror the posture of the two shameless ones, and her face was on fire. But speaking in a modest manner, she admired her beautiful gloves, which she was folding on a console.

After his coarse exploit, the impudent P. C. came to embrace me; and his abashed companion imitating his example, embraced my young friend, saying she was certain that she had not seen anything. C. C. modestly replied that she did not know what she could have seen, but a look she gave me made me guess all that she felt. As far as I was concerned, I let the reader imagine what my feelings were, if he knows a man's heart. How was it possible for me to stand such a scene in the presence of an innocent girl I worshipped, when I had to struggle against my own desires so as not to be overcome by them?

I was on hot coals; anger and indignation battling with the restraint I had imposed upon myself through the necessity to keep the object I treasured, caused in my body a general trembling.

The gentlemen who invented hell could not have failed to place in it this suffering, if they had known it.

The shameless P. C. had thought by his brutal action to give me a great proof of his friendship, making nothing of the dishonor of his mistress and modesty of his sister, whom he exposed to prostitution. I don't know how I had the will power not to strangle him.

The next day, when he visited me, I unmercifully reproached him with his conduct, and he tried to excuse himself by saying that he never would have done it, if he had not been certain that I had already treated his sister tête-à-tête as he had acted with his mistress in our presence.

My love for C. C. acquired every instant a new degree of intensity, and I had decided to risk everything to protect her from the unfair advantage her unworthy brother could have taken over her by placing her in the power of someone less scrupulous than I.

The matter seemed to me pressing. How horrible! What an unheard of seduction! What a strange way of gaining my friendship! And I saw myself forced to dissimulate with the being I despised most in the world!

I had been informed that he was up to his neck in debts, that he had been bankrupt in Vienna, where he had a wife and children, that in Venice he had compromised his father, who had been forced to drive him from the house, and who in pity pretended not to know he still lived there. He had seduced a married woman and caused a split between her and her husband, then after having spent all her money, exploited her body, not knowing what else to do with her.

His poor mother, whose idol he was, had given him all that she owned, even to her clothes. I expected to be importuned for a loan or guarantee, but I firmly resolved to refuse him everything. I could not stand the idea that C. C. should become the innocent cause of my ruin, and to be the tool of her brother in his debauches.

Impelled by an irresistible sentiment, by what is called a perfect love, the next day I went to see P. C., and after having told him that I adored his sister with the purest of intentions, I made him feel all the pain he had inflicted on me by forgetting all the amenities and that modesty which the most perfect libertine should consider if he has any pretensions to polite society.

"Even if I were forced," I said to him, "to forego the pleasure of seeing your angelic sister, I have decided not to consort with you any longer. But I warn you that I shall prevent her from going out with you to be used in some infamous bargain."

He apologized again for his drunkenness, and for his belief that my love for his sister did not preclude gratification. He begged my pardon, and weepingly embraced me. I was perhaps going to let him persuade me, when I saw his mother and sister enter. They expressed heartfelt thanks for my pretty present. I answered the mother that I loved her daughter only in the hope that she would give her to me as wife.

"In this hope, Madame," I added, "I shall speak to your husband as soon as I shall be in a position to assure her maintenance to render her happy."

Saying this, I kissed her hand, while the emotion caused tears to run down my cheeks. These tears were sympathetic, and made the good mother weep. After having thanked me affectionately, she left me alone with her daughter and son, who seemed frozen to marble. There are in the world many mothers of that stamp. They are so good themselves, and have so little knowledge of other than virtuous motives that they suspect no deceit, and their faith in a person who seems to them honest makes them ready victims.

What I had told the mother astonished the daughter, but her astonishment increased, when she heard what I had said to her brother. After a moment's reflection, she told him that with anyone else but myself she would have been ruined, and that she would not have forgiven him had she been in his lady's place, for his behavior was as dishonorable to her as to him. P. C. was weeping, but the traitor was master over his tears.

It was the day of Pentecost. As there was a lull in the round of gayeties, he told me that if I wanted to meet him the next day at the same spot as on other days, he would bring his sister, and that as honor did not permit him to leave Mlle. C. alone he would leave us in all freedom.

"I will give you my key," he said, "and you shall bring my sister back after you have supped wherever you please."

With this he gave me the key, which I did not have the courage to refuse, and then he left us.

Soon after he left I went out, telling my friend that we would go on the morrow to the garden of the Zucca.

"The decision of my brother," she said, "is the most honorable he could make."

I was punctual at the rendezvous, and burning with love I foresaw what was going to happen. I had taken the trouble to buy a box at the opera, but awaiting the evening we went into the garden. As it was a feast day, there were several small groups at separate tables, and not wishing to mingle with the crowd, we resolved to remain in an apartment which was rented to us, not caring to see the opera except at the end. By reason of this, I ordered a good supper. We had seven hours before us, and my charming friend assured me that we should not be bored. She got rid of her mask, and came to sit on my knees, saying that I had conquered her by the manner in which I had treated her after that awful supper. But all our arguments were accompanied by kisses, which by and by turned into fire. "Did you see," she said, "what my brother did to his lady? I only saw in the mirror, but imagined what it could have been."

"Were you not afraid that I would treat you in the same manner?"

"No, I assure you. How could I have feared that, knowing how well you love? You would have so humiliated me that I could not have loved you any more. We shall reserve ourselves for the time of our marriage; shan't we? You cannot imagine my joy when I heard you explain yourself to my mother! We shall always love each other. By the way, what is the meaning of the words which are embroidered on the garters?"

"Is there a motto? I didn't know it."

"Oh, yes, it's in French. Kindly read it to me."

Sitting on my knees, she unclasps one garter, while I unclasp the other. These are the two lines which I should have read to her before offering her the gift:

> "Envoyant chaque jour le bijou de ma belle,
> Vous lui direz qu'Amour veut qu'il lui soit fidèle."

> Lucky garter! what you see above,
> Tell it to be always true to love.

These verses, without doubt rather free, seemed to me well turned, amusing and full of wit. I burst out laughing, and laughed again when to satisfy her, I had to translate to her the meaning. As it was a new idea for her, I had to enter into certain details which put us on fire.

"I shall not dare show my garters to anybody," she said, "and I am grieved."

As I was thoughtful, she went on:

"Tell me what you are thinking about."

"I think that these garters have a privilege which I shall perhaps never have. How I would like to be in their place! I shall perhaps die of this desire, and I shall die unhappy."

"No, my dear, for I am in the same predicament, and I am certain I shall live. Anyhow, we can hasten our marriage. On my part, I am ready to give you my troth tomorrow, if you wish it. We are free, and my father will have to consent."

"You are quite right. Honor would force him to do so. Nevertheless, I must give him a mark of my respect by asking your hand, then our hour will soon arrive. It will be eight or ten days."

"So soon? You will see that he will answer that I am too young."

"And very likely he will tell the truth."

"No, for I am young, but not too young, and I am quite certain that I can be your wife."

I felt as in a furnace, and all further resistance to the fire which burnt me seemed impossible.

"You whom I cherish," I said, "are you quite certain that I love you? Do you believe me capable of being faithful to you? Are you sure that you will never repent of being my wife?"

"I am more than certain, my heart, for you could not wish my unhappiness."

"Well then! Let us be married this instant. God alone shall be witness of our oath, and we could not have a more loyal one, for he knows the purity of our intentions. Let us give each other our pledge, let us unite our destinies, and be happy. We shall strengthen our sacred knot with the consent of your father, and with the religious ceremonies as soon as possible; meanwhile, be mine, be all mine."

"Dispose of me, my own! I promise to God and to you, from this moment on, and as long as I live, to be your faithful wife. I shall speak thus to my father, to the priest who shall bless our union, to everybody."

"I make you the same promise, my beloved, and I assure you that we are wholly married. Come into my arms, complete my happiness!"

After having tenderly embraced her, I notified the mistress of the casino not to bring us our food until we called her and not to interrupt us.

Meanwhile my charming C. C. had thrown herself on the bed quite dressed, but I told her that troublesome veils would frighten love, and in less than a minute I made of her a new Eve, beautiful and naked as if she had just come out of the hands of the supreme artist. Her skin as soft as satin, was of a dazzling white, enhanced by the superb ebony hair which I had arranged over her alabaster shoulders. Her slender waist, her rounded hips, her perfectly moulded breasts, her rose lips, her animated complexion, her large eyes from which emanated at once sweetness and the sparkle of passion, everything in her presented consummate beauty to my greedy eyes. The perfection of the Mother of Love ornamented, with all that modesty adds in attraction to the features of a beautiful woman!

Beside myself, I began to doubt the reality of my happiness, or that it could not become perfect by a complete gratification, when love bethought himself, in so serious a moment, to furnish me with matter for laughter.

Finally as if overcome by the pleasure of the eyes, she pressed me tenderly against her breast and exclaimed:

"Oh! my dear, what a difference between you and my pillow!"

"Your pillow, my heart? But you jest; explain yourself."

"It's childish. Will you be angry?"

"Angry! How could I, in the sweetest moment of my life?"

"Well! For several nights I could not go to sleep without holding my pillow in my arms. I caressed it, and called it my dear husband. I imagined that it was you, and when a sweet enjoyment had rendered me still, I went to sleep, and in the morning I found my great pillow between my arms."

My dear C. C. became my wife heroically for the excess of her love had rendered even her suffering delicious. After three hours passed in the most delightful playfulness, I got up and called for our supper. The repast was frugal but delicious. We looked at each other without speaking, for what could we say which was worthy of what we felt? We found our happiness extreme, and we enjoyed it in the certainty that we could renew it at will.

The hostess came to ask if we wished anything, and wanted to know if we would not go to the Opera which was said to be so beautiful.

"Have you never been there?"

"Never. It is too expensive for people like ourselves. My daughter is so curious that she would, God forgive me, give herself away for the pleasure of going there once."

"She would pay dearly for it," said my little wife, laughing. "My darling, we could make her happy at less cost to her, for it certainly hurts."

"I was thinking that, darling. Here is the key to the box; you can make her a gift of it."

"Here," she said to the hostess, "here is the key to the box at the theatre St. Moise. It is worth two sequins. Go in our stead and tell your daughter to keep her rose for something better."

"So that you can enjoy yourself, mother, here are two sequins," I said to her, "let your daughter have a good time."

The good woman, astonished at the generosity of her hosts, ran to her daughter, while we persuaded ourselves of the necessity of going to bed again.

The hostess came up again with her daughter, a beautiful blonde, quite appetizing, and who was eager to kiss the hand of her benefactors.

"She will go at once with her lover," said the mother. "He is there, but I shall not let her go alone, for he is a buck! I shall go with them."

"Very well, my good woman, but on your return let the gondola which will take you back wait for us, we shall use it to return to Venice."

"What! You are going to stay here until our return?"

"Yes, for we were married today."

"Today! God bless you!"

Exhausted in enjoyment and happiness, we were going to sleep, when our hostess came to inform us that the gondola awaited us.

I got up at once, in the hope of laughing at what she would have to tell us about the opera, but she let her daughter do that, and went to prepare us some coffee. The blond girl helped my friend dress, but from time to time she looked at me in such a manner as to lead me to believe she had more experience than her mother suspected.

There was nothing less discreet than the eyes of my charming mistress. They carried the unmistakable marks of her first exploits. But she had had to sustain a battle which positively made her other than she was before.

We partook of the very hot coffee, and I told our hostess to prepare a delicate dinner for us the next day; then we departed.

It was at the first peep of dawn that, to deceive the curiosity of the gondoliers, we landed at the square Saint Sophie, and we parted happy, contented, and certain that we were quite married.

NOTE—The benefactor of Casanova, M. de Bragadin, did in fact ask Mlle. C. C. in marriage for his young pupil. This is one of the very rare instances when Casanova pushed his love so far. Luckily, the father refused his consent and hastened to lock his daughter up in a convent.

Chapter VII

A NOVEL LOVE CURE

NEXT day Righelini took me to see the lodgings he had spoken of. I liked them and rented them at once, paying the first quarter in advance. The house belonged to a widow with two daughters, the eldest of whom had just been bled. Righelini was her doctor and had been treating her for nine months without being able to cure her. As he was going to attend her now I went with him into her room. I could have thought it was a statue that met us. In my surprise I exclaimed, "Beautiful! but a hue as of Parian marble."

Then the statue smiled what would have been a divine smile if there had been any red in her cheeks.

"Her pallor need not surprise you," said Righelini. "She has just been bled for the hundred and fourth time," at which I could not restrain a gesture of astonishment.

This beautiful creature was eighteen years old and her courses did not function, so she was near expiring three or four times a week and the only way to relieve her was to open her veins.

"I want to send her to the country," said the doctor; "fresh air and exercise will do her more good than all the medicine in the world."

After I had been assured that my quarters would be ready for occupancy that very night I went out with Righelini who informed me that really the only remedy this girl needed was a robust lover.

"But, my dear doctor," I said, "could you not be her dispenser as well as her physician?"

"Too much risk. I might be forced to marry her, and I fear marriage worse than fire."

I was no more disposed to marry than was my friend the doctor, but I did not mind playing with fire a little, seeing that I was to be constantly exposed. The reader will see how I operated the miracle which restored the glow of health to the beautiful sufferer.

After supping with M. de Bragadin I went to my lodgings. I was surprised to find the balcony of my bedroom occupied. A young lady with a pretty figure got up when she saw me and excused herself for the liberty which she had taken.

"I am the statue you met this morning," she said. "We do not light the candles at night because the mosquitoes are so bad, but whenever you wish to retire we will close the windows and withdraw. Permit me to introduce my younger sister. Mother has gone to bed."

I answered that the balcony was always at their service. As it was early yet I begged them to let me put on my dressing gown and keep them company. Her conversation was delightful. She entertained me agreeably for two hours, at the end of which time the younger sister lighted a candle and they bade me good night.

By the time I went to bed her beauty had taken complete possession of my imagination. I simply could not persuade myself that she was an invalid. She spoke with force, she was gay, cultivated, and unusually witty. I did not understand by what fatality she had remained uncured in a city like Venice, if Righelini's unique theory was correct, for in spite of her misfortune she appeared to me well able to attract a lover, and I believed her sensible enough to submit readily to the most agreeable remedy the medical faculty has ever prescribed.

The next day I rang on rising and the younger sister entered. She said that there were no servants and for the time being she would look after me. I did not wish to be waited upon by my servant from M. de Bragadin's household, as I felt freer without him. After she had attended to some of my wants I asked her how her sister was feeling.

"Quite well," she said. "For all she is so pale she isn't really inconvenienced except when the breathless spells come on. She has a very good appetite and sleeps as soundly as I do."

"Who is playing the violin?"

"The dancing master. He's giving my sister a lesson!"

I completed my toilet in haste so as not to miss the sight. It was charming. She was graceful and active, but the old instructor allowed her to turn her toes inward. All this young and beautiful girl needed was the spark of Prometheus, the color of life, for her snowy pallor was truly distressing. The teacher requested me to dance a minuet with his pupil, and I complied, asking him to play larghissimo.

"That will tire the signorina too much," he said.

She hastened to answer that she was quite strong and would be glad to dance as I suggested. She did very well but at the end she was obliged to throw herself on a sofa.

"In the future, my dear teacher," she said to the old man, "I don't want to dance any other way. I believe this movement will do me good."

When the teacher left I told her that the lessons were too short and that her master was permitting her to acquire bad habits. I placed her feet, shoulders, and arms properly, taught her to offer her hand gracefully, to bend the knees in time; in short I gave her a lesson in due form, then seeing her somewhat fatigued I begged her to sit down and went out to pay a visit to M. M.

In eight or ten days my conversations with the daughter of my hostess, conversations on the balcony which generally lasted until midnight, and the deportment lesson I gave her every morning, produced two natural results: the first that she did not get out of breath any more, and the second that I fell in love with her. Though the cure had not been consummated she nevertheless had not needed to be bled again.

Righelini came to visit her as usual and seeing how much better she was looking he prophesied that before autumn nature would come to her assistance and obviate the necessity of keeping her alive by artificial means. Her mother looked on me as an angel sent by God to cure her daughter, and the latter felt a gratitude which with women is only a step from love.

I made her dismiss her old dancing teacher and I soon had made a first rate dancer of her. At the end of ten or twelve days I was starting to give her her lesson one morning when all at once she felt out of breath and fell as if dead into my arms.

I was frightened, but her mother, who was used to seeing her in that state, sent for a surgeon at once, and her sister came to unlace her. Her firm breast, which did not need any color to be perfect, enchanted me. I covered it, saying that if the surgeon saw it uncovered he would miss his stroke. Divining what rapture there was in my gesture she gently pushed me away with a beseeching look which impressed me profoundly.

The surgeon arrived and bled her arm. Almost at once she came back to life. Nearly four ounces of blood were taken, and when her mother told me they never took more I grasped the principle of this method of treatment. Four ounces of blood twice a week was two pounds a month, the quantity she would have lost in the normal way if certain veins had not been obstructed. Thus the physician was merely assisting nature to establish an equilibrium.

The surgeon had just left when she said, to my great surprise, that if I could wait a moment in the hall she would return and finish the lesson. This in fact she did, and danced as if nothing had happened. Two of my senses could give me conclusive proof of the beauty of her breast and I was thoroughly inflamed.

When I came in early that evening I found her in her room with her sister. She said that she expected her godfather, who having been an intimate friend of her father for the last eighteen years came every day to pass an hour with her.

"How old is he?"

"He is over fifty."

"Is he married?"

"Yes. It's Count S. He loves me like a dear father, the same as when I was a child. His wife comes to see me sometimes and invites me to dinner. Next autumn I am going to the country with her and I hope the fresh air will do me good. My godfather knows that you live with us and he is glad you do. He does not know you, but if you wish to you can make his acquaintance."

This speech tickled me. Without asking indiscreet questions I was put in possession of desired information. This rascal, whose friendship was obviously affected by love, was the husband of the countess S. who had taken me to the convent of Murano two years before. The count was most polite. He thanked me in the tone of a father for befriending his goddaughter and begged me to do him the honor of dining at his house the next day, when he would be overjoyed to present me to his wife. I accepted with pleasure, for his invitation bespoke the true gentleman, and after his departure I delighted my beautiful pupil by praising him.

"My godfather," she said, "has the keeping of all the documents relating to our inheritance, which amounts to forty thousand ecus. The fourth of this sum belongs to me, and my mother has promised my sister and myself to divide her share with us."

So this girl would bring fifty thousand current Venetian ducats to the man who married her. I fancied that she wanted to interest me in her fortune and that she was trying to force my respect by showing herself chary of her favors, for when I permitted myself any liberties she checked me with arguments which I dared not answer. I must manage her accordingly.

Towards evening, having taken a gondola, I was escorting the demoiselle home. I became direct and attempted to caress her. I was piqued when she responded with reproaches, so instead of going in with her when we landed at the house I went on to Tonine and passed most of the night there. The next day I got up too late for a lesson and when I tried to excuse myself she said she did not mind in the least. In the evening I tarried long on the balcony but my belle did not appear. I did not like this nonchalant treatment and next day I got up early and went out. I did not return until night. She was on the balcony, but I kept a respectful distance and spoke only of indifferent matters.

In the morning I was awakened by a great noise. I got up and hastily donning my dressing gown I went to her roof to see what had happened. I found her dying. Pretense was useless. I felt a real and tender concern. In the intense heat of early July my beautiful patient was covered only by a thin bed sheet. She could not speak to me, but in her sad eyes there was something imploring. I asked her if she had palpitation of the heart and applied first my hand and then my burning lips to her breast. The effect was as that of the electric spark, and she heaved a long sigh which did her good. She was not strong enough to push away my amorous hand. Emboldened I pressed my ardent lips to her dying mouth, kindling her with my breath. She made an effort to repel me, and her looks, in lieu of her vanished voice, told me how offended she was. I drew back and a moment later the surgeon entered. As soon as the vein was opened she breathed more freely and wanted to get up the instant the operation was over.

I begged her to stay in bed, and her mother coming in agreed with me. I finally prevailed by saying that we would not leave her a moment and that I should have my dinner served to me here. Then she put on a corset and begged her sister to cover her with a silk shawl, for she could be seen as through a veil of crepe. I gave my orders for dinner and when alone with her again I sat at the head of the bed burning with passion. Taking her hand and covering it with kisses I told her that I could surely cure her if she would love me.

"Alas!" she said, "I don't dare. Who could really love me in return?"

I did not let the opportunity pass. Redoubling my gallant protestations I was rewarded by a sigh and a voluptuous look. I put my hand on her knee, begging her to leave it there and promising not to demand anything further.

"Leave me alone!" she said, drawing up like a tragedy queen. "This will make me faint again."

"No, my darling, no," I cried impetuously, "it will make you get well!" and my kisses choked back the reply that was at her lips.

I was heartily glad to be near the goal of her favor with the expectancy of certainly curing her if the doctor was not mistaken. I spared her shame by speaking as discreetly as I could, and declaring myself her lover I promised not to require anything further than what she thought necessary to foster my affection.

They served a very good dinner and she ate with relish, then saying that she felt quite well she got up, and I dressed to go out. Returning early in the evening I found her alone on the balcony. There, tête-à-tête with her, using the language of the eyes and the language of sighs, greedy of her charms which the light of Phoebe rendered yet more alluring, I communicated to her the heat that consumed me, and pressing her lovingly to my breast I met with a response so eager and unconstrained as to prove to me that she believed she was receiving a favor as well as granting one.

Her sister came out to tell her that it was late, but received the reply, "Go to sleep. The cool night air is good for me, and I want to enjoy it awhile longer."

As soon as we were alone we went to bed as if we had done nothing else for a year. We passed a delightful night, I animated by love and the desire to cure her, she by the most ardent passion and the most affectionate gratitude. At dawn she embraced me with deep feeling, and, then, her eyes moist with happiness, she got up and went to her own room for some sleep. I needed rest as much as she did, and on that day a dancing lesson was out of the question.

Transported as we were we did not once neglect to take all due precaution. After three weeks of delicious nights I had the gratification of seeing her completely cured. Without doubt I would have married her if toward the end of the month a mishap had not befallen me.*

* Casanova is arrested and imprisoned in the Doge's palace.

Chapter VIII

FLIGHT FROM THE PIOMBI

ONE can entertain no very high opinion of the writers of anonymous letters, but it was grave imprudence on my part to ignore these missives entirely, as they ought to have shown me that I was in danger.

A certain Manuzzi, who passed as a jeweler and was really a spy in the pay of the state inquisitors, scraped up an acquaintance with me on the strength of an offer of obtaining me some diamonds on credit. He thus managed to get me to receive him at my lodgings. Looking over my books at random he alighted on some manuscripts treating of magic. I was foolish enough to enjoy his surprise and began to show him some treatises on the elementary spirits. My readers, I hope, will not do me the injustice to think I gave the slightest credence to these fairy tales. I kept them simply as curiosities, purely for the fun I got out of seeing what absurdities a shallow brain can contrive.

A few days later the spy came to see me again and said that a book collector, whom he was not at liberty to name, was willing to give me a thousand sequins for five of my manuscripts but wished first to make sure they were authentic. Manuzzi promised to return them in twenty-four hours, and I, suspecting nothing, let him take them along. He brought them back promptly the next day and told me the collector pronounced them forgeries. A few years afterward I learned that Manuzzi had carried them straight to the secretary of the inquisition which thus had evidence that I was a powerful magician.

During that fatal month everything conspired against me. Mme. Memmo took it into her head that I was converting her sons Andrea, Bernardo, and Lorenzo to atheism. She went to see old chevalier Antonio Mocenigo, who also had a grudge against me for having, as he claimed, led astray his nephew Signor Bragadin by cabalistic means. The charge was serious, and an auto da fe was not impossible. Holy Church was concerned, and she is a savage beast when antagonized. However, as it was not convenient to get me locked up in one of the ecclesiastical prisons my case was to be left to the inquisitors of state.

An ambassadorial secretary whom I came to know several years later told me that a professional denouncer, accompanied by two witnesses, who also were doubtless in the pay of the tribunal, had accused me of believing only in the Devil. As though such an absurd faith, if it could possibly exist, did not necessitate belief in God also. These three honest men testified on oath that when I lost money gambling I did not blaspheme as a true believer would have done, and that never was I heard to execrate the Devil. I was accused of eating meat every day and of never going to mass, and I was strongly suspected of being a freemason. In addition it was said that I frequented the society of foreign ministers and was evidently selling for great sums the state secrets I was crafty enough to worm out of the three patricians who were known to be my patrons.

All these charges, not one of which had the slightest foundation in fact, served the dread tribunal as a pretext for treating me as a public enemy and grand conspirator. For some weeks persons in whose counsel I had a good deal of confidence had been advising me to get out of the country, because the tribunal was considering me. That was enough, for in Venice the only persons who can live in peace are those of whose existence the inquisition is unaware. In the month of July *Messergrande* * was ordered to apprehend me dead or alive. I returned early one morning, and supposing everybody to be still in bed I was taking out my key to let myself in, when to my surprise I found that the door was wide open and the lock broken. I entered and found everybody up and the landlady voicing bitter complaints.

Messergrande and his myrmidons had entered the house by force and turned everything upside down. He claimed to be hunting for a trunk full of salt, which was strictly contraband. A trunk had been delivered the day before, but it belonged to Count S. and contained nothing but linen. Messergrande had examined the trunk, paid a visit to my room, and departed without saying anything.

The landlady wished full reparation for this outrage, and I told her I would speak to Signor Bragadin about it that very day. After a three or four hours' nap I went to his palace, told him the whole story, and asked him to institute immediate and drastic proceedings. I pointed out to him plainly the right my hostess had to claim a satisfaction proportionate to the offense, since the law guaranteed the tranquillity of a family whose conduct was above reproach.

What I said troubled my friends profoundly, and good old Signor Bragadin, calm but pensive, told me he would give me an answer after dinner.

De la Haye dined with us, and during the mournful repast said never a word. I ought to have been able to see the significance of my friends' demeanor on this occasion, but I was under the spell of an evil genius which forbade me the use of my ordinary faculties.

My intimacy with these men had been a matter for universal surprise. Everybody agreed that the association was unnatural, and that I must have brought it about by sorcery. The three gentlemen were devout and virtuous in the extreme. Nothing was further

* Captain of the watch.

from me than piety, and I was the most thorough-paced libertine in Venice.

"Virtue," said the wiseacres, "can be tolerant of vice, but cannot make alliances with it."

After dinner Signor Bragadin led me into his study, followed by our friends, whose presence could never be counted an intrusion. He told me nonchalantly that instead of thinking of punishing Messergrande for breaking into my lodgings I had better be making plans for flight to a place of safety.

"Trunk full of salt or trunk full of gold, my dear fellow," he said, "mere pretext. It is you they were after. Your guardian angel has caused them to miss you once, and now you must fly. Tomorrow will perhaps be too late. I was state inquisitor myself for eight months and I know how the arrests ordered by the tribunal are made. One doesn't break into a house to look for a box of salt. It is just possible they knew you were out and timed their coming so as purposely to give you a chance to get away. At any rate, my son, give heed to me and start this instant to Fusina, and then as quickly as possible to Florence, and remain there until I write you that it is safe for you to return. If you need money I will give you a hundred sequins for your immediate necessities. Absolutely, prudence requires that you go."

In my blind obstinacy I replied that as I had done nothing to be arrested for I did not fear the tribunal, and though I recognized the wisdom of his advice I could not follow it.

"The dread tribunal," he said, "can hold you for crimes real or imaginary without giving you any notion of the charge. Ask your oracle whether you ought to take my advice or not."

Knowing that he was poking fun at my superstitious regard for Ariosto I said that I would dispense with a consultation to which, to soften my refusal, I said I had recourse only when in doubt. Then as a real reason I told him that flight would be a sign of fear, which would declare my guilt, for an innocent person is as free from fear as from remorse.

As a last resort he tried to persuade me to stay all night and at least the next day in his palace. The palace of a patrician is inviolate. The archers cannot cross the threshold without a special order from the tribunal, and this order is never given. I am still ashamed of myself for having refused the offer of the worthy old gentleman to whom I owed so much love and gratitude. I could have spared myself an ordeal and my friend a slight which he felt rather keenly.

I was moved when I saw Signor Bragadin weeping, and I nearly accorded to his grief when I had refused to his arguments and to good sense.

"I pray you," I said, "spare me the heart-rending sight of your tears."

Controlling himself immediately he made a few light remarks, then with a smile which was all affection he embraced me, saying, "Perhaps, my friend, I am destined never to see you again, but *fata viam invenient.**"

I embraced him tenderly and went out. His prediction came true. I never saw him again. He died eleven years after this parting.

I left the palace quite unperturbed. I went home, consoled the landlady, kissed her daughter, and went to bed. This was early in the evening, July 25, 1755.

Next day at peep of dawn there came the terrible Messergrande into my room. I woke and heard him ask, "Are you Giacomo Casanova?" in the same instant. To my, "Yes, I am Casanova," he responded with a command to rise, dress, hand over all my papers and follow him.

"On whose authority do you give this order?"

* Fate finds (leads) the way.

"On the authority of the tribunal."

My secretary was open and all my papers were scattered about on the table I used for a desk.

"Help yourself," said I to the emissary of the dread tribunal, indicating the litter with my hand. He swept it into a sack, which he gave to one of his myrmidons, then he told me I must deliver up all the bound manuscripts I was known to have. I pointed out to him the place where they were kept, and now my eyes were opened. I saw that I had been betrayed by the perfidious Manuzzi, who, as I have related, had got me to receive him at my lodgings and then had pretended to have found a collector interested in purchasing manuscripts like these. There were *"The Clavicle of Solomon,"* the *"Zecor-ben,"* a *"Picatrix,"* a ponderous treatise on the planetary hours, and the conjurements necessary for holding colloquy with demons of any grade. The persons who knew I had these books thought me a powerful magician, and I was not displeased to be so considered.

Messergrande also took the books which were on my dressing stand, Petrarch, Ariosto, Horace, a manuscript of *"The Military Philosopher"* which Matilde had given me, *"The Carthusian Porter,"* and Aretino. This latter Manuzzi must have denounced, because Messergrande asked me particularly for it.

While Messergrande was thus ransacking my manuscripts, books and letters, I was methodically dressing, neither rapidly nor slowly. I washed, shaved, combed my hair, put on a ruffled shirt and my new coat, without saying a word and without quite knowing what I was doing. Messergrande, who never lost sight of me for an instant, did not seem to think it odd that I should be arraying myself as for a wedding.

When we went out I was surprised to see as many as forty archers in the antechamber. The state had done me the honor to think such numbers necessary to secure my person when as a matter

FLIGHT FROM THE PIOMBI

of fact, according to the saying *Ne Hercules quidem contra duos*,* two would have been sufficient. It is singular. In London, where everybody is brave, only one man is employed to arrest another, while in my dear fatherland, where everybody is a coward, thirty or forty are required. I suppose the poltroon transformed into an assailant is shakier than the poltroon assailed, and that when he assailed the coward by nature becomes a brave man by circumstance. Certainly it is not rare in Venice for one lone man to defend himself against twenty archers and end by escaping after wounding several. I remember to having aided a comrade in Paris to get away from forty pikesters. We put the whole dastardly pack to rout.

Messergrande set me on board a gondola and in the midst of an escort of four sat down beside me. When we arrived at his house he offered me a cup of coffee, which I refused, then he took me to a room and locked me in. I passed four hours there in sleep, waking up every fifteen minutes to make water. Extraordinary phenomenon. I had not been suffering from strangury, the heat was oppressive, and I had not supped the evening before. I knew from past experience of arbitrary despotism that oppression had on me the effect of a powerful narcotic; I was now to learn that sudden, intense surprise is diuretic. I surrender this discovery to the physicians. Perhaps some sage will succeed in making it of benefit to suffering humanity.

Toward the twenty-first hour ** the chief of the archers entered and said that he had orders to conduct me into the Piombi. Without a word I followed. We got into a gondola and after a thousand detours through the by-canals we came out into the Grand canal and disembarked at the prisoners' quay. After climbing several flights of stairs we crossed an enclosed bridge. This bridge, over the canal called the *rio di Palazzo,* connects the prisons with the

---
* The strength of Hercules is naught against two.
** 2 p.m.

doge's palace, and is known as the "bridge of sighs." At the end is a gallery. We came out into a chamber, through this into a second chamber. Here I was presented to an individual in the robe of a patrician, who said, after scrutinizing me, *"E quello, mettetelo in deposito."* (Put this man into a temporary cell.) The patrician, "the prudent Domenico Cavalli," secretary of the inquisition, apparently was ashamed to speak Venetian in my presence, for he pronounced the decree of my detention in good Tuscan.

Messergrande then handed me over to the warden of the Piombi, who stood there dangling an enormous bunch of keys. Followed by two archers the warden took me up two flights of stairs, then along a gallery, unlocked a door into another gallery, then into yet another gallery at the end of which he unlocked yet another door leading into a garret six fathoms in length, two in width, imperfectly lighted by a dormer window high overhead. I thought this was to be my prison, but I was mistaken. Taking a huge key the jailer opened a great door sheathed in iron, three and a half feet high, with a round hole eight inches in diameter in the middle.

He ordered me to enter. At that moment I was contemplating with a great deal of interest an iron machine solidly set into the wall. This machine had the shape of a horseshoe. It was an inch thick and about five inches across from tip to tip. I was puzzling over the use to which this horrible instrument might be put when the jailer said to me with a smile:

"I see, signor, that you would like to know what that is for. Well, I will tell you. When Their Excellencies order that anyone be strangled he is seated on a stool facing away from the collar. Then his head is pushed back so that the collar goes half way round his neck. A silk band is fastened across his throat, and passing through these two holes is connected to the axle of this wheel. The wheel is turned until the sufferer has yielded his soul—to our Lord, because, God be praised, the confessor is beside the wretch to the very end."

"Very ingenious, and I fancy, signor, that you have the honorable duty of turning the wheel?"

He made no reply but motioned me to enter my cell. To do so I had to stoop half over. He locked me in, then asked me through the grating of the door what I wanted to eat.

"Why, I hadn't thought of it," I replied, and he went away, carefully locking the innumerable doors after him.

Overwhelmed, stunned, I put my elbows on the sill of the door grating. The grating was two feet square, with six iron bars an inch thick cut by a cross bar in the center so as to form sixteen openings each five inches square. These openings would have let in plenty of light, because the dormer window was in the wall opposite my door, though at some distance, but a great quadrangular beam, the main support of the roof, entered the wall just under the dormer and though permitting an intercepted light to stray into the garret admitted none to my cell. Groping about, with head bowed, for the ceiling was but five and a half feet high, I found that my dismal domicile formed three quarters of a square six fathoms by six fathoms. The fourth quarter contiguous was a sort of alcove large enough to hold a bed, but I found no bed nor table nor chair nor furnishing of any kind, except a tub, whose use the reader can imagine, and a plank set into the wall, a foot wide and four feet above the floor. On the plank I placed my Padua silk mantle, the new coat thus inauspiciously inaugurated, and my white-plumed hat trimmed with Spanish point lace.

The heat was unbearable, and mechanically, driven by instinct, I repaired to the little grating which was the only place where I could lean my weight on my elbows. The dormer was now concealed, but there was daylight in the garret and I could see rats of a terrifying size running about quite at their ease. These hideous animals, the sight of which I abhor, came right up under my grating without seeming in the least afraid. A visit would have frozen my blood, so I hastened to push the sliding shutter, closing the round hole in the middle of the door. Falling into profound revery, leaning on my elbow all the while, I spent the rest of the day there, silent and motionless.

At the sound of the clock striking the twenty-first hour I arose. I began to feel uneasy. Was I to have nothing to eat and nothing to sleep on? My jailers ought at least to bring me a chair and some bread and water. I had no appetite—need I say?—and never in my life had I had such a dry, bitter taste in my mouth. I supposed that surely before nightfall somebody would appear, but when I heard the twenty-fourth hour strike I became furious and threw myself against the wall, kicking, hammering, and accompanying with loud cries all the vain disturbance which my strange situation moved me to make. After more than an hour of this violent exercise, when still nobody had come, when there had been not the slightest indication that anybody could have heard my outcry, I subsided in the uncanny darkness, and closing the grating for fear the rats would jump into my cell, I cast myself at full length on the floor.

The stroke of midnight wakened me. How frightful the wakening when it makes one sigh for the illusion of oblivion! I could not conceive that I had passed three absolutely painless hours. Lying on my left side, without altering my position, I reached out for my handkerchief, which I remembered to have put in my right hand pocket. I felt about——

God!

My fingers closed upon another ice-cold hand.

Fear electrified me from head to foot, and my hair stood on end. Never in my life have I experienced such terror unspeakable. I lay there three or four minutes in a sort of paralysis, not only motionless but incapable of thinking. Recovering somewhat and persuading myself that the hand was only a figment of my troubled imagination, I reached again, and again I touched that dead hand. I uttered a piercing cry and rolled over in horror.

Soon, becoming calmer and thinking myself capable of rational reflection, I decided that while I slept my oppressors had placed a corpse beside me. I was sure it was not there when I first lay down. I suppose, thought I, it is the corpse of some unfortunate whom they have strangled, and they wish in this way to give me a hint of the fate in store for me. The thought infuriated me. All my terror was turned into rage. I reached out again as if to defy their atrocious barbarity. In endeavoring to rise I supported myself on my elbow and was made to realize that all this panic was caused me by my own left hand, which had been benumbed by the weight of my body and the hardness of the floor—this last a poor substitute for eiderdown. The circulation had stopped and the member had lost all warmth, sensation, and power of movement.

This adventure, in spite of the element of the comic in it, did not amuse me at all. On the contrary it gave rise to the darkest forebodings. I perceived that I was in a place where, if the false appears true, the true must equally appear false, where the understanding must lose half its power, and where tottering reason must sway continually between chimeras, whether of crazy hope or of frantic despair.

At half past the fifteenth hour the profound silence of this hell of living humanity was broken by the creaking of the bolts of the many doors through which one must successfully pass to reach my cell.

"Have you had time to think what you want to eat?" cried my jailer in a raucous voice through the wicket.

One is fortunate when the insolence of an infamous creature shows itself only in the guise of raillery.

I answered that I wanted broth with rice, a roast, some bread, wine, and water. I perceived that the lout was astonished not to hear the complaints he expected. He went out and returned fifteen minutes later to tell me he was surprised that I did not want a bed and the necessary furnishings.

"For," he added, "if you've got an idea that you were put here for only one night, you're sadly mistaken."

"Bring me everything that you think necessary."

"Where shall I go for your belongings? Here's pencil and paper. Give me full instructions."

In writing I indicated where he could find my shirts, stockings, wearing apparel of all kinds, then I noted down the books which Messergrande had taken from me, and added a request for paper, pens, etc. The oaf did not know how to read, so I ran over the list, which of course was to be shown to the secretary of the inquisition.

"You'd better erase half of that," he said. "You can't have the books, paper, pens, mirror, nor razor. And now give me some money to buy your dinner."

I had three sequins. I gave him one and he went out. He was an hour serving seven other prisoners in this same section of the building, so widely were they separated to prevent communication.

Toward midday the jailer reappeared, followed by five turnkeys who acted as domestics to the prisoners of state. He brought in my dinner and some furnishings for my cell. The turnkeys placed the bed in the alcove and set my dinner on a little table along with my table service, consisting of an ivory spoon, because forks, knives, or any sharp implements were prohibited.

"Order what you want to eat tomorrow," he said, "for I can come here only once a day, at sunrise. The illustrious signor secretary ordered me to tell you that he will send you approved books, but that those you asked for are forbidden."

"Thank him for the favor he has done me of putting me alone."

"I will do as you wish, but it won't help you to go cracking jokes like that."

"I am not joking. I think it is much better to be alone than to be associated with scoundrels."

"Scoundrels, signor! You shock me. We have only honest men here, though they have had to be separated from society for reasons known only to the illustrious inquisitors. You have been put alone to punish you more—and you want me to convey your thanks?"

"Oh, I did not understand."

After the jailer had gone I placed my table close to the door to have a bit of light, then I sat down to dine. But all I could swallow was a few spoonfuls of soup. After I had fasted nearly forty-eight hours no wonder I was nauseated. I passed the day in my armchair, without rancor, wondering, resignedly, what kind of books would be graciously sent me.

I did not close an eye all night. The rats were making a horrible racket and every quarter of an hour there came the deafening boom of the bell of Saint Mark, which sounded as if it were right in my cell. I doubt whether the majority of my readers have any idea of the greatest of my torments, the thousands of fleas rioting over my whole body. These little insects sucked my blood with an indescribable rapacity, and their incessant biting gave me convulsions, caused me spasmodic contractions, poisoned my blood.

At peep of dawn the jailer—Lorenzo was his name—appeared, and had the turnkeys make my bed and sweep and scrub. One of the myrmidons brought me water to wash with. I wanted to go out into the garret, but Lorenzo told me this was not permitted.

I lived from day to day. Each night I hugged the delusion that the following day would see me a free man, and every morning I was undeceived. I took it into my poor head that infallibly I should be liberated the first of October, the day on which the new inquisitors would be inaugurated. According to this fine calculation my detention was only for the duration of the present inquisition, and that was why I had never been visited by the secretary, who otherwise would certainly have had to interrogate me and convict me and announce my sentence. Reasonable because natural, but false because this was the Piombi where the natural does not exist.

The last of September I passed a sleepless night in my extreme impatience to see the new day appear, so sure did I feel that I was to recover my liberty. The reign of the scoundrels who had imprisoned me was expiring, but when day dawned Lorenzo came as usual and announced no change. For nearly a week I was in a rage of despair. Then I concluded that for reasons impossible to determine I was to spend the rest of my life in the Piombi. Frightful. But I merely laughed. I need remain in servitude no very long time. I would succeed in escaping or getting killed.

At the beginning of November I formed seriously the project of escaping, by force, from a place where I was kept by force, and this thought became my sole idea.

One day while the turnkeys were scrubbing my cell I was standing in the garret. Looking up I saw the beam, without being dislodged, move slowly toward the right, then in a series of compensating movements, slow and intermittent, relapse into its former position. Having at the same moment lost my balance I realized that there had been an earthquake. Lorenzo and the turnkeys, coming out of my cell at that moment, said that they had felt the floor shake. Four or five seconds later there was another tremor and I could not keep from crying, *"Un altra, un altra, grand Dio, ma piu forte!"* (Again, again, great God, but harder!)

The turnkeys, frightened by what seemed to them the impiety of a desperate madman, fled in horror. After their departure I reflected that I was calculating the overthrow of the doge's palace as compatible with the recovery of my liberty. The collapse of this immense edifice must land me dead or alive in the place Saint Mark, where at the worst I should be crushed beneath the enormous mass of the ruins. In a situation similar to mine one sets liberty above all things and life at nought or at little. Truth to tell, my mind was beginning to be affected.

The oscillation of the doge's palace was an aftermath of the earthquake which destroyed Lisbon.

That the reader may understand my escape from such a place as the Piombi I must make him acquainted with the locality. The Piombi, where state prisoners are kept, is the garret of the doge's palace, and is called Piombi, "Leads," because of the great plates of this metal covering the roof. The only access is through the palace portals, over the "bridge of sighs," of which I have spoken, then through the room where the state inquisitors assemble. Only the secretary has the keys, which he entrusts to the jailer only during the short time, early in the morning, necessary for ministering to the needs of the prisoners. This visit is made at the break of day, because later the turnkeys coming and going would be a disagreeable sight to those who have business to transact with the chiefs of the council of ten. The only way to the prison leads through the room, called the *Bussola*, where the council meets.

The prison is divided into sections by the supports of the roof. On the side of the prison facing west there are three sections, and I was in one of these; on the side facing east there are four. The roof on the west side drains into a courtyard. From the eastern roof there is a gutter which drops perpendicularly into the canal called the *rio di Palazzo*. On that side the cells are quite airy and one can stand erect in them, as was not the case in my prison, known as the Trave on account of the enormous beam cutting off the light. The floor of my cell was directly above the ceiling of the room in which the inquisitors assemble at night after the day session of the council of ten, of which all three are members.

Knowing the locality perfectly and being well acquainted with the uniform habits of the inquisitors, I saw that I could hope to escape only by piercing the floor, but how was I to get instruments brought into a place where any communication from the outside world, whether visit or letter, was forbidden? To corrupt a turnkey I should have needed a great deal of money, and I had none. Supposing the jailer and two turnkeys should pemit me to strangle them, for I had no other weapons than my hands, there was still a third turnkey on guard before the gallery door which opened only for a comrade who had the pass word. In spite of all the obstacles my sole thought was still of flight.

At last I obtained permission to spend half an hour every day in the garret. I thus got some needed exercise and chanced, incidentally, on what was to bring about my escape eleven long months later. In the corner of this rat run I saw a quantity of old utensils scattered about the floor to right and left of two great chests. Among other miscellaneous objects were a waming-pan, a kettle, a fire shovel, tongs, some old candle sticks, and—a syringe! I wondered what specially privileged prisoner had had the use of these.

What interested me most was a straight iron bar as thick as your thumb and about twenty inches long. I touched nothing, for I had as yet no definite project, but now in the course of my daily turn about the garret I began to examine the rubbish heap more attentively. One of the chests was filled with good writing paper, cardboard, uncut quills, and balls of cord. The other chest was nailed shut. A piece of polished black marble an inch thick, six inches long, and three inches wide, caught my eye. I picked the thing up without quite knowing what I should do with it, and concealed it in my prison, taking care to cover it with my shirts.

New Year's day 1756 I received some presents. Lorenzo brought me a dressing gown trimmed with fox fur, a silk coverlet warmly padded, and a bearskin laprobe. I received them with joy, for the cold was now as intolerable as the heat had been in August. He told me from the secretary that I had at my disposal six sequins a month, with which I might buy whatever books I pleased, and even the banned Leyden Gazette. The presents were from Signor Bragadin, who had also used his influence to procure me the dispensation in the choice of books. I asked Lorenzo for a scrap of paper and a pencil and wrote, "I am grateful to the generous tribunal and the virtuous Signor Bragadin."

Lorenzo told me that Signor Bragadin had presented himself before the three inquisitors with tears in his eyes, and prostrating himself had begged the mercy of having this mark of his constant love brought to me if I was still among the living. The inquisitors had been too deeply moved to refuse.

I immediately wrote out the titles of the books I wanted. One fine morning while walking in my garret I looked long and thoughtfully at the bar of which I have spoken. It would make a perfect offensive and defensive weapon. I picked it up and brought it, hidden under my dressing gown, into my cell. As soon as I was alone I took my piece of black marble and began to rub the bar with it. It was an excellent whetstone and in no very great while I had made considerable impression.

I used saliva in the place of oil and worked a week filing the end of the bar pyramidally into eight facets, each an inch and a half long, terminating in a perfect point. I thus procured a stylus as nicely proportioned as if it had just come from the tool maker's. My first care was to hide it where even the most thorough search would fail to reveal it. My choice finally fell upon my armchair.

I was certain that the chamber under my cell could be no other than the one in which I had confronted Signor Cavalli. I knew this chamber was opened every morning and I did not doubt that when I had bored through the floor I could let myself down by a rope plaited from bed sheets and made fast to the bedstead. I would remain hidden under the great table of the tribunal, and in the morning as soon as the door was opened I would come forth and before I could be followed I should have reached a place of safety. I reflected that there would probably be a guard in this chamber, but my stylus should soon rid me of him. The floor might be double, in which case I should get into difficulties. I might then be two months in breaking through, and how was I to keep the turnkeys from sweeping during all that time? If I simply told them not to, I should arouse suspicion, because I had hitherto been very particular about requiring this service every day in an endeavor to deliver myself from the fleas.

I began by alleging no excuse. Lorenzo became inquisitive. I pretended that the dust made me cough so violently that I feared to injure myself.

"I'll have them scrubbed," he said.

"Worse and worse, signor Lorenzo, for the dampness would surely give me pneumonia."

But I did not dare yet to start work. After another week the brute ordered his myrmidons to sweep. He had the bed carried into the garret and on pretext of looking for dirt he lighted a candle. Obviously the rascal was aware that something was up. I feigned complete indifference, and far from renouncing my project I was pondering how I might carry it through.

Next morning I pricked my finger and staining my handkerchief with the blood I awaited Lorenzo in bed. As soon as he arrived I told him I had had so violent a cough that I had broken a blood vessel and must see a doctor. The doctor came and wrote out a prescription. I told him Lorenzo was the cause of my disaster because he positively would sweep. The doctor reproached him, and as if on instructions from me, began to tell us of a young man who had just died from inhaling dust stirred up by sweeping. Lorenzo swore by all the gods he had only meant to do me a service, and promised that this should not happen again. I laughed within myself, for the doctor could not have done better even if I had given him the word. The turnkeys present were overjoyed and promised faithfully to sweep only the cells of prisoners who provoked them and ill treated them.

When the doctor was gone Lorenzo asked my pardon and assured me that all the other prisoners were in the best of health, although he had their cells swept regularly.

"But I must quit endangering their lives. You know I consider them all as my children."

The long winter nights were unspeakably tedious, for I was obliged to pass nineteen mortal hours in the dark. On the cloudy days which in Venice are not rare, the light from the window was not strong enough to read by. The possession of a miserable kitchen lamp would have rendered me happy, but how was I to go about procuring such a treasure?

I itemized the raw materials necessary to make a lamp. I needed a reservoir, wicks, oil, flint, steel, tinder, and matches. For a container I could use the porringer in which my eggs were cooked. Pretending that ordinary oil disagreed with me I had the jailer bring me some Lucca salad oil. My cotton counterpane provided wicks. Feigning a troublesome toothache I told Lorenzo that I had to have some pumice stone. As he did not know what that was I said a gun flint would do. If soaked all day in vinegar and at the end of that time applied to the tooth it would stop the ache.

Lorenzo said, "Well, you've got plenty of vinegar," and tossed me three or four flints which he had in his pocket.

My stout steel belt buckle would do to strike the spark from the flint. Remained only the sulphur and the tinder. I was at my wits' end. Fortune finally came to my aid.

I had had a kind of rash which in drying up had left red spots on my arms that itched at times. I got Lorenzo to ask the doctor the remedy. In a note which had had to pass the secretary the doctor advised: "Fast a day and take four ounces of sweet almond oil, and the skin will heal. Or apply an ointment of flour of brimstone, but the latter is dangerous."

"Damn the danger," I said to Lorenzo. "Buy me the ointment. Or bring me some sulphur and I'll make the ointment myself. Have you any matches? Give me some."

He had a few in his pocket and handed them over.

Now for several hours I racked my brains trying to think of something that would serve as tinder. I had no pretext for wheedling any out of Lorenzo. I suddenly remembered that I had told my tailor to put some touchwood under the armpits of my coat to keep the perspiration from spoiling the goods. This coat, worn only once, was before me. My heart palpitated. The tailor might not have followed instructions. I wavered between hope and fear. I had only to take a step to find out, but the step was decisive, and I dared not move. Finally I approached, and feeling myself unworthy of this boon I fell on my knees and prayed God fervently that the tailor might not have disregarded my order. After this piteous prayer I took the coat, ripped open the lining, and found—the touchwood. I was delirious with joy.

The materials were now at hand and I soon had a lamp. Consider the satisfaction I felt at having, so to speak, created light in the lap of darkness. Consider too the satisfaction of transgressing the orders of my infamous oppressors. No more night for me—no more salad, either. I am very fond of salad, but I did not regret the sacrifice.

I fixed on the first Monday in Lent as the day on which to begin the difficult operation of boring through the floor. I rightly judged that the disorders of the carnival would bring a good many new arrivals, and consequently the turnkeys would be in and out all the time.

FLIGHT FROM THE PIOMBI

Sunday at noon I heard the creaking of the bolts and saw Lorenzo making for my cell followed by a fat man whom I recognized as the Jew Gabriel Scholon, notorious for his dexterity in ruining the young spendthrifts who came to him for money.

A fortnight after Easter I was delivered of my unwelcome cellmate, and now I began to work in earnest. I first drew my bed aside and after lighting the lamp I threw myself flat on my belly with my stylus in my hand and a napkin at my side to collect the chips as I chiseled away at the plank. At first the bits of wood I detached were no bigger than a grain of wheat, but soon I was able to drive deeper. After six hours' work I knotted my napkin and put it aside to be emptied in the morning behind the heap of papers in the garret. Then I put my bed back in place.

Next day I got through the upper plank, which I found to be two inches thick, and started on the second beneath. It took me three weeks to cut through three layers of boarding, and then I thought myself lost, for I was confronted by a stratum of marble mosaic. My stylus made no impression on the cement and I was completely discouraged. Then I remembered that according to Livy, Hannibal in crossing the Alps chopped his way through rocks that he had first had softened with vinegar. I surmised that Hannibal had used not *acetum,* but *aceta,* which in the Latin of Padua might very well be the same as *ascia.* Besides, who can guarantee the accuracy of a copyist? I did none the less empty a bottle of vinegar into the cavity, and next day, whether because of the treatment or of the renewed strength I was able to apply to the work after a night's repose, I began to crumble the mosaic to pieces.

The hole was now ten inches deep, and I was having difficulty getting a prise on my chisel. My work was completed the 23rd of August. I had seen daylight from the inquisitorial chamber before, but had had to dig around one of the beams of the ceiling.

At midnight precisely I heard the bolts creaking. I thought

death was upon me. I could feel my heart beating three or four inches above the spot where this organ is known to be located. Giving myself up for lost I threw myself into my armchair and waited. Lorenzo, entering the garret and sticking his head through the grating cried out to me in joyous tones, "Congratulations, signor, on the good news I bring you!"

Thinking at first that he was announcing my release—for what else could be good news?—I trembled. I knew that the discovery of the hole would have meant the revocation of my pardon. Lorenzo entered and told me to follow him.

"Wait until I dress."

"No need of that. You are only moving from this dark old cell to another one that is light and quite new. You'll have two windows, through which you can see the half of Venice, and you'll be able to stand up straight."

This was too much. I felt faint.

"Give me some vinegar," I said, "and go and tell the illustrious secretary that I thank the tribunal for this mercy and that I supplicate them to leave me here."

"Signor! have you gone mad? They wish to take you out of hell to put you into heaven, and you refuse! Come, come, you must obey. Rise. I will give you my arm, and I'll have your books and clothes brought down later."

I was soon inside my new cell. Lorenzo had had my armchair placed there before me, and he now went away to see about the rest of my effects.

I heard precipate steps, and soon the jailer was before me, grimacing and foaming with rage, and blaspheming God and all the saints. He began by ordering me to hand over the axe and the tools with which I had cut through the floor, then he demanded which of the turnkeys I had bribed to smuggle them in to me. I coolly told him I did not know what he was talking about. At this response he ordered his villains to search me. Rising with a resolute air I ripped open my shirt and said menacingly, "Do your duty!" but not one of them touched me.

They examined my mattress, gutted the straw tick, and ran their hands over the cushions of the armchair. They found nothing.

"You think you can put us off by keeping still?" Lorenzo roared. "We shall find the means of making you speak."

"If I am taken before the torturers," I replied, "I shall tell them that you supplied me with everything I used, and that you have it now."

This threat made his followers smile. Obviously he was not beloved. He stamped and fumed and tore his hair and rushed out like one possessed. His henchmen returned and brought me all my belongings with the exception of my stone and my lamp. I did wish they could have brought the hole.

After this the jailer tried to conciliate me. He was a family man and valued his neck.

I told him to buy me the works of Maffei. This expense displeased him, though he did not dare say so. He was making a good profit by economizing with my allowance. He asked me what I wanted with more books since I already had so many.

"I've read them all," I said, "I want something new."

"There is a prisoner here who will lend you books if you are willing to lend him yours. You can save money that way."

"I don't suppose he has anything but novels, and I don't like them."

"They are all scientific books. If you think you are the only smart man here you're mistaken."

"All right. Here is a book which I will lend your smart man. Let us see what he will send me in return."

I had given him the *Rationarium* of Petau. Five minutes later he brought me the first volume of Wolff. I was satisfied with the exchange and to Lorenzo's delight I said I could get along without Maffei. I was thinking less of the advantage of having something intelligent to read than of the opportunity for carrying on correspondence with a fellow captive who might second me in my project of flight. I opened the book the minute Lorenzo had gone. I was agreeably surprised when I found written on a blank page a smooth paraphrase in six verses of these words of Seneca, *Calamitosus est animus futuri anxius.** I made six others on the spur of the moment, and here is the expedient to which I had recourse in transcribing them. I had let the nail of my little finger grow very long to serve me as an ear pick. I cut it to a point and made a pen of it. I had no ink and was thinking of pricking my finger and writing with my blood when I methought me that the ooze of the walls would do just as well—and I certainly had plenty of it. Besides the six verses I wrote a catalogue of my little library and placed it in the back of the volume of Wolff.

It is worth knowing that in Italy books are generally bound in parchment and in such a manner that when a book is open the back forms a pocket. On the title page I wrote, *Latet.*** I was impatient to get the correspondence under way, so when Lorenzo appeared I told him I had read the book and that I begged the prisoner to send me another.

In the second volume of Wolff I found a note containing these words:

"We may congratulate ourselves that the avarice of an ignorant jailer has secured to us a privilege unexampled in this place. There are two of us. The writer is Marino Balbi, a monk of noble birth. My companion is the count Andrea Asquino d'Udine of Friuli. He charges me to let you know that all the books he possesses, a list of which is herewith enclosed, are at your service."

* Worry about the future brings calamity.
** Something hidden.

FLIGHT FROM THE PIOMBI

After glancing over the catalogue I wrote who I was, how I had been arrested for what crime I knew not, and how I hoped soon to be free myself. Balbi replied in sixteen pages, giving me the history of all his misfortunes. He had been imprisoned four years ago because he had had the favors of three young girls, each of whom had borne him a child. In perfectly good faith he had successively had the brats baptized under his name. The first time he had been let off with a reprimand from his abbot, the second time he had been threatened with excommunication, and the third time long suffering Mother Church had had him locked up. The abbot sent him his dinner every morning. He told me in his letter that the abbot and the tribunal were tyrants but had no authority over his conscience and that nothing could stifle the voice of nature which spoke to him in behalf of these innocent creatures. He finished with these words: "My abbot is in no danger of erring as I have done. He cares only for choir boys."

I knew my man. Eccentric, sensual, thoughtless, ungrateful. Out in the world I should not have responded to a man of this character, but in the Piombi I had to ally myself with whomever I could. I found in the back of the volume pencils, pens, and paper, which put me in a position to write at my ease.

I was starting to answer when there came to me a suspicion that this correspondence might be a ruse of Lorenzo's to make me tell who had furnished me with instruments and what I had done with them. I wrote that I had made the opening with a stout knife which was now hidden on the sill of the corridor window. My mind was soon set at rest, because Lorenzo after three days had not visited the window sill, as he would not have failed to do had the letter been intercepted.

When my suspicions had been completely dissipated I reasoned thus, "I must obtain liberty at any price. I have an excellent boring tool but I can not possibly use it, because every morning they sound the wall of my cell by striking on it with a bar. They don't tap the ceiling, though. So if I am to get out of here it is through the ceiling that I shall have to make my opening. I cannot bore from beneath, for it is not the affair of a day. I need an aid. He can escape with me."

I had no embarrassment of choice. The monk was thirty-eight years old, and though he was not rich in good sense I thought the love of liberty, that most imperative of the soul's demands, would give him enough resolution to execute the instructions I should give him. I must begin by taking him completely into my confidence.

I wrote to him that I had a pointed iron bar twenty inches long, that by means of this instrument he should pierce the ceiling of his cell, penetrate the wall which separated us, and then break through the floor over the ceiling of my cell.

"When we have got that far your work will be over and mine will begin. I will set you and Count Asquino free. Meanwhile have Lorenzo get you about forty saints' pictures, big enough to paper the entire surface of your cell. These religious images will arouse no suspicion in Lorenzo and they will serve to cover the opening which you will make in the ceiling. If you ask me why I do not do this, I must reply that I cannot because I am held suspect."

I told Lorenzo to buy me a folio Bible which had just appeared. It comprised the Vulgate and the Septuagint. I hoped to be able to place my stylus in the back of the binding of this great volume to be smuggled to the monk, but when I received the folio I saw that it was shorter than the bar by two inches.

This is what I did. I told Lorenzo that I wished to celebrate St. Michael's day by sending a plate of macaroni and cheese to the person who had been so kind as to lend me books. I should like to prepare the dish myself. Lorenzo told me the signor wanted to read the big book that cost three sequins. This was preconcerted.

"Very well," I told him, "I will send it along with the macaroni. Only, bring me the biggest plate you have in the house, for I mean to do this on a grand scale."

He promised me as big a plate as I could wish. I wrapped my bar in paper and placed it in the back of the Bible, taking care that one end should protrude no further than the other did. I was sure that Lorenzo in carrying the Bible under a great dish of macaroni would not look at the extremities, because he would have his attention concentrated on the edges of the dish to keep from spilling grease on the book. I notified Father Balbi of everything, recommending that he be adroit in handling the plate and take care above all to receive the two objects together and not one after the other.

On the morning designated, Lorenzo came earlier than usual with a sauce pan full of boiling hot macaroni and all the ingredients necessary for the seasoning. I melted a quantity of butter and after coiling the macaroni around the plate I lavished on the butter until the strands were fairly afloat. The platter was enormous, a good deal wider than the book on which I had set it. All this was done at the door of my cell with Lorenzo outside.

He said he had better carry the plate in first and come back after the book, but I said that would spoil the gift. It must all go together. He was sorry I had used so much butter and said, with a wry face, that he was not responsible for the damage.

I watched him until he was inside the vestibule of the other cell. The monk blew his nose three times as a signal that all was safely arrived in port, and Lorenzo came a moment later to confirm what I already knew.

Balbi set to work without delay. The 16th of October at the tenth hour, while I was occupied in translating an ode of Horace, I heard steps overhead and three light raps, the signal agreed upon to assure us that we had made no miscalculation. He worked all day and next morning wrote me, "The excavation is so far advanced that I shall need only about four hours to finish."

The same day, a Monday, at the twenty-first hour, while Father Balbi was working, I heard sounds at the door of the hall adjoining my cell. I felt my blood run cold, but I had the presence of mind to rap twice, our signal of alarm, at which Balbi was to get back into his cell and put everything in order. Less than a minute later Lorenzo opened my door and begged my pardon for giving me the company of a very hard case. This was a man of forty or fifty, little, thin, ugly, ill-dressed, wearing a round black wig. Two guards were loosing his bonds while I examined him. Lorenzo brought him a pallet, told him the tribunal granted him ten soldi a day, then locked us up together.

He began to narrate a host of miracles, to which I listened with the patience of an angel. I asked if he had dined. He said he was starving. I gave him all I had and he devoured rather than ate, drank all my wine, and as soon as he had become drunk he began to weep and then to talk about anything and everything quite incoherently.

He was a police spy, evidently imprisoned for calumny. He took an inordinate pride in his profession and boasted that he would sacrifice his own father to duty. Intensely ignorant and bestially superstitious, this Judas was not quite right in his mind. His name was Francesco Soradaci.

I wrote at night, as I had taught myself to do, to inform Balbi of this unfortunate turn of affairs and to tell him to discontinue work until I gave him the word.

After Soradaci had twice been before the secretary and twice returned I saw that I should not soon be rid of him. I had Lorenzo bring me crucifixes and a couple of bottles of holy water. Then I furiously taxed the loathsome creature with having attempted to betray me to the tribunal. I heaped upon him terrifying maledictions the while. All day I lay on my bed motionless, speechless, pretending not to hear the cries and protestations of my infamous cell mate. I was playing a rôle in the induction to a comedy which I now had completely blocked out in my mind. That night I wrote Balbi to come at the nineteenth hour, not a minute earlier nor later, finish the excavation, and to work four hours, not a minute more.

"Our liberty," I told him, "depends on this rigid observance. However, you have nothing to fear."

This was the 25th of October, and the time during which I must execute or forever abandon my project was not far distant. The state inquisitors, the secretary as well, went every year to spend the first three days of November in some village on the mainland. Lorenzo, profiting by the absence of his masters, would not fail to get drunk every night, and sleeping longer than usual he would not appear in the Piombi till late. I felt that prudence required me to choose this time for my escape, which would thus not be noticed until nearly noon.

I was in the state of mind in which one seeks in a verse of Virgil or of the Bible fatidic confirmation in his hazardous undertaking. I took the *Orlando furioso* of Messer Ludovico Ariosto. My heart beat as rapidly as if I really had implicit faith in this oracle. I opened the book, thumbed it at random, looked down, and read:

Fra il fin d'ottobre e il capo di novembre.

"Between the end of October and the beginning of November" there is only the instant of midnight, and it was precisely on the stroke of midnight October 31st that—but you shall see. Let this circumstance instruct the reader who has not yet become too knowing that many remarkable deeds would never have been accomplished if they had not first been prophesied.

I put in the whole morning working on the fanaticism of Soradaci. I told him to come and have something to eat. The traitor was in bed pretending to be ill. He would not have dared approach me if I had not called him. He rose and groveling toward me, he kissed my feet, wept great scalding tears, and told me that unless I withdrew my curse he would surely die within the day, for he already felt the effects of the vengeance of the Holy Virgin which I had called down on him. My care was now to make him hope for mercy. First I must feed him and get him drunk.

With face transfigured I said, "I announce good tidings of great joy. The Virgin has appeared to me in a vision and ordered me to forgive you. You shall not die but be delivered out of prison along with me. 'Soradaci,' said Our Lady, 'is piously devout in telling his rosary. You must forgive him, and in recompense for your generosity I will order one of my angels to assume the form of a human being and descend from heaven to break the roof of your prison and to free you within five or six days. This angel will begin his work at the nineteenth hour precisely and work until half an hour before sunset, for he must return to heaven in the light of day. When you issue forth accompanied by my angel you must lead Soradaci to liberty with you and take care of him, on condition that he renounce his nefarious calling of spy. Declare to him my will.' At these words the Virgin disappeared and I woke."

Controlling my mirth and keeping my sanctified expression, I scrutinized the traitor's face. He was stupefied. I took my book of hours, sprinkled the cell with holy water, and pretended to pray before the image of the Virgin, which I kissed from time to time.

An hour before the time fixed for the miraculous visitation I had dinner. I took nothing but water, and Soradaci drank all the wine and made his dessert on garlic. This was his favorite dish, a veritable confection for him, and served not ill to increase his excitability. When I heard the first strokes of the nineteenth hour I threw myself on my knees, ordering him in a terrible voice to do the same. He obeyed me with a frightened look in his eye. When

I heard the slight noise of Balbi passing through the wall, I said, "The angel is come," and lying prone I gave Soradaci a vigorous whack to force him to assume the same posture. Balbi made a great noise breaking the floor, and for a quarter of an hour I lay prone, uncomfortable as I was. In any other situation I should have laughed heartily at the sight of that beast, scared motionless, but now I did not laugh, for I could not forget my meritorious intention of frightening him into stark, staring madness. I rose to a kneeling posture, permitting him to imitate me, and I spent three hours and a half leading him in an antiphony. Every once in a while he fell asleep, more on account of the fatigue of his position than of the monotony of the prayer, but he never interrupted me. Sometimes he hazarded a furtive glance at the ceiling and with stupefaction written large on his countenance he wagged his head toward the image of the Virgin; all of which was comic in the last degree. When I heard the clock strike half past the twenty-third hour I said in solemn tones, "Prostrate yourself, the angel is ascending."

Balbi went back into his cell and we heard no more. Rising, fixing the wretch with my gaze, I saw that he was perturbed, indeed terrified. I was exultant. I amused myself for a moment talking with him to see how he would account for what had taken place. He wept floods of tears, and his conjectures were extravagant beyond words, for his ideas had neither substance nor sequence.

I saw Lorenzo for the last time the morning of the 31st of October. I gave him the book containing the note telling Balbi to come at the seventeenth hour to break through the ceiling. I could now anticipate nothing untoward. Lorenzo himself had told me that the inquisitors and the secretary had gone to the country. Hence no new arrival could be lodged on me, and I had Soradaci at my mercy.

After Lorenzo had gone I told Soradaci that the angel would come at the seventeenth hour and open the ceiling of our cell.

"He will bring scissors," I said, "and you shall trim his beard and mine."

"Will the angel have a beard?"

"Yes, as you shall see. After this operation we shall climb out, break through the palace roof, and descend into the place Saint Mark, and from there we shall go to Germany."

He did not answer. He dined alone. My mind and heart were too full to permit me to eat. I had not even been able to sleep.

The clock struck. The angel appeared. Soradaci would have prostrated himself, but I told him it was unnecessary. In three minutes the excavation was made, a chunk of timber fell at our feet, and Balbi dropped into my arms.

"Your labors are done," said I, "now mine begin."

We embraced and he gave me my bar and a pair of scissors. I told Soradaci to clip our beards. It was impossible to keep from laughing at this besotted creature. He gaped at the angel, who, to be sure, looked more like a devil. Though quite beside himself, Soradaci played the barber to perfection.

Impatient to reconnoiter, I told the monk to stay with Soradaci, whom I would not leave alone, and out I went. I found the hole in the wall narrow but succeeded in getting through. I was over the count's cell. I entered and cordially embraced the estimable old man. I saw that he was in no physical condition to surmount the difficulties of a flight across slippery lead-covered roofs which sloped at a sharp angle. He asked me what my plan was and told me he thought I was acting somewhat rashly.

"I ask only," I said, "to go forward to liberty or death."

"If you think," said he, pressing my hand, "to pierce the roof and make your way across the leads, and then get down somehow, I do not see how you can succeed unless you have wings. As I have not the temerity to accompany you, I shall remain here and pray God for your safety."

I went up under the main roof, keeping as close as I could to where the eaves ought to be. Where the angle of roof and joist was narrowest I perched myself on a rafter. I tapped the timbers with the end of my bar and had the luck to find them half rotten. At every stroke the woodwork crumbled and fell in dust about me. Seeing that I could surely make a big enough hole in less than an hour I returned to my cell and was four hours cutting up sheets, covers, mattress, and tick, and plaiting them into ropes. I was careful to make the knots myself, and to assure myself of their firmness, for a single loose knot might cost our lives. A leader worthy of success could not think of delegating such an important task to unreliable subordinates.

When the rope, about a hundred yards in all, was made, I bundled up my coat, mantle, shirts, stockings, and handkerchiefs, and with my two confederates passed into the count's cell. The good man first congratulated Soradaci on having a cell mate like me who was so soon to restore his liberty. Soradaci's blank look made me laugh. I exerted no effort to restrain myself, for I had cast aside my tedious rôle of Tartufe. The villain was obviously convinced that I had deceived him, but he could make nothing of it. He could not see how I had got word to the pretended angel to come and go at fixed hours. He listened attentively, and, I suspected, hopefully, as the count warned us that we were going forward to our doom.

I told the monk to get his bundle ready while I went and knocked a hole through the eaves.

At the second hour after sunset I had, unaided, effected an opening. I had pulverized the timbers and the fracture was twice as big as necessary. I could get at the lead plate entire. I could not pry it up alone because it was riveted. The monk helped me, and by forcing the bar in between the gutter and the plate I succeeded in loosening the plate, then by putting our shoulders to it we bent it up high enough to permit our bodies to pass. Sticking my head through the hole I saw to my great disappointment that there was a bright new moon in its first quarter. That was a mischance to be endured with patience. We must wait until the moon had gone to illuminate the antipodes. On such a superb night the whole fashionable world would be promenading in the place Saint Mark. I must not expose myself on the roof because my shadow lengthening out over the square would attract attention and betray me to Messergrande and his myrmidons, the only police in Venice.

The moon would set at the fifth hour and the sun would rise at half past the thirteenth. We should have seven hours of perfect obscurity in which to act, and though the task was hard, seven hours was time enough.

I told Balbi we might spend three hours talking with Count Asquino.

"Go first and tell him I want him to lend me thirty sequins. I've absolutely got to have them. They're as necessary as my crow bar."

He went to execute the commission. Five minutes later he came back to tell me to go myself, that the count wanted to speak to me alone.

The poor old man began by telling me gently that I did not need money to get over the roof, that he had no money anyway but did have a large family, that if he gave me money it would be thrown away, for I must inevitably perish; and he added a host of futilities of the same sort to disguise his avarice. My reply took half an hour. My reasons were excellent, but of the kind which since the world began have ever failed of effect against this most obstinate of the passions. It was a case for *Nolenti baculus*,* but I was not cruel enough to use violence on an unfortunate old man. I finally told him that if he would fly with me I would carry him on my shoulders as Aeneas did Anchises, but that if he meant to stay behind and pray for us his prayer would have no value in the sight of God

* The rod for him who refuses.

when he refused to back it up with the least of material aids.

He responded by bursting into tears. I was moved. He asked if two sequins would be enough. I told him I needed everything I could get. He gave them to me, begging me to give them back if after I had made a tour of inspection about the roofs I saw that the wisest course would be to return to my cell. I promised, somewhat surprised that he should think me capable of turning back.

I called my companions and we placed all our equipment up under the eaves. I divided the hundred yards of rope I had prepared, then we returned and spent two hours chatting, recalling, not unpleasantly, the vicissitudes of our enterprise. The first proof Balbi gave me of his noble character was his repeated complaint that I had deceived him, because I had assured him that my plan was perfected and safe, when it was nothing of the kind. He told me bluntly that if he had known how matters stood he would not have got me out of my cell. The count, with all the gravity of his threescore years and ten, also told me that the wisest thing I could do was to abandon a project which could not possibly succeed and would only jeopardize my life.

From time to time I put out my hands to see if Soradaci was still there, for he said never a word. I laughed as I wondered what he could have been revolving in his mind since he had had it made plain to him that I had deceived him. At half past the fourth hour I told him to go and see in what part of the sky the moon was. He obeyed, and coming back he told me that in an hour and a half it would no longer be visible, and that a thick mist was rising which would make the leads very slippery.

"Just as long," I said, "as the mist is not oil, I do not care. Make your cloak into a bundle and take your equal share of the rope."

As I spoke I was joyously surprised to find him throwing his arms about my knees, kissing my hands, and weeping, supplicating, beseeching me not to lead him to his death.

"I am sure," he said, "to fall into the canal. I can't be of any use to you. Leave me here and I'll spend the whole night praying St. Francis for you. Kill me now if you must, for you shall never get my own consent to follow you."

The dolt did not know that he was filling my cup of happiness to overflowing.

"You are right," I said. "You may stay here, but only on condition that you invoke your saint. And now go and get all my books. I want to give them to the count."

Great must have been his relief. He obeyed without a word.

My books were worth at least a hundred ecus. The count told me he would give them back to me when I returned.

"You will never see me again," I replied. "You may rely on that. These books will cover the loan you have made me. As for that scoundrel I am glad he hasn't the courage to follow me. He would be a vexatious encumbrance. Moreover, he isn't worthy to share with Balbi and myself the honor of such a glorious escape."

"True," said the count. "I only hope that tomorrow he shall not have cause to felicitate himself."

But it was time to set forth. The moon was no longer in the sky. I fastened about Father Balbi's neck his half of the ropes over one shoulder and his bundle of clothes over the other. I did the same for myself, and both of us, in our waistcoats, with our hats on, went to the opening.

*E quindi uscimmo a rimirar le stelle.**

I came out first. Father Balbi followed. Soradaci, who had accompanied us as far as the opening under the eaves, was ordered to get the lead plate back into its normal shape and then go pray his Saint Francis. On all fours, I grasped my bar firmly and thrusting it in where plate joined plate I raised a kind of cleat at each suture.

* Thence issuing we beheld again the stars.

FLIGHT FROM THE PIOMBI

Successively gripping each cleat with my fingers I scrambled up to the summit of the roof. The monk was clinging with his right hand to the belt of my breeches. I was thus carrying and hauling at the same time, and that on a high-peaked roof made slippery by mist.

Halfway in this perilous climb the monk told me to stop. One of his packages had become undone and fallen, but he thought it had not yet got past the ledge of the gutter. My first impulse was to give him a kick and send him after his bundle, but by the grace of God I had enough self-control to restrain myself. I asked him if it was the ropes he had lost. He said it was his wearing apparel, but that done up in them was a manuscript which he had found in the garrets of the Piombi and with which he expected to make his fortune. I told him that he must be resigned, that a single backward step might cost us our lives. The poor monk sighed, and with him clinging fast to my belt I continued to climb.

After struggling up over fifteen or sixteen plates with extreme difficulty we arrived at the peak of the roof. I sat down astride and Father Balbi followed suit. Back of us was the little island of San Giorgio Maggiore, and facing us, two hundred paces away, was the cathedral of Saint Mark with its many cupolas. Saint Mark is a part of the doge's palace, and is, properly speaking, only the doge's chapel. Certainly no monarch can flatter himself that he possesses a finer. I began by unburdening myself of my bundle and invited my companion to do the same. He placed his pile of rope under him the best he could. His hat was bothering him. He took it off, it twisted out of his hands, went rolling from plate to plate, cleared the gutter, and went to join his other effects in the canal.

If it had fallen to the left instead of to the right it would have landed in the courtyard of the palace, where the guards would have found it and immediately known that there must be somebody on the roof.

After looking about me for several minutes I told the monk to stay there without moving until I returned. With bar in hand I slid along astride of the roof peak. I spent almost an hour reconnoitering thoroughly but vainly. Nowhere in the eaves was there anything to which I could make fast a rope's end. I was in the greatest perplexity. My gaze finally rested on a dormer window on the side toward the canal and about two-thirds of the way down the slope. It was far enough from the place I had left to make me think that the attic which it lighted did not belong to the prison enclosure. The garret, inhabited or not, would be that of some apartment of the palace. At break of day I could probably find a door open. I was morally certain that the palace servants, even those attached to the doge's family, would, if they discovered us, hasten to facilitate our flight. Even if they recognized us as the greatest of sinners against the state they would not deliver us up to justice, so horrible was the inquisition in the eyes of all.

I must have a look at the front of the dormer. Letting myself slide gently straight down, I soon found myself astride of the dormer roof. Gripping the eaves I craned my neck and managed to see a little grating behind which was a leaded window with square glass panes. The window did not bother me, but the grating, frail as it was, seemed to present an impassable obstacle. Without a file I should never get it away, and I had only my bar.

I was beginning to lose courage when the simplest and most natural thing in the world gave me new hope. The bell of Saint Mark sounded midnight at that instant,

Fra il fin d'ottobre e il capo di novembre.

The sound of the bell was like the voice of prophecy, telling me to act and promising me victory. Stretched out prone, craning my neck to see what I was doing, I inserted my bar into the casement and in a quarter of an hour had pried the grating off bodily. Placing it intact beside the sill I had no difficulty in breaking all the glass of the window, though the blood was now flowing freely from a gash in my left hand.

With the aid of my bar, following my previous method, I regained the pinnacle of the roof and made my way toward the place where I had left my companion. I found him frantic. He heaped upon me the grossest insults for having left him alone so long. He assured me he awaited only the seventh hour to return to prison.

"What did you think had become of me?"

"I supposed you had fallen down one of these precipices."

"And you insult me instead of greeting me with joy?"

"What in the world have you been doing all this time?"

"Follow me and I will show you."

Picking up my bundle I made my way toward the dormer. When we were where we could see it I gave Balbi an exact account of what I had done and consulted him as to ways and means of getting into the window and down to the room below. It was a simple matter for one of us, because the other could let him down with the rope, but I did not see how the second was to descend afterward. A rope could not be fastened to the fragile casement. A blind leap in the dark would probably result in broken limbs, for there was no knowing the distance of the window above the floor. To this prudent statement, pronounced in a tone of the most friendly concern, my brute responded, "Let me down at any rate, and when I am below you will have plenty of time to think of a way of following me."

I confess that in the first impulse of rage I was tempted to bury my stylus in his chest. My good angel restrained me and I did not vouchsafe a word to reproach him for his base selfishness. On the contrary, at once undoing my bundle of rope I fastened a cord about his armpits, and making him lie prone, feet downward, I paid out the rope and let him down to the roof of the dormer. I then told him to get his head and trunk into the window and brace himself with his elbows. When he was in I slid along the roof as I had previously done. Lying prone on top of the dormer I got a good grip on the rope and told the monk to let himself go without any fear. Landing on the floor of the garret he undid the rope. I drew it up and measuring I found that the height must be more than fifty feet. It was too far to leap. As for the monk, safe after spending two hours in a position far from reassuring, he called to me to throw down the ropes and he would take care of them. As may be imagined I gave no heed to this absurd proposal.

Not knowing what was to become of me and awaiting inspiration I climbed again to the peak. My gaze wandered toward a corner, in the shadow of a cupola, which I had not yet visited. I went over and saw a terrace-platform covered with lead plates and adjoining a great skylight closed by two shutters. There was a tub full of wet mortar, a trowel, and a ladder which I judged long enough to get me down to the garret room where my companion was.

My decision was quickly formed. Fastening my rope to the topmost rung I dragged the awkward object to where I wanted it. Then I had to go about getting this heavy twelve-fathom ladder into the window, and the difficulties which I encountered made me regret having deprived myself of the help of the monk.

I had poked the ladder up to the dormer, with a third of its length jutting out past the gutter. I slid along the dormer roof, dragged the ladder to my side, attached the end of my rope to the eighth rung, then I held the ladder on a level with the sill and made a strenuous effort to swing it into the broken window. I got it in as far as the fifth rung, and there it caught against the ceiling. No force in the world would have made it penetrate further without breaking either the roof or the ladder. There was no help for it but to raise the other end; thus tilted, the ladder would topple in of its own weight. I could have placed the ladder crosswise of the window and fastened a rope to it, and thus let myself down without danger, but then I could not have pulled it in after me, and in the morning it would have indicated to Lorenzo and the archers where perhaps we should still be.

I did not wish to lose by negligence the fruit of so many fatigues and perils, and I must, to obliterate all traces, get the ladder entirely inside. Having no one to help me I had to go out on the marble coping to raise the end of the ladder. This was so dangerous that but for prodigious luck I should have paid for my temerity with my life. I let go the rope without fear that the ladder, jammed as it was, would fall into the canal. Then, gripping my bar, I slid gently down beside the ladder, and lay prone with my toes braced against the marble ledge of the gutter. In this position I forced the ladder six inches upward and forward, and the reader can see that its weight was thus considerably diminished. It must yet go two feet higher and further. After that I was certain that from the dormer roof I could with my rope swing the ladder all the way in.

In order to give the necessary elevation I rose to my knees. The effort I made in lifting the ladder threw me off my balance so that all of a sudden I felt myself launched off the roof as far as my chest and digging into the ledge of the coping for dear life with my elbows. Frightful moment, the inconceivable horror of which makes me tremble even yet. Only the natural instinct of self-preservation made me thrust out my elbows to arrest my flight. Miraculously, I am tempted to say, I was preserved. I had happily nothing to fear for the ladder. It had been pushed in more than three feet and rendered immovable by the nearly fatal shove.

Poised on the gutter, positively by my wrists and my groin, I saw that by wriggling I could get first one knee then the other over the ledge, and thus be quite out of danger, but my troubles were not yet at an end. The effort caused me such a powerful muscular contraction that I was assailed by a paralyzing cramp. I remained perfectly motionless till it had passed away. Previous experience had taught me that this was the only remedy. Two minutes later, having gradually renewed the effort, I got my knees over the gutter and firmly planted against the ledge. As soon as I had recovered my breath I cautiously raised the ladder so that it was at a perfect balance. I took my bar again and making fingerholds in the leads I scrambled back to the dormer roof and now had no difficulty letting the ladder down. My companion received the end of it in his arms. Then I threw my bundles into the garret and climbed down. The monk caught me, deftly enough, and took care to pull away the ladder.

Arm in arm we set about inspecting the dark hole we had got into. It was about thirty paces long by about twenty wide. At one end we found a door barred with iron. That augured ill, but I seized the latch, it yielded to the pressure and the door opened. Trying to cross this new enclosure we bumped into a table surrounded by stools and armchairs. We groped about till we found the windows. We opened one and looked out. Nothing was to be seen by the light of the stars but the precipices between the cupolas. I did not for a moment entertain the thought of climbing down the wall. I merely wished to reconnoiter, for I could not recognize what part of the building I was in. I closed the window and we went out of the room and back to the place where we had left our baggage.

Exhausted beyond measure I keeled over on the floor, and placing the bundle of rope beneath my head, I sank into deep, sweet slumber. I slept three hours and a half. I was awakened by the expostulations of the monk, who was violently shaking me. He told me the twelfth hour had just sounded. He did not see how a man could go to sleep in a situation like ours.

As soon as I had cast my eyes about me I cried, "This place is not a prison, at any rate. There must be an exit easy to find."

Then we went to the end of the room opposite the iron door and in an out of the way corner I thought I recognized a door. I groped around and finally got my fingers into a keyhole. I inserted the point of my bar and after three or four twists the lock gave. We found ourselves in the archive chamber. I discovered a little stone staircase. At the bottom was another, yet another, and at the end I was confronted by a glazed door, which I opened. Now I was in a room which I knew well. It was the ducal chancery. I opened a window. I could easily have dropped to the ground, but then I should have found myself in the labyrinth of little courtyards surrounding the cathedral of Saint Mark. God preserve me!

Descending two more flights of stairs we were checked by a great door which was locked. At a glance I could see that without a battering ram or a charge of powder we could not get through. I sat down calmly, telling the monk he might as well do the same.

"My work is done," I said, "what follows is up to God or to Fortune.

"*'Abbia chi regge il ciel ruca del resto,*
"*'O la Fortuna, se non tocca a lui.'**

"I do not suppose the caretakers of the palace will come to sweep today nor tomorrow, as both are saints' days. If anyone does come I shall run out the moment the door opens, and you must follow right in my tracks, but if nobody comes I shall not stir, and if I starve to death, so much the worse for me."

I was frightfully bruised all over. Tearing up some handkerchiefs I bandaged myself the best I could. I put on my unworn dress coat, my white stockings, a lace-frilled shirt with two similar ones over it, put some stockings and handkerchiefs in my pockets, and tossed the rest into a corner, after throwing my mantle over the

---

* *"Let heaven's ruler care for what remains,*
Or Fortune, if it be not His concern."

shoulders of the monk. He looked as if he had stolen it. I must have presented the aspect of a gallant who having been to a ball had spent the rest of the night in a brothel and been ill used.

Thus attired, with my white-plumed, lace-trimmed hat on my head, I opened a window. I was observed by some idlers in the courtyard, who, wondering what a man dressed as I was could be doing there, went to notify the doorkeeper. I was vexed at having allowed myself to be seen. I did not know that the circumstance had served me better than I could have planned.

The clanking of keys was heard. I rose, somewhat agitated, and putting my eye to a crack in the door I saw a man in a periwig, without hat, slowly mounting the stair, quite alone, dangling a great bunch of keys. In a tense whisper I told the monk to keep his mouth shut, to stand right behind me, and to do as I did. I held my bar in my right hand hidden under my coat. I was praying that this man might not offer resistance and force me to murder him.

At sight of me the attendant stopped as if petrified. I precipitated myself down the stair, the monk after me. Without seeming to be running, but proceeding very rapidly I took the magnificent Giant staircase, paying no attention to Father Balbi's iteration of, "Go into the cathedral."

The door of Saint Mark's was not twenty paces away, but for years the churches in Venice had not been places of refuge for criminals. The monk knew that, but fear dulled his wits.

I went straight to the quay and stepped into the first gondola I found. I said in a loud voice to the gondolier on the poop, "Get another rower and take me to Fusina."

As soon as we had doubled past the custom house the gondoliers began to ply vigorously the waters of the canal Giudecca through which we must pass to go either to Fusina or to Mestre. The latter was my actual destination. When we were well out into the canal

I called to the rower on the poor, "Do you think we can get to Mestre in less than four hours?"

"But, signor, you said you wanted to go to Fusina."

"You're drunk. I said Mestre."

The second rower told me that I was mistaken, and my fool of a monk, Christian zealot and great lover of truth, chimed in and echoed that I was in the wrong. I could have kicked him, but reflecting that he could not help his natural stupidity I laughed heartily, saying that I might have made a slip of the tongue, but that my intention was to go to Mestre. The master gondolier said he was ready to take me to England if I wanted him to.

"Bravo. Go to Mestre."

"We shall be there in three quarters of an hour, for we have the wind and the current with us."

At Mestre I found neither postilion nor horses, but there were plenty of fast traveling coaches, and I made a bargain with the driver of one of them. He had us at Treviso in an hour and a quarter.

Chapter IX

M. DE CHOISEUL AND M. DE BERNIS

IT will be remembered in what relation I had stood to the French minister in Venice. Naturally my first thought was to look him up. He was then on the crest of the wave of fortune, and I knew him well enough to be sure that I could count on him.

As I could not expect to see him without an appointment I wrote a letter and carried it in person to the Bourbon palace. The Swiss took my letter and address. That was all I wanted, so I came home.

I retired early, but I was impatient to see what the minister would write in answer to my note. I did not have to wait long. I received a brief reply at eight o'clock. I could visit him at two that afternoon.

I was punctual and was received by His Excellency in the most engaging manner. M. de Bernis expressed himself as perfectly satisfied that I had carried off the prize, and as well pleased that he was able to be of service to me. He told me that when M. M. had informed him of my escape he had expected me to come directly to Paris, where, he flattered himself, my first visit would be to him. He showed me the letters in which M. M. described my imprisonment and my flight. All the circumstances were pure invention. M. M. was excusable, as it was not easy to obtain an exact version, and she could only tell the story as she had heard it. The charming nun wrote that as she despaired of ever seeing again either of the two men whose love was her sole interest in life, her existence

was a burden to her and she regretted her inability to seek solace in religion.

"C. C. comes to see me often," she continued. "Alas, the dear girl is quite unhappy with her husband."

I told M. de Bernis that our friend's account of my escape from the Piombi was quite inaccurate and that I would take the liberty to write him out the detailed facts. He encouraged me to keep my word and promised to send a copy to M. M. At the same time he placed in my hand, with all the delicacy in the world, a roll of a hundred louis, saying that he would bear me in mind and as soon as he had anything to offer he would hasten to let me know.

Being now in funds I thought at once of my apparel. As soon as I had made necessary purchases I set to work and in a week had my story ready to send to my generous protector. I authorized him to have as many copies made as he saw fit and to use them in whatever way seemed to him best calculated to interest all persons who could be useful to me.

Three weeks later the minister wrote me to come and see him. He had spoken about me to M. Erizzo, the Venetian ambassador, who had said that he would not molest me, but that, not desiring to antagonize the State Inquisitors, he could not receive me. I was not displeased. He was perfectly right, and I could not have used him, anyway. M. de Bernis then told me he had given my story to Mme. de Pompadour. She remembered me, and he promised to introduce me to this powerful lady at the first opportunity.

His Excellency added, "You might, my dear Casanova, present yourself to M. de Choiseul and to Comptroller-general De Boulogne. You will be well received, and with a little diplomacy you can derive profit from the latter. He will give you useful information, and you will notice that the good listener is the man who obtains favors. Try to think up some method of increasing the royal revenues. Nothing complicated, nothing chimerical, you understand. Write it out, and if your summary is not too long I will give you my opinion of it."

I came away from this satisfactory interview grateful but perplexed. My financial mind was not working and I beat my brow in vain. I could think of nothing that did not necessitate new taxes and odious measures, and I rejected each scheme after I had considered it from every angle.

I went first to see M. de Choiseul, as soon as I heard that he was in Paris. He received me while dressing, that is, he was writing while his valet did his hair. He was polite to the extent of interrupting himself several times to ask me a question, but while I was answering, his Excellency continued writing as if I did not matter, and I doubt very much if he could have grasped the sequence of my speech. Although sometimes he seemed to be looking at me, it was apparent that his eyes and his thoughts were not busy with the same object. In spite of this manner of receiving, at least of receiving me, M. de Choiseul was a man of great charm.

When he had finished his letter he said to me in Italian that M. de Bernis had related to him part of the story of my escape.

"Tell me," he added, "just how did you manage it?"

"Monseigneur, the recital is rather long. It would take at least two hours, and your Excellency appears to be busy."

"Give me a condensed account."

"As short as I may make it it would take two hours."

"You may reserve the details for some other time."

"In this story the details are the only interesting part."

"Oh, surely everything can be condensed as much as one desires without detracting from the interest."

"Very well. It would be ungracious for me to make any further objection. Know then that the state inquisitors imprisoned me in the Piombi, that at the end of fifteen months and five days I succeeded in boring a hole through the roof, that through a skylight, after overcoming all manner of obstacles, I reached the chancery, the door of which I smashed, that after this exploit I descended to the square of Saint Mark, thence to the quay where I took a gondola to the mainland, and that finally I made my way to Paris, where I have the honor to make my obeisance."

"But . . . what is the Piombi?"

"Monseigneur, to explain that will take at least fifteen minutes."

"How did you bore a hole through the roof?"

"I could not tell you that in less than half an hour."

"Why were you imprisoned?"

"That is a long, long story, monseigneur."

"I believe you are right. The interest of the story lies only in the details."

"As I have taken the liberty to observe to your Excellency."

I had been almost infuriated by the manner in which M. de Choiseul had received me, and my temper had asserted itself, but the rest of our conversation, and especially the amicable tone of his last words, calmed me, and I came away, if not satisfied, at least without rancor.

Chapter X

THERESE DE LA MEURE

SOON a cab stopped at the door, and a moment later a fat woman of a certatin age entered with an extremely pretty girl, followed by a pale man dressed in black with a round wig. After effusive greetings the niece of the Pope presented her cousin, the count of Sixtimes. This name seemed to astonish the old lady, but the Lambertini woman passed over her comments in silence. Nevertheless the visitors found it strange that a man who was completely ignorant of the national language should have the hardihood to remain in Paris and make himself ridiculous by persistently jabbering away, with the greatest assurance, in absurd French that nobody could understand.

After a few moments of frivolous conversation the pretended niece of the Pope proposed a game of brelan. She asked me to join, but when I refused she did not insist and asked her dear cousin to be her partner.

"He does not know one card from another," she said, "but it does not matter. He will learn. I shall teach him."

The younger woman, of whose beauty I had taken particular note, likewise knew nothing about cards. I offered her a seat beside the fire and asked if I might have the honor of her company. She assented graciously. The old woman with whom she had come laughed, saying I should have difficulty finding subjects on which her niece could converse.

"She came out of a convent only a month ago," said the old lady.

I assured her I did not think it would be difficult to entertain such an amiable person, and the game having begun, I sat down beside the pretty niece. For some moments I had contented myself with admiring her, when she asked who that good looking man was who spoke so amusingly.

"That is a nobleman of my country who has had to leave because of an affair of honor."

"He speaks a queer jargon."

"True, but in Italy the French language is not often used. It will not take him long to learn, so as not to be a laughing-stock. I am sorry to have brought him here, as in less than twenty-four hours they have spoilt him."

"How?"

"I dare not tell you. Your aunt would probably think it bad taste."

"I haven't the slightest intention of giving her the opportunity to judge. But do you think my question bold?"

"No, mademoiselle, far from it. Since you ask me I will not make a mystery of the matter. Mme. Lambertini has taken a fancy to him. He passed the night with her, and to commemorate the satisfaction he rendered she has given him the nickname of 'Count of Sixtimes.' That's all. I am sorry, because my friend is not a libertine."

It will seem surprising that I should have dared to speak in such a manner to a young girl who had just come out of a convent. I should have been shocked, myself, if I had been able to conceive of the possibility of finding a decent girl in the house of the Lambertini.

I gazed into the eyes of my beautiful interlocutor. I saw her redden with shame, but this seemed to me a dubious sign. One can judge my amazement when two minutes later I heard her ask:

"But, monsieur, what is the connection between sleeping with madame and the name of Sixtimes?"

"Mademoiselle, the matter is quite simple. My friend has accomplished in one night the duty which a husband needs often six weeks to fulfill."

"And you believe me foolish enough to report our conversation to my aunt? Don't be uneasy."

"There's another thing I am angry about."

"You shall tell me in a moment."

I need hardly explain what forced the charming niece to absent herself for a few moments. When she returned she placed herself behind her aunt's chair and gazed fixedly at Tiretta. Then she came back with sparkling eyes and sitting down beside me again she said:

"What is the other thing you are angry about?"

"Dare I tell you all?"

"You have said so much already that it seems to me you ought to have no scruples whatever."

"Well, then, know that today, right after dinner, in my presence, he and she——"

"Oh, it's evident that you're jealous."

"Never! I was humiliated by this display of bad taste."

She had been standing behind her fat aunt five minutes when the latter lost a brelan. Not knowing on whom else to vent her exasperation she said to her niece, "Go away, you little goose, you bring me bad luck. Moreover you show your lack of breeding by leaving this gentleman who has been kind enough to keep you company."

The lovely niece made no reply and came back to me smiling.

"If my aunt," she said, "knew what you have been saying she would not accuse me of being impolite."

"I cannot tell you how mortified I am. I should like to prove to you my repentance, but I can do so only by going away. If I go away will you take it in bad part?"

"If you go away my aunt will say that I am a big fool, that I bore you."

"Then you wish me to stay?"

"You cannot go away."

"Just a month ago my aunt took me out of the convent where I had been ever since I was seven years old."

"And how old are you now?"

"Seventeen. They wanted me to take the veil, but not feeling any inclination for the mummeries of a convent, I resisted."

"Are you angry with me?"

"I ought to be, but I admit that it was my fault. I beg you to be careful."

"No, but don't be vexed with me for what has happened. I would never have dared to come to this point had it not been for the feeling I conceived for you at first sight."

"Shall I take that as a declaration of love?"

"Yes, divine friend. It is audacious on my part, but it is sincere. If it did not come from the heart and from emotion not to be repressed, I should be unworthy of you and of myself."

"Shall I believe what you say?"

"Yes, with all confidence. Tell me if I may hope that you will love me."

"I don't know anything about it. All I know is that I ought to hate you, because in less than an hour you have given me a range of experience that I oughtn't to have until after I am married."

"Are you angry?"

"I ought to be, although I cannot tell you how enlightened I feel upon a matter about which I had not dared to think till now."

She allowed me to take her hand, and I covered it with kisses. This moment, so agreeable to me, was interrupted by the entrance of M. Le Noir, who came to see if the niece of the Pope had anything to say to him. M. Le Noir, a man of a certain age, of a simple and modest appearance, begged everybody to remain seated. Mme. Lambertini having presented me, he asked me if I was the artist of that name. When he heard that I was the elder brother he complimented me on the lottery and congratulated me on the good opinion M. Duverney had of me. But he was most interested in the cousin whom Mme. Lambertini presented under his real name of Count Tiretta, for his new dignity would not have had great weight with M. Le Noir. I told him that the count had been particularly recommended to me by a personage I thought a great deal of, and that he had been forced temporarily to leave his country on account of an affair of honor. Mme. Lambertini added that she wished to lodge him, and that she did not want to do it without knowing if M. Le Noir found it convenient.

"Madame," said this respectable man, "you are sovereign mistress in your own home and I shall be enchanted to see monsieur le comte in your company."

As M. Le Noir spoke Italian perfectly, Tiretta left the game and the four of us sat before the fire where my new conquest had an opportunity to display her wit. M. Le Noir was a man of good sense and wide experience. He got her to talking about her convent, and when she told him her name he spoke of her father, whom he had known quite well. Her father had been a councilor in the parliament of Rouen and had enjoyed a great reputation in his lifetime. My new conquest was taller than the average, her hair was of a beautiful blond shade, her features regular, and her expression, in spite of the vivacity of her eyes, was of modesty and candor. Her dress showed up the lines of her beautiful figure. Although M. Le Noir said not a word about all these perfections it was easy for me to observe that in his way he appreciated them as keenly as I did.

This gentleman left us at eight o'clock sharp. Half an hour later the fat aunt went away with her delightful niece and the pale man who had come with them. I soon took leave accompanied by Tiretta, who promised the niece of the Pope to be her guest beginning with the morrow, and he kept his promise.

Three or four days after this arrangement was made I received from Mlle. de la Meure—that was the name of the beautiful niece—a letter addressed to my office. It read as follows:

"My aunt, sister of my late lamented mother, is devout, jolly, rich, avaricious, and unjust. She does not love me, and not having succeeded in making me take the veil, she wants to marry me to a rich merchant of Dunkirk whom I don't know, but I would have you observe that she does not know him any more than I do. The matrimonial agent lauds him to the skies, as he naturally would, because a merchant has to praise his merchandise. This gentleman must content himself with an income of barely twelve hundred francs a year for the rest of his life, but there is surety that at his death he will leave me 150,000 francs. I must tell you that by the will of my deceased mother my aunt is obliged to hand over to me 25,000 ecus on the day of my marriage.

"If the conversation that has taken place between us has not made me in your eyes a despicable object, I offer you my hand and my heart with 75,000 francs and a similar sum at the death of my aunt.

"Don't answer me, as I should not know how and through whom I could receive your letter. You shall answer me by word of mouth Sunday at Mme. Lambertini's. That gives you five days to think over the most important thing. As far as I am concerned, though I don't know quite whether I love you, I do know that I must give you the preference over any other man because you love me. I feel that there is much I must do yet to win your esteem, as there is much you must do to win mine, but I am certain that you could render my life agreeable, and that I could always be faithful to my duties as wife. If you consider that the happiness to which I aspire coincides with your own, I warn you that you will need a lawyer, for my aunt is avaricious and inclined to haggle. Should you come to a decision you would have to find a convent where I could take refuge, before anything else could be done, for otherwise I should be exposed to ill treatment. If, on the contrary, the proposition I have made does not suit you, I ask you a favor which you cannot refuse, and which will earn you my profound gratitude. You will try not to see me any more, taking care to avoid the places where you think I may be. Thus you will help me to forget you, and that is the least you can do for me. You must realize that I can be happy only by becoming your wife or forgetting you. Adieu. I am certain to see you Sunday."

I was moved by this letter. I felt that it was dictated by virtue, honor, and wisdom. I discovered in the mind of the charming girl more merit even than in her person. I blushed at the thought of trying to seduce her, and I should have considered myself worthy of the rack if I had refused her hand, which she offered with so little loss of dignity. Moreover, greed, although of second consideration, did not cease prompting me to view with complacency the prospect of a fortune superior to any that I could reasonably pretend to. Nevertheless the idea of marriage, for which I felt no vocation, made me tremble. In knew myself too well not to foresee that regular married life would become intolerable to me and that with the best intentions in the world I could bring only sorrow to any woman who should place the care of her happiness in my hands.

My hesitation to make up my mind during the four days she had given me convinced me that I was not in love with her. In spite of all, so great was my weakness that it became impossible for me to decide, as I ought to have done, to reject her offer, and still less could I tell her so with a frankness which would only have done me credit in her sight.

During these four days my mind was entirely absorbed in a single train of thought. I was bitterly sorry to have outraged her, for I felt towards her respect and esteem, but try as I might I could not bring myself to offer the only honorable reparation. The idea that she should hate me was unbearable, but to fetter myself odious; in fine I was in the state of mind usual when a man is forced to make a decision and cannot.

Fearing that my evil genius would lead me to miss the rendezvous by going in spite of myself to the Opera or somewhere or other, I decided to dine at Lambertini's, still in a state of irresolution.

The pious niece of the Pope was at mass when I arrived at her house. There I found Tiretta amusing himself playing the flute, but as soon as he saw me he laid the instrument aside and came to embrace me. He paid me back the money which I had spent for his coat.

"You are in funds, my friend. I congratulate you."

"Condole with me rather, my dear fellow, for it is stolen money, I am sorry to say, although I am not party to the theft."

"Stolen money?"

"Yes, they cheat here, and they have taught me the game. I share their ill-got gains out of some kind of false delicacy. My hostess and three or four women of her ilk ruin the dupes. This profession revolts me, and I feel that I shall not endure it long. Sometime or other I shall kill somebody or somebody will kill me, and in either case I'm a dead man. Therefore I am thinking of getting out of this cut-throat den."

"I advise you to do so, my friend. What's more, I urge you emphatically to do so, and better today than tomorrow."

"I don't want to break off suddenly. M. Le Noir is a gentleman and a good friend to me, and he believes me to be the cousin of that wretched woman. As he does not know what her infamous business is he would suspect something and probably abandon her if he learned why I left. In five or six days I shall find a pretext, and then I shall come to your house."

Mme. Lambertini complimented me for having invited myself to dinner like a friend. She announced that Mlle. de la Meure and her aunt would be with us too.

I asked if she was as satisfied as ever with my friend Sixtimes, and she answered that although the count did not always tarry in his estate she felt as ever enchanted.

"Moreover," she added, "as a good sovereign I do not demand too much from my vassals."

I complimented her and we continued the banter until the arrival of the guests.

Mlle. de la Meure could hardly hide the pleasure she felt at seeing me. She was dressed in half-mourning and was so beautiful in this costume which enhanced the whiteness of her skin, that I am still astonished that that moment did not decide my fate.

Tiretta, who had left us to dress, rejoined us, and as there was no reason why I should conceal my partiality for the lovely girl I showed her all possible attention. I told the aunt that I found her niece so pretty that I would give up bachelorhood if I could find such a companion.

"My niece, monsieur, is sweet and true, but she has neither wit nor religion."

"Never mind the wit," said the niece, "but as for religion, such an accusation was never brought against me in the convent."

"I can well believe that. They were Jesuits there."

"But what of it, my dear aunt?"

"My dear niece, we all know the Jesuits and their adherents are without religion. That is to say, they have not found grace. But let us talk about something else. I am only anxious that you shall please the man who is to be your husband."

"But, madame, is mademoiselle on the eve of marrying?"

"Her future husband will arrive at the beginning of next month."

"Is he a barrister?"

"No, monsieur, he is a well-to-do merchant."

"M. Le Noir told me that mademoiselle was the daughter of a councilor, and I did not imagine that you could wish to contract a misalliance."

"It won't be one, Monsieur. After all, what is a misalliance? The future husband of my niece is noble, for he is an honest man, and I am sure that it depends only on her to be happy with him."

"Yes, admitting that mademoiselle loves him."

"Oh, love comes in time."

As this conversation could but be painful to the young person who listened without a word, I changed the subject and spoke of the great throngs which would be present at la Grève for the execution of Damiens. As I found them quite curious to witness this horrible spectacle I offered them a large window where we could see everything. The ladies accepted eagerly and I promised to fetch them in time. I had no window but I knew that in Paris, as everywhere, with money one can get whatever one wants.

After dinner, under pretext of business, I went out and having taken the first cab that came along, in fifteen minutes I had rented for three louis a good window on a first floor. I paid in advance and took good care to get a receipt.

Having done this I hastened back to the company and found them engaged in a game of piquet. Mlle. de la Meure, who did not know the game, was bored looking on. I went to her, and wishing to talk we withdrew to the other end of the room.

"Your letter, my charming friend, has made me the happiest of mortals. In it you have shown a mind and a character which must assure you the worship of all men of good judgment."

"I am interested only in the love of one man. The esteem of the others will suffice."

"You shall be my wife, my angelic friend, and I shall bless to my last day the happy insolence to which I owe the preference reserved to me over so many others. Not a man would ever have refused you, even without the fifty thousand ecus, which are nothing in comparison to your personal qualities and your sensible way of thinking."

"I am very glad that you have such a good opinion of me."

"How could it be otherwise? Now that you know my feelings, be not precipitous, but trust me."

"Remember my situation."

"I cannot forget it. Give me time to get a house, to furnish it and to get into a position to be judged worthy of you. You must remember that I am still living in a furnished room, that you have relatives, and that I should be ashamed to appear as an adventurer when taking such an important step."

"You have heard that my future husband is coming soon."

"Yes, that fact did not escape me."

"When he is here you may be certain things will be done in a hurry."

"But not so quickly that in less than twenty-four hours I could not deliver you from all tyranny in such a way that your aunt would even know that I was taking a hand. I can assure you, my darling, that the minister of foreign affairs, as soon as he learned that I was to be your husband, would find you a safe refuge in one of the best convents in Paris. He will even find you a lawyer, and if the will is clear your aunt will soon pay your dowry and give you security for the rest of the inheritance. Be at rest and let the merchant of Dunkirk come. At any rate you can count on me not to leave you in the lurch. You won't be in your aunt's house the day when the contract is to be signed."

"I place the matter entirely in your hands. But I do wish you would not lay so much stress on an incident which does very little credit to my modesty. You just now said that I would never have put it up to you to marry me or cease seeing me if it had not been for the liberties which you took last Sunday."

"Was I wrong?"

"At least in one respect. You must realize that to propose to you point blank would have been a very imprudent act if I had not had some more powerful reason. Our marriage could have come about in another manner, for I now feel free to tell you that in any case I would have given you the preference over anyone else."

I did not feel comfortable, and taking her hand I kissed it many times, tenderly and respectfully. I am convinced that if at that instant we had had before us a notary public or a priest authorized to give us the nuptial blessing I would have not hesitated to marry her.

The 28th of March, the day of the martyrdom of Damiens, I went early to the house of Mme. Lambertini to get the ladies. As there was barely room for us in the carriage I had the privilege of taking my charming friend on my knee, and we drove to the square of la Grève. The three ladies, squeezing as much as they could, pressed up to the window sill, leaning on their elbows so as to permit us to look over their heads. This window had two steps beneath it, and the ladies were standing on the upper one. We had to stand on the same step, as we were not enough taller than they to see from the lower one. I give these details that the reader may divine others about which I must be silent.

We had the endurance to remain four hours watching this horrible spectacle. The torture of Damiens is too well known to be described here. For one thing it would be too long. For another, such horrors outrage nature. Damiens was a fanatic, who thinking to perform a good deed deserving of a heavenly reward had attempted to assassinate Louis XV, and although he only scratched the king he was tortured as if the crime had been consummated.

During the torture of this victim of the Jesuits I was forced to turn my eyes away, and to stop up my ears to keep from hearing his heartrending cries when he had only half of his body left; but the Lambertini woman and the fat aunt never moved. Was not that an evidence of their innate cruelty? I made believe I was convinced when they told me that the horror inspired by the attempt of the monster had prevented them from feeling any pity for him at the sight of the unheard-of suffering he was made to undergo.

Finally we left, and having dropped the niece of the Pope at her door, I begged to have Tiretta's company for a few hours. I escorted Mme.*** to her house in the rue Saint-Andre-des-Arcs, when she asked me to see her the next day, as she had something to tell me. I noticed that she did not salute my friend when she left us. We went to dine at Laudel's at the hotel de Russie, where we had excellent fare at six francs apiece.

At the table my friend informed me that he had quarrelled with Mme. Lambertini and was changing his lodgings at once. I asked him why and received this reply:

"On my word. Here's what happened. Last night a young man employed in the revenue department was brought in to supper by an old, rascally Genoese woman. After he had lost forty louis playing, he threw the cards at my hostess' head and called her a thief. In an unguarded moment I grabbed the candle and extinguished it on his face, almost putting his eyes out. Luckily I caught him in the jaw. He drew his sword. I had already drawn mine, and if the Genoese woman had not thrown herself between us murder would have followed. The unlucky fellow seeing his cheek in the mirror became so incensed that the only way to quiet him was to return him his money. They gave it back to him in spite of my protests, for the restitution could only be construed as a tacit confession that the money had been won from him by cheating. That caused a very bitter quarrel between the Lambertini woman and myself after the departure of the young man. She said that nothing would have happened and that we should still have the forty louis if I had not interfered; and that she was the one who had been insulted, not I. The Genoese woman added that with coolness we could have kept him for quite awhile, but that now God only knew what he would do with his face disfigured. Annoyed by the infamous speeches of these two prostitutes I told them to go to, but my hostess mounting the high horse permitted herself to say that I was merely a scoundrel. If M. Le Noir had not entered I would have taught her a lesson, for I had already grabbed my stick. At the sight of M. Le Noir they told me to be quiet, but I was excited, and turning round towards the honest man I informed him that his mistress had insulted me, that she was only a prostitute, and that I was not her cousin, nor for that matter any kin to her at all, and that I would go away the same day. Finishing this hasty speech I locked myself in my room. In a few hours I shall get my things and tomorrow morning I shall breakfast with you."

Tiretta was all right. He had a noble soul, and a few youthful peccadilloes need not cause him to wallow forever in a mire of vice. As long as a man has not committed a felony, as long as his heart is not an accomplice of his head, he can return with honor to the path of duty. I would say as much for woman if prejudice permitted it, and if woman did not act much more through her heart than her head, anyway.

We separated after dining well and drinking some delicious sillery. I spent the rest of the evening writing.

The next morning I was out on some errands, and at noon I went to call on the afflicted devout lady, whom I found with her charming niece. For awhile we talked about the weather, then she told her niece to leave us, as she wished to speak to me alone. I was ready for the scene and waited for her to break the silence which no woman in her place would think of neglecting to maintain for several minutes.

"I am a very lonely woman. My husband has been dead for some years and I still desire the advantages of marriage. Your friend Tiretta interests and amuses me. I could come to love him and to find in him affection, and the satisfaction of those natural desires, which I am at present denied."

I promised that I would act as the go-between but she made me promise that I would not let Tiretta know of this conversation.

The reader does not have to be told that I gave Tiretta a faithful account of my conversation with the dowager. If some timorous souls should protest against my breach of faith I shall retort that there was a "mental reservation" in my promises, and those of my readers who have some acquaintance with the teachings of the children of Ignatius will realize that this consideration made me perfectly comfortable.

Everything being satisfactorily arranged with my friend, we went to the opera the next evening, and from there we proceeded on foot to the house of the lady.

"I never sup," she informed us, "but if I had known that you were coming I would have taken care to prepare something."

After having imparted all the gossip I had heard in the foyer, on pretext of business I begged to be allowed to leave my friend in her keeping for a few moments.

"Should I be a quarter of an hour late, my dear count, don't wait for me. Take a cab and go home, and we shall see each other tomorrow."

Instead of going out I went into the next room, which had an entrance on the corridor. Two minutes later I saw the charming niece come in, carrying a candle and agreeably surprised to see me.

"I don't know if I am dreaming," she said, "but my aunt told me not to leave you alone, and to inform the chambermaid not to enter unless she rings. Your friend is with her, and she has ordered me to speak in a low voice, as he is not supposed to know that you are here. May I know the reason for this strange procedure?"

"Then you are curious?"

"I confess that I am. All this mystery is enough to rouse anybody's curiosity."

"You shall know all, my angel, but it's cold here."

"My aunt has given orders to start a good fire. She has become generous all of a sudden, even lavish, for as you can see there are some candles."

"Is that unusual?"

"Decidedly so."

As soon as we were in front of the fire I began to relate the whole adventure, to which she listened with all the attention a young girl is capable of giving in such a matter. She was indeed surprised.

"Oh, it's all so preposterous! I don't believe a word you say. My dear aunt is too much in love with the salvation of her soul. Moreover, how do you expect this young man to be in love with her or pretend to be when he has before his eyes a face like my aunt's? Let us pass over his mad act. He did not see her. Have you ever seen a more disgusting face than my aunt's? A blotchy complexion, eyes which distil molten wax, teeth and a breath to discourage the bravest of the brave. She is hideous."

"Dear heart, these are only bagatelles for a strapping fellow twenty-five years old. At that age one is always prepared. It's different with me. I can become manly only through charms like yours, which I wish to possess legitimately."

"You shall find in me the tenderest of wives, and I feel certain to succeed in capturing your heart so as not to lose it."

An hour had passed in this agreeable conversation, and Tiretta was still closeted with the aunt. This promised well, and I judged that the affair had become serious. I said as much to my charming companion and suggested that she might offer me something to eat.

"I can give you," she said, "only bread, cheese, ham, and some wine which my aunt says is delicious."

"Bring it all, right away, for I am starving to death."

She quickly prepared a table and got out two plates and all the food she could lay her hands on. There was some delicious Roquefort cheese, and ham glacé which was excellent. There was enough to satisfy ten healthy persons, but the fact is, though I don't know how we did it, everything disappeared along with a bottle of Chambertin which I can still taste. Pleasure sparkled in the eyes of my beautiful mistress. Chambertin wine and Roquefort cheese are excellent fare to restore love or to bring a nascent love to a head.

"You are not curious to know what your aunt has been doing the last two hours, alone with M. Sixtimes?"

"Maybe they are playing cards. I will peep through the keyhole. I can see nothing but candles with wicks an inch long."

"I told you so. Give me a blanket. I shall lie down on this sofa, and do you, my dear friend, go to bed. But show me your bed."

She showed me her little room, where I saw a pretty bed, a small praying-stand, and a large crucifix.

"Your bed is too small for you, dear heart."

"No, not a bit, I am quite comfortable."

While saying these words she lay down at full length.

"What a charming wife I shall have! Don't move. Let me admire you as you are."

My hand pressed a small corset, veritable prison of two globes which seemed to complain of their captivity. I go further, I unlace her—for where does desire stop?

"My friend, I cannot defend myself, but then afterwards you will not love me any more."

"All my life."

My flame kindled hers, and having lost control she opened her arms, making me promise to respect her, and what do we not promise? Is there time to pay attention to promises in these delirious moments? The inborn modesty of women, the fear of consequences, a certain instinct which reveals to them the natural fickleness of men, may induce them to ask these promises at first; but where is the woman, if she is very much in love, who will think of demanding of her lover to respect her, at that moment when love has absorbed every faculty of reason, at that instant when all life is concentrated in the fulfillment of an all-devouring desire? She is not to be found.

We had been for four or five delicious hours on the sofa. She left me, started a good fire, then went to her room, and I remained on the sofa and slept a profound sleep until noon. I was awakened by Mme. *** who appeared in grand disarray.

"You are still sleeping, monsieur Casanova?"

"Good morning, madame. Well, what has become of my friend?"

"He has become mine."

"Really, madame?"

"Yes, I am very happy."

"I am really charmed. Where is he?"

"He has retired. You will find him at home, but don't tell him that you passed the night here or he will think that you have passed it with my niece. I am infinitely obliged to you, and I am in need of your indulgence, and especially of your discretion."

"You can count entirely on it, for I owe you my gratitude for having forgiven my friend."

"And why not? That dear man is really above mortals. If you knew how he loves me! It is so gratifying to think that he is going to be my lodger for a year. He will be well lodged, well fed, and everything."

"A charming arrangement, and I take it that the price of board has been fixed?"

"That can be arranged as between friends, and we shall not have recourse to arbiters. Today we are leaving for La Villette, where I own a pretty house, for you must understand that in the beginning one must act in such a manner as not to give evil tongues a chance to wag. There my friend shall have all that will make him comfortable, and you, monsieur, every time that you give us the honor of your presence, you shall find a pretty room and a good bed. I am only worried about one thing, and that is that you will be bored with my niece, who is very flighty."

"Your niece, madame, is charming. Last night she provided for me a delicious supper and entertained me till three o'clock in the morning."

"Really. I wonder where she got it, there was nothing to eat in the house."

"I do not know, madame, but she gave me a delicious supper and we ate it all. Then after having entertained me she went to bed, and I have slept very comfortably on this excellent sofa."

"I am delighted that everything has turned out to your satisfaction as well as mine, but I should never have thought my niece had so much sense."

"She has a great deal, madame, at least in my eyes."

"You are a connoisseur. Let us go and see her. She has locked herself in. Open the door! Why do you lock yourself in, you little prude? Monsieur is a perfect gentleman."

The lovely niece opened the door, begging our pardon for not being dressed. But what had rendered her so beautiful? She was dazzling!

"Look at her," said the aunt, "she is not bad at all. It's a pity she is so silly. You did well to offer supper to the gentleman. I thank you for being so thoughtful. I have been playing cards all night, and when one plays one does not think of anything but the game. I had quite forgotten you were here, and not knowing that the count was in the habit of supping, I had ordered nothing, but in the future we shall sup. I have taken that boy as a boarder. He has an excellent character and a great deal of wit, and I am certain that it will not take him long to learn French. Get dressed, my dear niece, for we must pack our things. This afternoon we go to La Villette, where we shall stay all through the spring. Listen, my dear niece, it's quite unnecessary for you to relate this adventure."

"I? my dear aunt! Have I said anything the other times?"

"The other times! Do you see how idiotic the girl is? With her 'other times,' would not a person imagine that this is not the first time such a thing has ever happened to me?"

"You misunderstand, my dear aunt. I meant to say that I never talk about your actions at all."

"That's right, my niece, but you should learn to express yourself properly. We shall dine at two o'clock. M. Casanova will please us by dining with us, I hope, and we shall depart after dinner. Tiretta has promised to be here with his trunk and it will go along with our luggage."

Promising to come at the set time I saluted the ladies and went home quickly, as I felt a woman's curiosity to know how the great affair had been settled.

"Well," I said to Tiretta when he met me, "now you are established. Tell me immediately what happened."

"My dear fellow, I have sold myself for one year, at twenty-five louis per month, including a good table, good lodgings, etc."

"I congratulate you."

"If you think congratulations in order."

"There are no roses without thorns. She tells me that she is very happy."

"I am certain your time has been better employed than mine."

"I have slept like a king. Get up and get dressed. I am to be one of the dinner party and I want to see you depart for La Villette, where I shall visit you sometimes, as your sweetheart has told me that there will be a room there for me."

We arrived at two o'clock. Mme. —— was dressed as a young girl and made a strange appearance, but Mlle. de la Meure was as beautiful as the sun. Love had unfolded her being and pleasure had given her a new life. We dined well, for the good lady had put coquetry into the making of the dinner as well as into her toilette.

At least about the meal there was nothing to take exception to. But everything about the hostess herself was unspeakably ridiculous.

At four o'clock they left with Tiretta, and I spent the evening at the Comédie Italienne.

* * * * *

Casanova visits the little house at La Villette and passes some happy nights with Therese. Then the merchant of Dunkirk, the fiancé, having arrived, the young girl demands that Casanova either leave her or marry her. But these quick decisions never suit the adventurer. He wishes to continue possessing a charming mistress without marrying her. He awaits with serene confidence the pretty Therese in his room at night.

* * * * *

I was fifteen minutes in my room in the sweet hope of seeing my mistress appear in her pretty negligée, when suddenly she entered, completely dressed. That surprised and worried me.

"You are astonished to see me dressed," she said, "but I have something to say to you before I disrobe. Tell me frankly if I must consent to this marriage."

"How do you like the gentleman?"

"He does not displease me."

"Then consent."

"That's enough. Goodbye. From this moment our love ceases and our friendship begins. Go to bed. I shall do likewise. Goodbye."

"No, stay here. Our friendship shall begin tomorrow."

"No, not even if it kills me and you too. It is hard for me, but this is final. If I must become the wife of another man I must assure myself that I shall be worthy of him. Perhaps I shall be happy. Don't detain me. Let me go. You know how I love you."

"Kiss me, at least."

"Impossible."

"You are crying?"

"No. In God's name let me go!"

"Dear heart, you are going to your room to weep. I am in despair. Remain. I will be your husband."

"I cannot consent now."

She freed herself with an effort and fled. I was filled with shame and remorse. I could not sleep. I hated myself, and I did not know in which I was more guilty, in having seduced her or in having turned her over to the other man.

The next day I remained to dinner, in spite of my heartbreak. I must have made a sad appearance. Mlle. de la Meure sparkled with wit. She entertained her future husband with a display of so much charm and good sense that it was easy to see that he was enchanted. As I had nothing to say I pleaded, as usual, a toothache so as not to have to talk. Sad, distraught, and sick after the sleepless night I had passed, I confessed to myself that I was hopelessly in love and desperately jealous. Mademoiselle did not address a single word to me, did not favor me with a single look. She was right, but I was far from doing her justice then. I thought dinner would never come to an end. Never have I sat through anything so painful.

As we left the table Mme. —— went into her room with her niece and future nephew, and Mademoiselle came out an hour later asking to be congratulated, because in a week she would be married and right after the ceremony she would accompany her husband to Dunkirk.

"Tomorrow," she added, "we are all invited to dinner at M. Kornman's, where the contract will be signed."

I don't know why I did not fall dead on the spot. My suffering was indescribable. Soon it was suggested that we should go to the Comédie Française, but under the pretext of business I returned to

Paris. I was feverish all the way, and when I got home I went to bed. Instead of finding the rest I needed, all the torments of remorse assailed me and I experienced the agonies of the damned. I thought that I must prevent this marriage or die. Convinced that Mlle. de la Meure loved me I imagined that she would not resist if I told her that her refusal would cost me my life.

Filled with this idea I got up and wrote her the most powerful appeal which stormy passion ever inspired. Having relieved my pain I went back to bed and slept till morning. As soon as I awoke I sent for a messenger and promised him twelve francs to deliver my letter. He returned with a voucher within an hour and a half.

My letter was in an envelope addressed to Tiretta, on which I had written that I would not go out until I had received an answer. It came four hours later and read as follows:

"It is too late, my dear friend. You have decided my fate. I cannot withdraw. Don't confine yourself at home. Come to dine at Kornman's and be sure that in a few weeks we shall both be happy to have carried off a great victory. Our love, too soon satisfied, will be forgotten. I beg you not to write again."

Chapter XI

MADEMOISELLE X. C. V.

MME. X. C. V. of Greek origin, was the widow of an Englishman who had left her with six children, four of whom were girls. On his death bed, unable to resist the tears of his wife, he embraced Catholicism, but the children could not inherit a capital of forty thousand pounds sterling left by the deceased in England unless she declared herself of the Anglican faith. The family had just returned from London, where the widow had fulfilled all the formalities required by the English law. How powerful is self-interest! However one should not be too severe upon people who in this case merely conformed to prejudice consecrated by the laws of nations.

We were then at the beginning of the year 1758. Five years before, in Padua I had fallen in love with the eldest daughter while playing in amateur theatricals with her, but a few months later in Venice X. C. V. found it expedient to exclude me from her daughter's society.

The daughter made up for this insult by writing me a charming letter which I sometimes delighted to read again. I must confess, that at that period it was easy to be patient under this grievance as I was busy with my beautiful nun M. M. and with my charming C. C. Nevertheless, Mlle. X. C. V., although barely fifteen years old, was a perfect specimen of beauty, all the more ravishing as in addition to attractive features she possessed the advantage of a cultured mind, which is often more seductive than physical perfection.

Count Algarotti, chamberlain to the King of Prussia, was her tutor and several young patricians were eager to capture her heart. The preferred swain was then the heir of the Memmo de San Marcuola line. This young man died within the year as procurator of St. Mark.

My surprise can be imagined when I saw Mme. X. C. V. and her brood again after I had lost track of them.

Mlle. X. C. V. recognized me at once and pointed me out to her mother, who beckoned me with her fan. I went to visit them in their box.

She received me in the kindest manner, saying that we were no longer in Venice and that she hoped I would not refuse her the pleasure of seeing me often at the hotel de Bretagne, rue de Saint-André-des-Arcs. I told her that I did not wish to remember Venice, and when her daughter joined her mother in inviting me, I promised to visit them.

I found Mlle. X. C. V. had become more beautiful, and my love, after lying dormant five years awakened with a power which I can only compare to the degree of perfection which the object of my love had attained in this space of time. They told me that they would remain six months in Paris before returning to Venice. I informed them that I planned to settle in this capital, that I had just come from Holland and that having to go to Versailles the next day, I could not present my respects till the day after. I likewise offered them my services making them understand that if necessary I was capable of rendering important ones.

Mlle. X. C. V. said that what I had achieved in Holland ought to endear me to France, that she had always hoped to see me again, and that my famous flight from the Piombi had rejoiced them greatly.

"For," she added, "we have always loved you."

"I have not always been aware of such a feeling on your mother's part," I told her in a whisper.

"Don't let us speak about it," she said in a low voice, "we learned all the details of your marvelous escape through a sixteen-page letter which you wrote to M. Memmo. It made us tremble alternately with joy and fear."

"And how did you hear of my stay in Holland?"

"We were informed of it yesterday by M. de la Popelinière."

M. de la Popelinière, general revenue agent, whom I had met seven years before in his house at Passy, entered the box as Mlle. X. C. V. was mentioning his name.

After having paid me a slight compliment, he told me that if I could get twenty millions for the India Company he would make me a revenue agent.

"I advise you, Monsieur Casanova," he added, "to become a Frenchman, before it is known that you have made half a million."

"Half a million! Monsieur, I wish it were so."

"You cannot have made a lesser profit."

"I assure you, monsieur, that this affair is going to ruin me if they cheat me out of my percentage."

"You are right to talk like that. At any rate everybody is anxious to meet you, as France owes you a great debt. You are responsible for a lucky upward trend of the state funds."

The next day I went to the hotel de Bretagne to pay my first call to Mme. X. C. V. This lady, who did not like me, received me with a great deal of kindness. In Paris and in good luck I could only be something superior to what I was in Venice. Who does not know that glitter fascinates the sight and usurps the need of merit? In the company of Mme. X. C. V. there was an old Greek named Zandiri. His brother, who was the maître d'hôtel of M. de Bragadin, had just died. I condoled with this brute. He made no answer. I was compensated for this foolish coldness by the fuss the whole family made over me. Mademoiselle, her sisters, and her two brothers all showered kindness upon me. The oldest was only fourteen years old, a charming lad, who surprised me by the independent spirit which he showed at every turn. He sighed for the moment when he should be master of his fortune so as to be able to dedicate his life to debauchery. This he would take to like a duck to water.

Mlle. X. C. V., besides being an accomplished beauty, had the nonchalant and easy manner of the best society, as well as talents and substantial knowledge which she never exhibited except at the proper time and then unpretentiously. It was hard to approach her without feeling for her the most affectionate tenderness, but she was no coquette, and I soon convinced myself that she gave no hope to those who did not please her. She could be cool without being rude and all the more so as she was indifferent to opinion.

Within an hour she had captivated me. I confessed as much to her, and she told me that she was glad of it. She took the place Esther * occupied a week before, but I confess candidly that Esther lost out because of absence. As to my affection for the daughter of Silvia, it was of a kind which did not prevent my falling in love with others. In the heart of a libertine, a love without solid nourishment dies of inanition, as women with some experience well know. The young Balletti was inexperienced and consequently unaware of this need.

Monsieur Farsetti, a Venetian nobleman, commander of the order of Malta, a man of letters, who was interested in abstract sciences besides writing Latin verses, arrived at one o'clock. As they were

* Casanova had with her a long but quite platonic love intrigue. There is in Dux, in the archives of Waldstein, a collection of exquisite letters written by this delightful Manon.

going to sit down Mme. X. C. V. hastened to order a plate laid for him. She also asked me to remain for supper, but I declined the honor that evening. M. Farsetti, who had known me quite well in Venice, barely looked at me, and I paid him back in the same coin without appearing to attach too much importance to the process. He smiled when Mademoiselle paid a compliment to my courage. She noticed it and as if to punish him she added that I had forced all the Venetians to admire me, and that the French were proud to claim me as their own. M. Farsetti asked me if my post as agent of the lottery brought good results. I answered with indifference, "All that is necessary to make my clerks happy." He understood the meaning of my answer and Mademoiselle smiled.

* * * * *

Casanova goes one evening to the ball of the Opera.

* * * * *

I was not masked. I was approached by a black domino. I soon recognized the masquerader as a woman. In a falsetto voice which intrigued me she told me many things known only to my intimates and as I wished to discover her identity I led her into a box. As soon as we were seated she took her mask off. I was quite astonished to see Mlle. X. C. V.

"I came to the ball," she said, "with one of my sisters, with my oldest brother and M. Farsetti. I just left them changing dominoes in a box."

"They must be worrying about you."

"I suppose so, but I don't intend to stay for the end of the ball."

Seeing myself alone with her and thinking I should be with her the rest of the evening, I began to speak of my old love. I told her that I felt it growing as strong as ever. She listened to me with great patience and did not even refuse my embraces. By the small resistance she opposed to my attempts, I judged that the critical moment was only postponed. Nevertheless on that evening I restrained myself and she seemed grateful.

"I have heard in Versailles, my dear young lady, that you are going to marry M. de la Popelinière."

"They all believe it and my mother wishes it. The old general revenue agent believes he already owns me; but he is mistaken for I shall never agree."

"He is old, but he is very rich."

"Very rich and very generous. He has promised a million as a dowry in case of childless widowhood, and all his fortune if I have a child."

"It won't be difficult for you to get all his fortune."

"I shall never enjoy it. I don't want to be unhappy with a man I am not in love with, whom I actually dislike, particularly as my heart belongs to someone else."

"To someone else? And who is this happy mortal to whom you have granted this boon?"

"I don't know if the one who has my love is happy. I love a Venetian and my mother knows it, but she insists that he who has my heart would make me unhappy and that he shall not be my husband."

"What a strange woman your mother is! She is always crossing your love affairs."

"I cannot blame her. She may be wrong, but she loves me. She would prefer to see me become the wife of M. Farsetti, who would willingly renounce his cross to be my husband, but I detest him."

"Has he already asked for your hand?"

"Formally, and the contempt I always show him does not discourage him."

"He is tenacious, but very likely your charms have fascinated him."

"Possibly, but I doubt if he has any feelings of delicacy and generosity. He is moonstruck, and full of malice and jealousy besides. After hearing me speak about you in terms which your merits justify, he had the impudence to tell my mother, in my presence, that she should not receive you in our home."

"He needs a lesson in politeness, but there are other ways to punish him. I offer you my services without reserve in anything that I can do."

"Alas! I should be spared great unhappiness if I could count completely on your friendship."

At these words she sighed. Set on fire, I expressed my devotion adding that I owned fifty thousand ecus which were at her service, and that I was willing to risk my life to have a claim on her heart. She answered by embracing me affectionately and gratefully. Our lips met; but I felt tears running down her cheeks, and I respected her while moderating the fire excited by her kisses. She begged me to see her often, promising to be tête-à-tête with me every time she was able. That was all I could wish for, and after I promised to dine with her the next day, we separated.

I remained another hour in the room, watching her and enjoying the happiness of having become her friend, then I returned to the Petite-Pologne.

The trip did not take long, for although I lived in the country I could reach any quarter of Paris in fifteen minutes. My coachman was skillful and my horses excellent, especially as they were not spared work. They had once been of the King's stable, real blood horses, and when I lost one, as happened sometimes, for one of the greatest pleasures in Paris is to drive too fast, I immediately replaced him at a cost of two thousand francs.

Having accepted an invitation to dinner with Mlle. X. C. V. I slept only a few hours and went out in a frock coat. I traversed the distance on foot. The snow was falling in large flakes, and I appeared before Madame all covered with white. She received me very well and laughingly told me that her daughter had related how I had been fooled. She said she had been happy to hear that I would please them by dining informally.

"But," she added, "today is Friday and you will have no meat. We have some excellent fish, though. While waiting for dinner, go and see my daughter, who is still in bed."

I did not have to be told twice. A woman is at her most attractive in bed. I found Mlle. X. C. V. sitting up. She was busy writing, but she stopped when she saw me.

"Yes, my dear friend, I am here because I am lazy and also because I am more free this way."

"I was afraid that you were not well."

"I am somewhat indisposed, but don't let us talk about it today. I am going to have some broth, as those who have foolishly prescribed going without meat on certain days did not have the politeness to ask my permission. It does not agree with my taste or my health, and I shall not get up even to dine, although thus I shall be deprived of the pleasure of being with you."

I told her that naturally without her the dinner would seem tasteless to me, and I did not exaggerate.

As the presence of her sister did not worry her, she took out of her pocketbook a letter in verse which I had written her when her mother had forbidden me the house.

She recited it from memory, then moved by it she wept.

"This prophetic epistle," she said, "which you entitled *The Phoenix,* has decided my fate, and it may be the cause of my death."

I had given it the title of *Phoenix,* for after having complained about the severity of my punishment, I foretold with a great deal of poetical license, that she would give her love to a mortal whose superior qualities made him a veritable Phoenix. I wrote a hundred verses to describe these imaginary physical and moral virtues, and assuredly the being who possessed them could well be worshipped, for he would be more likely a god than a man.

"Well, then," continued Mlle. X. C. V., "I fell in love with this imaginary being. Convinced that he must exist, I began to look for him, and after six months I thought I had met him. We were very fond of each other. Four months ago we parted. That was when my mother took the family to London. Since we have been here—it's now six weeks—I have received only one letter from him. Still I don't reproach him. I know it's not his fault. I am not free and cannot receive or send word."

This account confirmed me in my conviction that the most decisive actions of our whole lives often depend entirely on the most trifling things.

My letter was only a poetical flight of an indifferent sort. The being I depicted was impossible to find, as he was above all human perfection, but the heart of woman goes quickly and far. Mlle. X. C. V. took the matter literally, and having fallen in love with a chimera, she wanted to substitute for it a reality without thinking that her imagination must now take an enormous step backward. Nevertheless, when she thought she had found the original of the fantastic portrait which my muse had traced, she had no difficulty discovering in him all the qualities portrayed, as her love furnished them at will. Without my letter Mlle. X. C. V. would have fallen in love, but in another way, and the consequences of her love would have been different. Everything down here and maybe higher up, is a network of circumstance, and we are the authors of acts for which we are not responsible. All that happens to us is surely dictated by deterministic forces, and we are only the thinking atoms who go wherever the wind drives us. I realize that the reader will accuse me of subscribing to fatalism, but I have a right to my own opinion and I do not deny him the same right.

As soon as dinner was served I was called in. We had excellent fare, with fine salt water fish which M. de la Popelinière had furnished. Mme. X. C. V., a narrow-minded Greek, was naturally as bigoted and superstitious as could be. God and the devil are nearly allied in the mass of contradictions which is the brain of a vain, weak, voluptuous and timid woman.

A priest had told her that by converting her husband she prepared for herself eternal happiness, as the Holy Writ promised in no uncertain terms *a soul for a soul* to every creature who brought into the lap of the church a heretic or a pagan. Therefore as Mme. X. C. V. had converted her husband, she felt certain about her future. She had nothing more to do. Nevertheless she kept the fasts on the prescribed days. She liked fish better than meat.

As we got up from the table, I returned to the bedside of Mademoiselle. She held her own until nine o'clock, and I was sufficiently master over myself to keep my desires in check. I was conceited enough to imagine that her feeling was not less violent than my own, and I did not wish to appear less capable of self-control than she, although I knew then as I know today, that restraint is bad policy. Opportunity is like fortune: one must seize it by the forelock as soon as it appears or it will run away and not return.

Not having seen Farsetti at the table I suspected a rupture. I asked Mademoiselle about it, but she undeceived me by saying that her persecutor was a crazy visionary whom nothing could induce to go out of the house on a Friday. This mad man had had his horoscope cast by a gypsy. He had learned that his fate was to be killed on a Friday, and to prevent the danger he was threatened with, on that day he made himself inaccessible to everybody. People made fun of him, but he kept on, and they were right after all. Four years ago he died quietly in bed at the age of seventy. He thought this proved that man's destiny depends on his good behavior, prudence, and the care he takes wisely to avoid the evil foreseen. This is true in any case, but it doesn't apply to the matter of the horoscope. If the evils are unavoidable then forecasting them is a silly game. The horoscope is merely the interpreter of fate, which no precaution can alter.

The chevalier Farsetti was therefore a fool to think that he had proved anything. He would have convinced many people if he had gone out every day, and fate had willed at least that he should be killed on a Friday. Pico de la Mirandola, who believed in astrology, said, *"Astra influunt, non cogunt"*—The stars influence, they do not compel.—I have no doubt about it. But would it have been necessary to believe in astrology if Farsetti had been killed on Friday?

No, certainly not.

The day after my long talk with Mlle. X. C. V. my valet told me that a young man desired to deliver a letter into my own hands. I bade him enter, and asked him who had given him the message. He said that the letter would tell me all, and that his orders were to wait for an answer. This is what was written:

"It's two o'clock in the morning. I am in need of rest, but the difficulty I am in prevents me from sleeping. The secret I am going to confide in you, my friend, will cease to burden me as soon as I have deposited it in your breast. Confession will be a great relief. I am pregnant, and my position makes me desperate. I have decided to write you about it, as I feel it would be impossible to tell you by word of mouth. Kindly write me a line in reply."

One can imagine what I must have felt when I read this. I was petrified, and I could only answer:

"I shall be at your home at eleven o'clock."

There is really no misfortune which can be called very great, unless one loses one's head under the strain. The confidence which Mlle. X. C. V. manifested in me showed that she was at her wits' end and needed a guide. I considered myself favored in that she had thought of me in preference to anyone else, and I decided to help her even if I had to perish with her. Can one think otherwise when one is in love? Nevertheless I did not quite like the course she pursued. It was a case for speech or silence and the feeling which could make one prefer the pen to the tongue could only come of a false shame, which is but another word for faintheartedness. Had I not been in love with this amiable and unfortunate person, it would have been easier to refuse her my services by writing than by speaking to her. But I adored her.

"Yes," I said to myself, "she can count all the more surely on me as her misfortune brings her nearer to me." And a secret feeling, that was more convincing for being secret, whispered to me that if I had the luck to save her my recompense was assured. I know that many a strict moralist will upbraid me, but I doubt if he was ever in love, and I was desperately so.

I was punctual. I found my beautiful, sorrowful girl at the door of the hotel de Bretagne.

"You are going out? Where?"

"I am going to mass at the Augustins."

"Is it a feast day?"

"No, but my mother requires me to go every day."

"I shall escort you."

"Yes, give me your arm. We shall speak in the cloister."

Mlle. X. C. V. was attended by her chambermaid, who, however, was not in the way. We left her in the church and entered the cloister. As soon as we were inside Mademoiselle said:

"Have you read my letter?"

"Why, certainly, here it is. Take it back. You must burn it."

"No, I don't want it. Burn it yourself."

"I see that you trust me thoroughly, but I shall not take advantage."

"I am sure of that. I am four months gone with child, and I am desperate."

"Comfort yourself, we shall find a remedy."

"Yes, I place myself in your care. Try to bring about an abortion."

"Never, my dear. That would be wicked."

"Alas, I know, but it is not worse than suicide. Should it come down to the choice between the two, to destroy the unlucky testimony of my dishonor or to poison myself, I am ready to carry out the latter plan. You are my only friend, the arbiter of my fate. Speak. Are you angry that I have preferred you to chevalier Farsetti?"

Seeing me open-mouthed she stopped and took her handkerchief to dry her tears. I was heart-broken. "My dear lady," I said, "besides being wicked, an abortion is not in our power. If the methods employed to bring it about are not violent, their success is doubtful; if they are so, they endanger the life of the mother. I will never take the risk of being your executioner. But count on me. I shall not desert you. Your happiness is as dear to me as your life. Calm yourself and from this moment on imagine that I am in your place. Be assured that I will get you out of trouble and it will not be necessary for you to make an attempt on your life, which is as dear to me as mine. Meanwhile allow me to tell you that on reading your note I felt highly flattered that in an event of such importance you should have chosen me in preference to another. You are not mistaken in the trust you have placed in me, as there is nobody in Paris who loves you more affectionately than I do, and no one in the world can feel more keenly the wish to be useful to you. Tomorrow at the latest you shall begin to take the remedies which I shall prepare, but I warn you to be careful about keeping the secret, as it means infringing the most drastic laws.

It's a question of life and death. You have perhaps confided in somebody, to your chambermaid or to one of your sisters?"

"To no one but yourself, my friend, not even to the author of my misfortune. I tremble to think of what my mother would say or do if she were informed of my present state. I fear that she may guess it by looking at my waist."

"Your waist is as yet perfectly discreet. It has lost nothing of its shape."

"But each day will deform it more, and that is why we must hurry. You can find a surgeon who does not know me and you will take me to him. He can bleed me at will."

"I would not take such a risk as he might betray us. I will bleed you myself. That is easy."

"How grateful I am to you! I feel as if you were already giving me back my life. I want you to be kind enough to take me to a midwife to consult her. We could easily go there without being seen, during the first ball of the Opera."

"Yes, my friend, but that is not necessary, and this step might compromise you."

"Not a bit. In this enormous city there are midwives everywhere, and we cannot possibly be known if we keep our masks on. Be kind enough to do that. The advice of a midwife can be very useful to me."

I did not have the heart to refuse her this, but I induced her to wait until the last ball, as the crowd was as a rule larger, and we could go out in greater safety. I promised to wear a black domino and a white Venetian mask with a rose painted near the left eye. As soon as she saw me go out, she was supposed to follow me and get into the carriage I had taken. All this was done accordingly. We shall return to it.

After we had reached this agreement, I brought her home and dined informally there without paying any attention to Farsetti who was present too and who had seen me come in with her. We did not speak to each other. He did not like me and I held him in contempt.

I must relate an unpardonable blunder I committed. I have not forgiven myself yet.

Having promised to take Mlle. X. C. V. to a midwife, I ought, of course, to have taken her to an honest matron, as all we wanted to know was how the young woman should regulate her habits during pregnancy, but led by an evil genius I walked through the rue St. Louis toward the Tuileries and saw la Montigny going into her place with a pretty girl I did not know. Impelled by curiosity, I stopped my carriage and entered the resort.

After having had some fun, and still mindful of Mlle. X. C. V. I asked this woman to give me the address of a midwife. She pointed out a house at the Marais and said that there I should find the pearl of midwives. Thereupon she related a number of exploits which had made the creature famous and which were clear proof of rascality.

As I knew I was not going to see about an illegal operation I thought she might do. I took her address and as I had to go there at night, I went to look the place over the next day.

On the night of the last ball, Mlle. X. C. V. recognized me as agreed. Following me out she climbed into the carriage she had seen me take, and in less than fifteen minutes we arrived at the house of the infamous matron.

A woman about fifty years old received us cordially and at once placed herself at our disposal.

"I am ready to serve you," she said, "for fifty louis, half to be paid in advance for the purchase of the medicines and the rest as soon as they have had their effect. I trust your honesty as you trust mine. Give me first twenty-five louis and come back tomorrow or send for the medicines and the instructions as to their use."

"If my medicines," she added, "do not do their work, though they certainly ought to, I shall give you further directions. In any case, if I do not satisfy you completely, I shall return the money."

"I don't doubt it," I said, "but what, pray, are these other ways?"

"I shall show you how to destroy the foetus."

I could have answered that it was impossible to kill the child without mortally wounding the mother, but I did not feel like arguing with that ugly creature.

"If madame decides to take your remedies," I said, "I shall return tomorrow to bring the money needed to buy the medicines."

I gave her two louis and we left.

Mlle. X. C. V. told me that she thought this woman an accomplished rogue. Surely the fruit could not be destroyed except at the risk of killing the one who bore it.

"I have confidence only in you," she said.

I encouraged these ideas to keep her from rendering herself criminally liable, and I assured her that I should justify her confidence in me. All of a sudden, complaining about the cold:

"Should we have time to get warmed up at the Petite-Pologne?" she said, "I am very anxious to see your pretty dwelling."

This whim surprised and pleased me. The night being very dark, she could not see any of the exterior beauties. The interior had to suffice and imagination furnish the rest. I was careful not to impart my thoughts, as in love many should be hidden. The fact is I entertained the illusion that I was going to reach the moment of happiness. I ordered the carriage to stop at the Point-au-Change. We got out and took another at the corner of the rue de la Ferronière, promising the driver six francs extra if he drove us to my door in fifteen minutes.

I rang the bell with the air of proprietorship. La Perle opened the door and announced that there was nobody in. I knew that perfectly well, but it was a habit we had.

"Light a fire at once and give us something to go with a bottle of champagne."

"An omelet?"

"All right."

"Very well," said mademoiselle, "an omelet."

She was ravishing, and her laughing mien seemed to forecast a delicious moment. Sitting in front of a good fire I placed her on my knees. I covered her with kisses, which she returned affectionately, and I felt on the moment of success, when she begged me quietly and gently to moderate myself. I thought to please her by obeying, for I was convinced that she postponed my victory only to render it more beautiful, and that she should surrender after the champagne. I read love, trust and gratitude in her face, and I should have been sorry to have her believe that I required a reward in the shape of trifling complaisances and marks of affection. I was high-minded enough to wish for nothing but love.

We came to the last glass of champagne. We got up and half coaxing, half compelling, I got her on to a small couch, keeping her lovingly enclosed in my arms; but instead of surrendering she opposed my desires, first by sweet prayers, which as a rule makes one more enterprising, then by commands, and finally by force. That was too much. The idea of violence always was repugnant to me, as I believe that there can be happiness in amorous unions only in as much as there is perfect unanimity of trust and self surrender. I pleaded my cause in every possible manner. I spoke as a flatterer, then as a deceiver and lastly as a despised lover. Finally I told her that I was cruelly disappointed. I perceived that she was mortified. I fell on my knees and asked her forgiveness.

"Alas," she said in the saddest voice, "as I am no longer mistress of my heart, I am a thousand times more to be pitied than you."

She wept copious tears, her head drooped against mine, and my lips met hers, but the play was at an end. The thought of renewing the attack did not enter my mind. I would have rejected the idea with contempt. After a long silence, which we both required, she for the sake of smothering feelings of shame, and I to argue myself into control over a perfectly legitimate burst of temper, we put our masks on and returned to the opera.

On our way, she had the spirit to tell me that she would be obliged to renounce my friendship if I placed such a price on it.

"Love, mademoiselle, must bow to the demands of honor, and yours as well as mine forces me to remain your friend, if only to prove that you are unjust to me. I shall sacrifice myself and do for the sake of duty what I should like to have done for love. May I perish if I try in the future to get favors which I imagined you thought I merited."

We separated at the opera, where the enormous crowd made me lose her in a moment. The next day she told me that she had danced all night. She doubtless hoped to find in that violent exercise the remedy which she did not expect from medicine.

I returned home in bad humor, trying in vain to discover reasons for a refusal which appeared to me humiliating and preposterous. I could justify Mlle. X. C. V. only by adding sophistry to sophistry. In spite of all the imaginable conventions and prejudices, my common sense told me that I had cause to be nettled. I reflected on the bon mot of Populia who never permitted herself infidelities towards her husband except when pregnant.

I was angry at having proved conclusively to myself that I was not loved, and I thought it unworthy of me to continue to love a person whom I could not hope to possess. I went to sleep determined to revenge myself by leaving her to her fate, and thought mockingly what a different occasion she would soon have for heroics. My honor prescribed that I should not be anybody's dupe.

But sleep brings counsel. On awakening I found myself mollified and still in love. My last decision was to act generously towards the unlucky girl. There was no doubt that without me she was lost. Therefore I must continue helping her and show myself indifferent to her favors. The rôle was not easy, but I had the hardihood to play it to perfection, and later the reward came automatically.

The difficulty, the restraint only aggravated my love for the charming Anglo-Greek.

I visited her every morning, and as I was really interested in her state, my rôle became more natural. She could not mistake for something else my anxiety to get her out of her embarrassing position, and as I did not let her see that I was burning up for her, she could attribute to me only the most altruistic motives. She likewise seemed glad of my change of behavior, but her satisfaction may have been only apparent as I knew women well enough to guess that even without loving me she must feel piqued to see me so easily quieted.

One morning, in the middle of our frivolous and haphazard conversation, she complimented me on the strength I showed in controlling myself, then she added with a smile, that my passion and my desires could not have been very powerful as they had subsided in less than a week. I answered calmly that I owed my recovery less to the weakness of my passion than to the force of my self-respect.

"I know myself, mademoiselle," I said. "Without being too conceited, I believe that I am worthy to be loved. Naturally, after having convinced myself that you do not think me worthy of you, I felt humiliated and indignant. Do you understand, mademoiselle, the effect of this double feeling?"

"Alas, I know only too well. It is followed by contempt for the being who brought it about."

"That's an exaggeration, at least in my case. My indignation has only been followed by a return to reason and a plan of revenge."

"Of revenge! And of what kind?"

"I wanted to prove to you, while forcing you to have some regard for me, that although overwhelmed by my feelings, I could forego a prize so ardently desired. I don't know if I have succeeded completely but now I can contemplate your charms without a desire for them."

"And I imagine that you find the consummation of your revenge in the esteem you have won from me. But you are mistaken if you ever thought I had no respect for you. I respect you today, and I did a week ago. Never for one moment did I believe you capable of leaving me to my fate to punish me for having refused your transports, and I am glad to have judged you aright."

Then she spoke about the opiate which I had her take, and as she did not notice any change in her state and as her waist was getting bigger every day, she begged me to increase the dose; but I refused to listen to her demands, as I knew that more than half a dram might cost her her life. I forbade her likewise to be bled a third time, for without realizing what she was doing, she might hurt herself greatly. Her chambermaid, whom she had been forced to take into her confidence, had had her bled by a Saint-Côme student, the maid's lover. Then I told her that it was necessary to be generous with these people to assure herself of their discretion, but she answered that it was not in her power to do so. I offered her money and she said she would borrow fifty louis, which she needed for her brother. I did not have that sum of money on my person, but the same day I sent her a roll of twelve hundred francs with a note saying that I begged her affectionately to come to me whenever she needed help. Her brother received the whole sum and on that account thought himself empowered to ask me another favor. Thanking me the next day, he asked me

to help him in a much more important business. Young and debauched, he had gone into a brothel and come out of it in a bad shape. He complained bitterly of M. Farsetti who had refused him the loan of four louis, declining to mix in such ugly business, and he begged me to speak to his mother so that she would help him get well. I agreed, but when his mother heard about it she said that it was better to let him remain as he was, because it was the third time that he had got into that state, and it was better not to free him from his disease.

"As soon as he is well," she added, "it will be the same old story all over again."

She was right, for having been cured by a skillful surgeon at my expense, he fell a month later victim to his pet vice. This young man was made for shameless excesses, and at the age of fourteen he was an accomplished libertine. His sister was in her sixth month of pregnancy, and her despair increased with the thickness of her waist. She had decided not to get out of bed, and she tormented me. Believing me perfectly cured of the passion she inspired me with, she made me feel all the parts of her body so as to convince me that she could not risk showing herself to anybody. I played the rôle of a midwife with her, and it was mighty hard for me to appear calm and indifferent when the flame which devoured me was coming out at every pore. I could not stand it any longer. She spoke of killing herself with an air of conviction which made me tremble, as it proved a well thought out decision. I was in a position hard to describe, when luck relieved me in the most comical manner.

Seeing, as I said, this charming young lady several times a day in complete freedom, I was ever tempted, and ever restrained, and the fire which was smoldering in its ashes threatened to burst out. Her image pursued me incessantly, she was ever the object of my thoughts, and each day I felt more convinced that I should get no peace as long as I could not smother my passion in absolute possession of all her charms.

One day while visiting at her bedside her mother entered, followed by chevalier Farsetti, and after some insignificant remarks asked me to stay to dinner.

I was on the point of refusing, when Mademoiselle told me that she was going to dine with us. I accepted and we left the room to permit her to dress.

She joined us and appeared with a waist like a nymph. I was astounded. I could hardly believe my eyes, and was on the point of suspecting that she had deceived me, as I could not imagine how she had managed to hide to that degree the fullness which she had let me touch with my own hands.

M. Farsetti sat next to her and I sat next to the mother. At dessert Mademoiselle, who was thinking about the aroph, which she had been advised to use to help her out of her trouble, asked her neighbor, who was a great chemist, if he knew what it was.

"I think," answered Farsetti with a self-satisfied air, "that I know it better than anybody else."

"What is it good for?"

"You ask me too vague a question."

"What does the word mean?"

"Aroph is an Arabic word which I am not acquainted with. You must consult Paracelsus."

"This word," I said, "is neither Arabic nor Hebrew. It does not properly belong to any language. It's a contracted word which hides two."

"Could you," said the chevalier, "give us these words?"

"Nothing easier: *aro* derives from *aroma* and *ph* is the initial of *philosophorum.*"

"Is it Paracelsus," said Farsetti, piqued, "who has imparted to you this knowledge?"

"No sir, I owe it to Boerhaave."

"That's amusing," he said ironically. "Boerhaave does not say that anywhere, but I love to hear people quote with assurance."

"Laugh, Monsieur," I said proudly, "you are at liberty to laugh, no doubt, but this is the test, accept if you dare. I never quote wrongly, as do some who speak Arabic."

Saying this I threw a purse full of gold on the table, but Farsetti, though sure of his facts, answered with a disdainful air that he never betted. Mademoiselle, who enjoyed his embarrassment, remarked that that was the best way never to lose, and joked him about the Arabic word. Pocketing my purse, I made believe I was going out and sent my lackey to Mme. d'Urfé's to fetch Boerhaave.

Reëntering the room I amused the company until my Mercury returned with the book. I opened it and, as I had glanced over it the day before, I at once found the place of the quotation, and having presented it to Farsetti I begged him to ascertain for himself that I had not quoted with assurance but with certainty. Instead of taking the book he got up and left without saying a word.

"He went away angry," said the mother, "I wager that he will never come back again."

"I will bet the contrary," said the daughter, "tomorrow will not pass without his honoring us with his agreeable presence."

She guessed rightly. Farsetti from that day on became my sworn enemy and did not let any opportunity pass to convince me of it.

After dinner we all went to Passy to a concert given by M. de la Popelinière, and of course we had to stay to supper. Mlle. X. C. V. filled all my thoughts in spite of my pretended indifference and I could not but await with anxiety the moment when she could no longer conceal her state from her family.

Mademoiselle was all the time ravishingly gay. Quips and piquant anecdotes enlivened the repast, and fun was the god of the feast. We did not separate till midnight and before leaving

Mademoiselle found the opportunity to beg me to come to see her early as she had something important to say.

I complied religiously. I was at her home before eight o'clock. I found her very sad, and she said that she was in despair. La Popelinière was pressing the conclusion of the marriage and her mother kept persecuting her.

"She has given me to understand that I must sign the contract, and she announced that a modiste would come to take the measurements for my corsets and dresses. I cannot consent to that, as," she added gently, "it's impossible for a modiste not to notice my state. I have made up my mind to kill myself rather than marry before having been delivered and I suppose I must confide in my mother."

"Death," I said, "is an expedient which there is always time to make use of, and it shouldn't be resorted to except when all other means of escape have failed. It seems to me that you can easily get rid of La Popelinière. Confide your state to him. He is a man of honor. He will act without compromising you, as he is sufficiently interested to keep the secret."

"But then of what advantage will that be to me? And how about my mother?"

"Your mother? I take it upon myself to make her listen to reason."

"My friend, how little you know her! Honor would force her to make me disappear; but before doing that she would make me suffer pains to which death is preferable."

"Mademoiselle, I am unhappier than you are!"

Sitting up in her bed, she begged me to remain and asked, with tears in her eyes, how I could think myself unhappier than she. Affecting an air of sentimental pique, I answered that I felt too strongly her contempt.

"How cruel you are! How unjust!" she said weeping, "I can

see that you don't love me. You could triumph over my disgrace. I can only consider your action as revengeful and unworthy a generous man."

Her tears moved me and I threw myself on my knees.

"As you know that I adore you, Mademoiselle, how could you imagine in me a spirit of revenge?"

I pleaded for her forgiveness and all went on as before.

Three or four days later I found her thoughtful and evidently perturbed. She said that she had lost all hope of freeing herself from the burden before the term, and that her mother continued to persecute her. In a few days she would have to decide whether to make a declaration of her state or to sign the contract, but not being able to bring herself to do either she had made up her mind to run away and she wanted me to help her out.

My resolution to assist her was decisive, but I wanted to save appearances, as I should get into trouble if it were discovered that I had carried her away or had made it easy for her to leave the kingdom. At any rate we had never thought, either of us, to unite our destinies by an eternal knot. I left her thoughtful, and wandered towards the Tuileries where they were giving a sacred concert. The oratorio was composed by Mondonville. The words were by the abbe de Voisenen, to whom I had given the motive: *The Israelites on Mount Oreb.* This piece was a novelty and created a sensation. Descending from my carriage I saw Mme. du Rumain who was descending from her own carriage alone. I went up to her and was kindly received.

"I congratulate myself on finding you here," she said. "This is good luck. I am going to hear the new oratorio and I have two reserved seats. You must do me the favor to accept one."

Realizing the importance of such a flattering invitation I did not dare to refuse, although I had my ticket in my pocket. I respectfully offered my arm, and we sat down in the two best seats.

In Paris they do not talk when sacred music is being played, especially if the piece is new. Mme. du Rumain could therefore not judge of my state of mind by my enforced silence during the concert, but afterward my thoughtful air which was not usual with me, made her perceive that I was sad and worried.

"Monsieur Casanova," she said, "be kind enough to come to my house for an hour. I have two or three cabalistic queries to make. I am anxious to have you solve them, but you must hurry as I have a supper engagement in town."

One can guess that she did not have to insist, and as soon as I was in her home my answers were ready in less than half an hour. When I was through this amiable lady said in her kindliest manner: "What is the matter, Monsieur Casanova? You are not in your usual humor, and if I am not mistaken you are confronted by some great misfortune. Are you not weighing an important decision? I am not curious, but if I can be useful at court, you may count on my influence. I will go to Versailles tomorrow morning if the matter is pressing. I am welcome with all the ministers. Confess your troubles to me, and if I cannot ease them at least I shall share them. Have no fear that I shall betray your confidence."

This speech came like a call from heaven, and my good genius moved me to be entirely frank with the lady who had read my thought, and who expressed in clear terms her interest in my happiness. After looking at her a few moments in silent gratitude, I said:

"Madame, I am on the eve, perhaps, of ruin, but your kindness has brought back peace and hope. You shall know my situation. I will make you the depository of a secret which honor renders inviolate. I cannot doubt your discretion as well as your kindness. If afterward you think me worthy of counsel, I promise to follow it and I swear that I will never reveal its source."

After this speech, which gained me her undivided attention, I told her the whole affair in detail. I did not hide the name of the girl, nor suppress any of the circumstances which obliged me to watch over her welfare. I confessed that I had procured some remedies in the hope of removing the burden but without avail.

After this important admission I kept silent and Mme. du Rumain remained as if absorbed in her thoughts for a quarter of an hour. Finally she got up saying:

"I am expected at the house of Mme. de la Marq. I absolutely must go there as I am to meet the Bishop of Montrouge, to whom I have something very important to say, and I hope to be useful to you. Please come back the day after tomorrow at eight o'clock. You will find me alone. Meanwhile do not take any steps without having seen me. Adieu."

I left her full of hope and quite determined to be led by her counsel in this ticklish affair.

The Bishop of Montrouge, to whom she was going to speak about an important affair known to me, was the abbé de Voisenon, who took the title of Montrouge from the name of an estate which he visited frequently. It was near Paris and belonged to the Duke de la Vallière.

I saw Mademoiselle the next day and told her only that in a few days I hoped to be able to give her good news. I was pleased to see that she appeared resigned and trustful.

The day after, I did not fail to be at the house of my noble protector at eight o'clock. The Swiss smilingly said that I should find the doctor with Madame. This did not prevent my going upstairs and as soon as I appeared he took his leave. It was Herrenschwand, the fashionable doctor who treated all the pretty women in Paris and whom the unhappy Poinsinet put on the stage in the *"Circle"* a one-act skit of little merit, but successful because the personages were easily recognized.

"My dear, unhappy man," said Mme. du Rumain, as soon as we

were alone, "I have settled your business, and now it is your turn to keep a secret inviolate. After having seriously reflected on the case of conscience which you have confessed to me, I went to the Convent C——. The abbess is my friend. I confided the secret to her and I am certain that she is quite incapable of taking advantage of it. We have decided that she shall receive the girl in the convent and give her a good converse sister to take care of her at the time of delivery. You cannot deny," she added, with a smile, "that the convents are good for something, after all. Your protégée will go there alone with a letter for the abbess which I will give you and which she must send in through the gate keeper. She will then be shown to a comfortable room. She will not receive any visitors, and she will receive no letters that have not passed through my hands. The abbess will send me the answers which I shall deliver to you personally. You understand that she must not correspond with anybody but you, and you will have no news except through my mediation. In writing to her you must be careful always to leave the address space blank. I had to give the abbess the young lady's name, but I did not tell her yours as she did not ask me. Acquaint the young lady of all the arrangements and when she is ready let me know, and I shall give you my letter. Tell her not to take along anything that isn't strictly necessary. Diamonds or valuables, especially, must be left behind. You can inform her that the abbess will see her from time to time, and will be very friendly to her and give her edifying books to read. In a word she will be treated with distinction and have the best of care. Tell her also not to confide in any way in the sister converse who serves her; for although good and honest, a sister is a sister and the secret might not be kept. After the delivery she must go to confession and receive the sacrament at Easter. The abbess will give her a certificate in due form to present to her mother, who will be too happy at having her back again, to make any difficulty or to insist on the marriage—which, by the way, will serve as a pretext for the retreat."

Admiring Mme. Rumain's prudence, I thanked her profusely and begged her to give me the letter at once, as there was no time to lose. She kindly sat down before her desk and wrote the following:

"My dear Abbess:

"The girl who will present this letter to you is the one I had the pleasure of speaking to you about. She wishes to pass three or four months under your protection, in peace and prayers and she wants to be sure that when she returns to her mother, she will not be persecuted into contracting a marriage to which she cannot bring herself. This distasteful marriage is the reason for her resolution to keep away from her family for a while."

After having read me the letter she presented it to me unsealed so that Mademoiselle could read it. The abbess was a princess, consequently her convent was above all suspicion. When I received the letter from Mme. du Rumain's hands I felt so grateful that I knelt down before her. This generous lady was always useful to me as will be seen later.

Leaving Mme. du Rumain I went directly to the hotel de Bretagne, where Mademoiselle had only time to inform me that she was going to be busy all day but that in the evening at eleven o'clock she would go to the attic, where we should have all the time we wanted. I was delighted. I foresaw the happy culmination of a beautiful dream, now that I should have no more opportunities to find myself alone with her.

Before going out of the house I spoke a word to Madeleine, who promised to give notice to our Mercury to have everything in the best order.

I was exact to the rendezvous and I did not have to wait long for my belle. I told her not to forget to burn all the letters she had received from me, and to write me from the convent as often as possible, sealing the letters but leaving the address space blank. She promised to follow my instructions carefully and then I forced her to accept a roll of two hundred louis, which might be needed, although we did not foresee how. She wept, more pained by the embarrassing situation she thought I was in than by her own difficult position; but I reassured her, saying that I had a great deal of money and very powerful patronage.

"I will leave," she said, "the day after tomorrow at the appointed hour."

I promised to visit the hotel de Bretagne the day after the flight as if I did not know anything about it and to write to her everything that was said about her. Thereupon we embraced tenderly and I left.

* * * * *

In the convent Mlle. X. C. V. gave birth to a fine boy. She soon left Paris with her mother and became later a great lady in Venice.

Chapter XII

ABBE DE BERNIS AND JEAN JACQUES ROUSSEAU

THE Abbé de Bernis to whom I paid my respects regularly every week, told me one day that the comptroller general often inquired after me and that I was making a mistake in neglecting him. I had spoken to the abbé of a plan I had for the increase of the state revenues and he told me I need feel no hesitancy about laying my scheme before the comptroller. As the abbé had made my fortune I attached too much weight to his counsel to disregard it. Accordingly I went to see the comptroller, and relying completely on his good faith I submitted my proposition. It called for the promulgation of a law by virtue of which all inheritance not directly from father to son should furnish the state a year's total income. A legally certified donation to be enjoyed during the lifetime of the donor was subject to the same levy. The returns to the heir or beneficiary would be the same as if he secured full possession, principal and interest intact, one year after the actual date of transmission, so I thought the measure could hardly seem oppressive. The minister thought as I did, and saying that my plan offered no difficulty, placed it in his secret portfolio, furthermore assuring me that I was a made man.

A week later he was replaced by M. de Silhouette. I presented myself to this new minister, who told me coldly that when it was time to publish the decree he would inform me. The proposal became a law two years later, and when I declared myself its author and claimed my just reward I was held up to ridicule.

Soon afterward the Pope died and was succeeded by a Venetian, Rezzonico, who created my protector Bernis a cardinal. Bernis was exiled to Soissons by his gracious majesty Louis XV two days atfer receiving the red hat from his royal hands. Such is the friendship of kings.

The disgrace of my charming abbé left me without a protector, but I had gold, and this circumstance made me support the misfortune with resignation.

Bernis died a year ago in Rome. At the height of his glory as minister of France he had, in concert with the Prince von Kaunitz, succeeded happily in destroying all that Cardinal Richelieu had done to foment hatred between the houses of Bourbon and Austria. Italy had served as battleground every time the ancient rivals had one of their interminable quarrels to fight out, and the alliance of the two houses freed her from the horrors of continuous warfare. Rezzonico at the time of the treaty was bishop of Padua, consequently he was well able to appreciate the achievement of the noble abbé.

Distinguished as were his services Bernis was exiled from the court of Louis XV for telling the king, who had solicited the opinion, that the Prince de Soubise was not competent to take command of the armies. As soon as La Pompadour heard of this, and she had it from the king himself, she exerted her influence and had the prelate disgraced. There was general dissatisfaction, but it was vented in the composition of pointed verses and the new cardinal was soon forgotten.

That is characteristic of this nation. Flippant, witty, good-natured, she does not feel her misfortunes nor those of anybody else when once she has had a laugh out of them. At this time imprisonment in the Bastille awaited the authors of epigrams and songs which satirized the king and his ministers, or even his concubines, but the penalty did not prevent the wits from continuing to amuse society. Many thought it an honor to be persecuted for a clever epigram. A man whose name I have forgotten, but who was making a valiant bid for notoriety, appropriated some verses written by the son of Crebillon and had himself lodged in the Bastille rather than disown them.

Crebillon, who was not a man to deny his own productions, said to the Duc de Choiseul, "I wrote some verses which are identical to those, but it may have happened that the prisoner wrote them too."

This made everybody laugh and the author of the Sofa was not bothered.

The illustrious Cardinal de Bernis was ten years *in exule procul negotiis,* and profoundly unhappy, as I learned from him in Rome fifteen years later. I have heard people declare they would rather be minister than king. To me this seems absurd. It is as much as to claim that servitude is preferable to independence. In a despotic government under a weak or lazy king a master minister exerts a tremendous influence, but the position is not without its disadvantages.

Louis XV was never known to reinstate a disgraced minister, so Cardinal de Bernis was not recalled to court, but on the death of Rezzonico he was summoned to the papal conclave at Rome, in which city he remained the rest of his life as representative of France, enjoying the particular favor of Pius VI.

About the time of the abbé's disgrace Mme. d'Urfé expressed a desire to know Jean Jacques Rousseau. I went with her to Montmorency to pay the philosopher a visit, under the pretext of giving him some music to copy, a task which he performed admirably. He charged twice as much as other copyists did, but he guaranteed the perfect execution of the work. At that time this famous writer had no other means of livelihood.

We found a man of simple and modest appearance, in no way

distinguished, though he conversed sensibly and logically. Rousseau did not seem to me to have a winning personality, and he possessed none of the social graces. Mme. d'Urfé thought him rude. We had heard a good deal about the woman he lived with. We met her, but she paid little or no attention to us. When we left we entertained each other with anecdotes illustrative of the philosopher's eccentricity.

I must tell of the visit paid him by the Prince de Conti, father of the Count de la Marche. The amiable prince went alone to Montmorency to pass an agreeable day conversing with the already famous thinker. Rousseau was walking in the park. The prince accosted him and announced the intention of dining with him and staying all day so that they might discuss everything to their complete satisfaction.

"Your highness will have poor fare," said Rousseau, "but there shall be a place for you."

The philosopher left to give his orders and returned and walked with his guest two or three hours. When dinner time arrived the prince was conducted to the dining room. Noticing that the table was set for three he asked, "Who is going to dine with us? I thought we were to remain tête-à-tête."

"Our third party, monseigneur," said Rousseau, "is my alter ego, a being who is not my wife, nor my mistress, nor my servant, nor my mother, nor my daughter, and who is all these at the same time."

"That may be, my dear sir, but having come with the express purpose of seeing you alone I will not dine with your alter ego, whom you may have all to yourself."

So saying the prince saluted and left. Rousseau did not try to detain him.

Chapter XIII

VOLTAIRE

EVERYBODY wanted to give me a letter to M. de Voltaire. From this solicitude one would have believed the great man beloved of all, whereas he was universally detested because of his satirical turn of mind.

"How is it, mesdames," I asked, "is not M. de Voltaire amiable and gallant toward you who had the condescension to act his plays with him?"

"No, not in the least. When we rehearsed our parts he scolded all the time. We never could do anything to suit him. Sometimes it was a word mispronounced, sometimes an intonation wasn't spirited enough or passionate enough, or it was an inflection or a cadence, or what not? And when we played! The fuss he made because a syllable was added or dropped so a verse didn't scan properly. He frightened us. One of us had laughed in the wrong place; in Alzire one of us did not weep convincingly."

"He required of you that you should really weep?"

"Actually. He wanted real tears. He declared that an actor must shed real tears to make people weep. I told him one day that it was not my fault if his old verses weren't tragic enough."

"I am sure he only laughed?"

"Laugh? No, he sneered, for he is brutal and even insulting."

"But you overlooked these faults?"

"Not all. We drove him away."

"You drove him away?"

"Neither more nor less. He suddenly left the house he had taken and moved to where he is now. He does not visit us any more, even when we invite him."

"Then you invite him, although you have driven him away?"

"We cannot deprive ourselves of the pleasure of admiring his talent, and if we plagued him it was only to get even and to teach him how to behave."

"A deportment lesson to a great master!"

"Just so. When you meet him speak to him about Lausanne and see what he says. But he will laugh when he says it. That's his way."

After dinner we went to Voltaire's. He was getting up from the table as we entered. He was as if in the midst of a court of lords and ladies, so my presentation was very formal, but perhaps this circumstance was not a disadvantage to me.

"This," I said, "Monsieur de Voltaire, is the most momentous day in my life. I have been your pupil for twenty years, and I am truly overjoyed to see my master."

"Monsieur, honor me for another twenty years, and promise me at the end of that time to bring me my fees."

"Gladly, on condition that you wait for me."

This Voltarian sally produced a general laugh. I was glad of that because there is nothing like an amused audience to give a keenness to conversation, and I knew Voltaire would be on the alert to get back at me. For my part I did not mean to be taken by surprise.

Meanwhile two newly arrived Englishmen were introduced.

"These gentlemen are English," said Voltaire, "I wish I were."

I thought the compliment out of place, for it sounded as if he wanted these gentlemen to answer from politeness that they wished they were French, and if they did not feel like lying they were in an embarrassing situation. I think it is permissible for a man of honor to put his own nation first.

A little later Voltaire spoke to me again, saying that as I was a Venetian I must know Count Algarotti.

"I know him, but not because I am a Venetian. Seven-eighths of my countrymen are unaware of his very existence."

"But you know him as a man of letters?"

"I know him because I stayed with him for two months in Padua, seven years ago, and what particularly attracted my attention to him was his admiration for M. de Voltaire."

"That's flattering to me, but he does not need to be one's admirer to merit one's esteem."

"If he were not a good admirer Algarotti would never have made a name for himself. He began by admiring Newton, and now he has made it possible for the ladies to talk about light."

"Has he really succeeded in doing that?"

"Not so well as M. de Fontenelle with his 'Plurality of the World,' but still he has succeeded."

"That is a great deal. Should you see him in Bologna tell him that I await his letters on Russia. He can send them to Milan to my banker Bianchi, who will forward them to me."

"I shall not fail."

"They tell me the Italians do not care for his style."

"Indeed we do not. Everything that he writes teems with Gallicisms. His style is pitiful."

"I should think a few French phrases would improve your language."

"They make it unbearable. Imagine a page of French interspersed with Italian, even if M. de Voltaire had written it."

"You are quite right. Purity is essential to any language. That is what they criticize in Livy. They say his Latin reeks of 'Patavinity.'"

"When I began the study of Latin the Abbé Lazzarini told me he preferred Livy to Sallust."

"Is that the Abbé Lazzarini who wrote the tragedy 'Ulysses the Younger'? You couldn't have been very old at the time. I should like to have known him. I was quite well acquainted with Abbé Conti, who was the friend of Newton and whose four tragedies embrace all Roman history."

"I have also known and admired him. I was young then, and I felt highly flattered at being admitted to the society of these great men. It seems but yesterday, although it was many years ago. You see the realization of my inferiority in the presence of the great has never been to me a source of humiliation, nor is it at this moment. I could be the younger son of humanity."

"You could better be its dean. Is it indiscreet to ask you to what kind of literature you have dedicated yourself?"

"To none, but that may come later. Meanwhile I read as much as I can, and while traveling I study men."

"The fittest subject, surely, but the text book is too bulky. One gets at them more readily by studying history."

"Quite so, if history did not lie. One is never certain of the facts. It's a bore, too, and the study of the world through travel is amusing. Horace is my guide book. I can follow him everywhere."

"Algarotti memorized all of Horace. You love poetry?"

"It's my passion."

"Have you written many sonnets?"

"Ten or twelve which I like, and two or three thousand which I have never read a second time."

"Italy has a rage for sonnets."

"Yes, if the inclination to enhance the value of a thought by giving it a harmonious turn can be called a rage. The sonnet is difficult because of its rigid form. The thought must be coerced to fit the fourteen lines."

"It's the very bed of Procrustes. That is why you have so few good ones. As for ourselves, we have not a single good one, but that is the fault of the language."

"And of the genius of the French, who consider that in expansion a thought must lose its force."

"And isn't that your opinion?"

"Pardon me. It depends on the thought. A pithy saying, for example, is not sufficiently material for a sonnet; it belongs, in Italian as well as in French, in the domain of epigram."

"Who is the poet you admire most?"

"Ariosto, but I cannot say I love him better than the others, for he is my only love."

"Nevertheless you know the others?"

"I think I have read them all, but they pale before Ariosto. Fifteen years ago when I read the evil you said of him I declared that you would retract it after you had read him."

"I thank you for believing that I had not read him. I read him when I was young and had but a superficial knowledge of your language. Being prejudiced against him by Italian scholars who worshipped Tasso I was unfortunate enough to publish a judgment which I believed was mine, while I was merely echoing the thoughtless bias of those who had influenced me. I adore your Tasso."

"Ah, Monsieur de Voltaire, I breathe freely now. But, I beg of you, excommunicate the work in which you have ridiculed our illustrious artist."

"No need of that. My books are all on the index, but I will give you a proof of my retraction."

I was astounded. The great man, without missing a single verse, without the slightest mistake in prosody, recited from memory the two passages from the thirty-fourth and thirty-fifth cantos wherein the divine Ariosto sets forth the conversation of Astolfo with the apostle St. John. Then he pointed out the beauties of individual lines. The ablest of Italian commentators could not have shown more unerring insight. In a state of high excitement I gave the closest attention and was unable to find him at fault in a single detail. I turned toward the company exclaiming that I was overcome and that I would inform all Italy of this admirable performance.

"And I, monsieur," replied the great man, "shall inform all Europe of the reparation which I owe to the greatest genius she ever produced."

Eager for praise, which he deserved on so many counts, Voltaire gave me next day the translation he had made of the stanza which Ariosto begins with this verse:

> *Quindi avvien che tra principi e signor* . . .
> Whence happed that amid lords and potentates . . .

At the end of the recitation, which brought applause from all hearers, although none of them knew Italian, Mme. Denis, his niece, asked me if I thought the passage which her uncle had recited was one of the poet's best.

"The best, madame, but not the most beautiful."

"No, those could hardly be the lines which brought about the apotheosis of Signor Ludovico."

"He has been canonized? I did not know that."

Everybody laughed except myself. I was quite serious.

Voltaire, piqued at my ingenuousness, asked me, "You are thinking of some particular passage, to whose more than human beauty the poet owes the epithet of 'the divine Ariosto?'"

"Yes, I have the very passage in mind."

"Which one is it?"

"The last thirty-six stanzas of the twenty-third canto, in which the poet tells how Orlando went mad. Since the world began nobody knew how insanity came on, except Ariosto, who went mad at the end of his life. These stanzas inspire horror, Monsieur de Voltaire. I know they have made me tremble."

"Yes, I remember them. They show the awful power of love. I must read them again."

"Perhaps monsieur will be kind enough to recite them," said Mme. Denis casting a passing glance at her uncle.

"Gladly, madame," I said, "if you will listen with patience."

"You have taken the trouble to learn them by heart?" asked Voltaire.

"The pleasure, monsieur, for it gave me no trouble. Since the age of sixteen I have passed never a year without reading Ariosto two or three times, and the lines have quite naturally fixed themselves in my memory. I know the whole epic with the exception of the tedious genealogies and long-winded historical tirades which fatigue the mind without interesting the heart. Horace is the only poet whose verses are all engraved in my soul, in spite of the oft prosaic turn of his epistles, which are far inferior to those of Boileau."

"Boileau is too much given to eulogy, Monsieur de Casanova, let Horace be. As far as Ariosto is concerned, forty great cantos, that's too much."

"There are fifty-one, Monsieur de Voltaire."

The great man was silent, but Mme. Denis spoke at once.

"Let us hear, then, the thirty-six stanzas which make one tremble and which gained the author the title of 'the divine.'"

I launched out confidently, not reciting in the monotone adopted by the Italians, and for which the French justly reproach us. The French would be the best declaimers in the world if they were not constrained by the couplet rhyme, for of all peoples they most truly feel what they say. They have not the uniformly high-keyed intonation of my countrymen, nor the sentimental and exaggerated tone of the Germans, nor the listless manner of the English; they give to each phrase the tone and the voice which best suit the feeling to be conveyed, but the forced repetition of the same sounds makes them lose these advantages. With animated gestures I recited the beautiful verses of Ariosto in a well cadenced prose, modulating the intonations according to the feelings which I wanted to inspire. My hearers afterward said they felt the violence of my effort to restrain my tears, and when I came to the stanza beginning

> *Poichè allargare il freno al dolor puote,*
> Then might he loose the leash of his despair,

my tears flowed in such abundance that all the listeners wept aloud. M. de Voltaire and Mme. Denis embraced me but their embraces could not stop me, as Orlando to become mad was yet to see that he was in the same bed in which once upon a time Angelica had been found in the arms of the too happy Medoro, and I had to reach the next stanza. When I had finished Voltaire exclaimed, "I have always said it! The secret of making people weep is to weep yourself but the tears must be real, and before one can shed real tears the soul must be profoundly moved. I thank you, sir," he added, embracing me, "and I promise to recite the same stanzas and to weep like you."

He kept his word.

"It is surprising," said Mme. Denis, "that intolerant Rome has never placed his Roman divagation on the index."

"Not at all," said Voltaire. "Leo X stole a march by excommunicating all those who dared condemn it. The two great families of Este and Medici were interested in sustaining him. Without this protection it is quite probable that the one verse in which the poet says that Constantine's gift of Rome to Silvester *'puzza forte'*, 'stinketh vilely', would have sufficed to place the whole poem on the index."

"I believe," I said, "that the verse which created most scandal was the one in which Ariosto seemed to doubt the resurrection of the human race at the end of the world. Ariosto is speaking of the hermit who attempted to dissuade Rodomonte from seizing Isabella, widow of Zerbino. The giant, bored by the sermons, grabbed him and hurled him against a rock where in death he lay as if asleep, so that *'al novissimo dì forse fia desto'*: 'on the last day perhaps he will be wakened.' This *perhaps,* which to the poet represented only a bit of rhetoric, or a couple of syllables to fill out a verse, raised an outcry which without doubt amused Ariosto if he deigned to notice it."

"It is a pity," said Mme. Denis, "that Ariosto was not more economical with this kind of hyperbole."

"Not so, my dear niece. These are the grains of salt sprinkled most judiciously over the whole work and giving it its perfect savor."

We talked of a thousand different things pertaining to literature and finally of *L'Ecossaise,* which we had played at Soleure. They knew all about it. M. de Voltaire said that if I wanted to play at his home he would write to M. de Chavigny to invite my Lindane to come and assist me and that he would play the rôle of Montrose. I excused myself by saying that Mme. de M. was in Basle and that I was forced to leave the next day. At these words he protested loudly, stirring the whole company against me, and ended by saying that he would be insulted if I did not devote at least a whole week to him.

"Monsieur," I said, "I have come to Geneva only to have the honor of seeing you. Now that I have obtained this favor I have nothing else to do here."

"Have you come here to speak to me, or for me to speak to you?"

"Partially that I might speak to you, but much more that I might listen to you."

"Then stay at least three days longer. Come and dine with me every day and we shall have much to say and to hear."

The invitation was so pressing and so flattering that I could not refuse. I accepted and retired to do some writing.

The next day I again presented myself. I was silent during dinner, but at dessert M. de Voltaire, knowing I had no reason to be satisfied with the government of Venice, spoke to me on this subject. I disappointed his expectations by trying to prove to him that there is no country in the world where one could be more free.

"Yes," he said, "if you are willing to play the rôle of a deaf mute."

Seeing that the subject did not please me he took me by the arm and led me to the garden, which he said was his Creation. The wide promenade ended at the bank of a beautiful river.

"This," he said, "is the Rhone which I send to France."

"A present which does not cost you very much."

He smiled agreeably, then showed me the rue de Geneva and the Dent Blanche, which is the highest point in the Alps.

Reverting to the subject of Italian literature he spoke mistakenly but wittily about it, manifesting a great deal of knowledge and false judgment. I let him talk. He spoke of Homer, of Dante, of Petrarch. Everybody knows what he thought about these geniuses: his mistake was in writing the opinion. I merely told him that if these great men did not deserve the esteem of every scholar they would have descended long ago from the high pedestal where the approbation of centuries had placed them.

The Duke of Villars and the famous Dr. Tronchin came to join us. The doctor, tall, well built, good looking, had a fine manner and was eloquent without being a babbler. Favorite pupil of Boerhaave, he was a learned physician without professional jargon or charlatanry or the conceit of the pillars of the faculty. I was delighted with him. His treatment was based on a régime, and to order it he had perforce to be a philosopher. I was told that he had cured a consumptive of a secret disease by means of milk taken from a she donkey which had been subjected to thirty vigorous mercury rubs administered by four brawny porters. I did not believe this tale.

Villars, the governor of Provence, claimed my attention but impressed me less favorably. He had the face and demeanor of a woman seventy years old who might have been beautiful once and who still clung to her pretensions. His blotched cheeks were covered with rouge, his lips with carmine, and his eyebrows were dyed black. He had false teeth, an enormous wig which gave off a strong odor of amber, and a buttonhole nosegay which came up to his chin. He affected graceful gestures and spoke in a voice so soft that one could hardly hear what he had to say. Otherwise he was very polite and affable in the style of the regency, but all in all a supremely ridiculous being. They told me that in his youth and prime he had loved the fair sex, but when he lost his vigor he decided to become a woman and kept four minions, each one of them having the disgusting honor of warming his old carcass at night.

His back was eaten up by a cancer. According to nature's law he ought to have been buried ten years before, but Tronchin had kept him alive artificially by feeding his wounds with slices of veal. Without this nourishment the cancer would have died, carrying his corpse along with it. This method of treatment was a fair example of Tronchin's régime.

I escorted Voltaire to his bedroom where he changed his wig and put on a cap, for he was very liable to catching cold. On the table I saw the *Summa* of Saint Thomas, and among many Italian poets the *Secchia Rapita* of Tassoni.

"That," said Voltaire, "is the only tragi-comic poem of Italy. Tassoni was a monk, a wit, and a learned man as well as a poet."

"He might pass as a poet but not as a scientist, for he ridiculed Copernicus' theory of lunar eclipses."

"Where did he say such nonsense."

"In his academic speeches."

"I do not own them. I must."

He took a pen to make a note on the subject, then said, "Tassoni criticized Petrarch with a great deal of wit."

"Yes, and in so doing discredited his own taste, like Muratori."

"Here it is. You must admit that his erudition is enormous."

"*Est ubi peccat.*" *

Voltaire opened a door and I saw about a hundred big bundles of paper.

"That," he said, "is my correspondence. You see there as many as fifty thousand letters which I have answered."

"Have you copies of your replies?"

"Of most of them. The labor of copying my correspondence is entrusted to a valet who does nothing else."

"I know a great many publishers who would give a mint of gold to own this treasure."

"Beware of publishers when you have something to give to the public, if you have not begun already. They are highwaymen more to be feared than those of Morocco."

"I shan't have any dealings with them until I am an old man."

"Then they will be the curse of your latter days."

A propos of that I recited a verse from the *Macaronicon* of Merlino Cocci.

"What is that?"

"It's a verse from a celebrated poem written in twenty-four cantos."

"Celebrated?"

---

* That is where he sins.

"Yes, and justly, but to be able to appreciate it one must know the dialect of Mantua."

"I could probably read it if you would get me a copy."

"I shall have the honor of offering you one tomorrow."

"You would oblige me beyond measure."

Somebody came and dragged us back into the midst of the company, and we passed two hours discussing every possible subject.

Voltaire displayed the vast resources of his fertile intellect and charmed everyone, in spite of his caustic shafts which did not even spare those present, but he possessed the inimitable art of flinging his sarcasms so as not to hurt. The great man sped his witticisms with a winning smile, and laughter never failed.

He was lavish of his hospitality, and one ate well at the poet's, a rare circumstance with the confreres of Apollo, who are seldom, as he was, the favorites of Plutus. He was then sixty-six years old and had an income of a hundred and twenty thousand livres. Slanderers said that this great man had enriched himself by cheating his publishers. The fact is that he was not favored any more than the least of authors, and that far from having cheated his publishers he had often been their dupe. He can certainly not be said to have cheated Cramer, who made a fortune off him. Voltaire was able to become rich by other means than by his pen, and as he was greedy for fame he often gave away his works on the sole condition that they be printed and distributed.

In the short time that I was with him I was a witness of this prodigality. He gave away his *Princesse de Babylone,* a charming tale which he wrote in three days.

After a good sleep I awoke refreshed and wrote M. de Voltaire a letter in blank verse, which caused me more work than if I had attempted rhyme. I sent it with the *Macaronicon,* which, as I might have foreseen, he could not understand well enough to appreciate it.

At midday I went to see M. de Voltaire. He did not dine with us. It was not until five o'clock that he appeared, holding a letter in his hand.

"Do you know a Bolognese senator named Marquis Albergati Capacelli, and Count Paradisi?"

"I don't know Paradisi, but I know M. Albergati by sight and reputation. He is not a senator, he is one of 'the Forty' of Bologna, who, as you know, are fifty."

"Good heavens! That is a puzzling enigma."

"Do you know him?"

"No, but he has sent me the complete works of Goldoni, a translation of my *Tancrede,* and some Bologna sausages, and he is coming to see me."

"He won't come. He is not fool enough."

"Is it foolish for a man to come and see me?"

"Yes, for M. Albergati."

"Why, pray?"

"He knows he would lose too much. He cherishes the idea you seem to have of him, and once you were forced to realize his incapacity—goodby illusion! He is nothing more nor less than a kind gentleman with an income of six thousand sequins and a mania for the theater. He is a fairly good actor and has written some prose comedies which cannot stand representation or reading."

"Your account of him does not add to his stature."

"Nor diminish him to his actual proportions, I assure you."

"But tell me, how can forty be fifty in Bologna?"

"As, in Basle, midday can be eleven o'clock."

"I understand. As your Council of the Ten is of seventeen."

"Precisely. But the cursed Forty of Bologna are worse than our Ten."

"Why cursed?"

"Because not being subject to revenue levies they can commit any crime with entire impunity and get out of it by retiring outside the state and living on their incomes."

"They are blessed, not cursed. But to continue. Marquis Albergati, you say, is a man of letters?"

"He can write his own language but he is prolix and has nothing to say."

"He is an actor?"

"And a very good one, especially in his own pieces when he plays the lover."

"Is he good looking?"

"Yes, on the stage, but not elsewhere, as there is no expression in his face."

"Nevertheless his comedies please?"

"To understand them is to hiss them."

"What do you think of Goldoni?"

"More than I can say. Goldoni is the Molière of Italy."

"Why does he call himself the poet of the Duke of Parma?"

"Doubtless to prove that a clever man can have his weaknesses. as well as a fool. The duke probably knows nothing about it. Goldoni calls himself a lawyer too, but that is only a fancy of his. He is a good author of comedies, and nothing else. All Venice knows me as his friend, therefore I can speak intelligently about him. In spite of the fine sarcasm in his writings he is excessively good natured. He does not shine in society."

"That is what I have heard. They say he is poor and wants to leave Venice. That would not please the theatrical managers who produce his plays."

"There was talk of giving him a pension, but the plan has gone up in smoke. It was thought that as soon as he had a pension he would cease writing."

"Or perhaps it was as when a pension was refused to Homer in the fear that every blind man in Greater Greece would immediately apply."

We passed a very agreeable day. He thanked me effusively for the *Macaronicon* and promised to read it. He introduced me to a Jesuit who was in his pay and who was called Adam, "Not," said Voltaire, "the first among men." I was told later that they played backgammon together and that when Voltaire lost he threw the dice and dice box at Adam's head. If Jesuits everywhere were treated with as little consideration we should end by having only inoffensive Jesuits. That happy day is as yet far off.

On the way he said about shame, "This feeling, which prevents women from showing the parts they have been taught since childhood to keep covered, springs sometimes from innate modesty. Oftener, however, I think it is only skin deep and no protection against an aggressor who knows how to manage. The easiest way to overcome shame is to keep it from asserting itself, to turn it into ridicule and override it. Victory is certain. The effrontery of the assailant conquers the victim, who asks nothing better than to be conquered, and who almost always ends by thanking you for your victory. Clement of Alexandria, sage and philosopher, said that shame, which seems to have such deep roots in the mind of woman, dwells only in the linen which covers her and that when this is removed no trace of shame remains."

After ten hours of sweet and refreshing sleep I felt in a state to enjoy M. de Voltaire's society. I went to see him and was disappointed. That day it pleased the great man to be fault finding and sneering. He knew that I was departing the next day. At the table he began by saying that he thanked me for my present of the work of Merlino Cocci.

"You certainly offered it to me with good intentions," he said, "but I cannot thank you for having made me waste four hours reading a lot of nonsense."

I felt my hair bristle, but controlled myself and answered in a dispassionate tone that some other time he would perhaps outdo me in praising the poem. I told of several instances which had proved to me the inadequacy of a first reading.

"All right," he said, "but as far as this *Macaronicon* is concerned I leave it to you. I place it side by side with Chapelain's *La Pucelle*."

"Which delights every connoisseur in spite of some bad verses. With all his faults Chapelain was a poet."

My frankness probably shocked him. I knew of his prejudice against *La Pucelle*. I also knew that a smutty poem by the same name was being circulated and was supposed to be Voltaire's, though he disowned it. I thought that as the subject was tender he would change it, but he challenged me bitterly and I replied in kind.

"Chapelain," I said, "had the merit of making his subject agreeable without catering to popularity by the use of salaciousness or impiety. That is the opinion of my master Crebillon."

"Crebillon! You quote sound authority. But on what, if I may inquire, do you base your claim that my confrère Crebillon is your master?"

"In less than two years he taught me what French I know, and to give him a proof of my gratitude I have translated his *Rhadamiste* into Italian Alexandrines. I am the first Italian who has dared adapt this meter to our language."

"The first? I beg your pardon. This honor belongs to my friend Pierre-Jacques Martelli."

"I am sorry to be forced to tell you that you are in error."

"Indeed! I have in my room his complete works published in Bologna."

"I do not dispute your word, I am merely calling into question the meter employed by Martelli. You can have read of him only verses of fourteen syllables, without rotation of masculine and feminine rhymes. It is true he thought he was imitating your Alexandrines. His preface made me explode with laughter. Perhaps you have not read it?"

"Not read it, monsieur! I have a passion for prefaces, and Martelli proves that his verses have the same effect on Italian ears as Alexandrines on ours."

"It is precisely on that point that I find him ridiculous. This good man was badly mistaken, as I think I can prove to your satisfaction. Your masculine verses have twelve syllables and the feminine thirteen. All of Martelli's have fourteen except those whose final word ends in a long vowel. Kindly observe that Martelli's first hemistich is always of seven syllables, while in French it is always six. Your friend Pierre-Jacques must have been deaf."

"Then you followed carefully our rules of prosody?"

"Rigidly, in spite of the difficulty. You know, almost all our words end in a short syllable."

"What effect has your innovation produced?"

"Nobody was able to recite my verses, but I hope to convey the method when I recite them myself to our literary coteries."

"Do you remember any passages from your *Rhadamiste?*"

"I remember it all."

"A prodigious memory! I should like to hear a sample."

I recited a new rendition of the same scene which I had declaimed to Crebillon ten years before, and I thought M. de Voltaire listened with pleasure.

"One does not notice the slightest difficulty," he observed.

That was the most agreeable thing he could have said to me. In his turn the great man recited a passage from his *Tancrede,* which had not yet been published, I think, and which afterward was justly pronounced a masterpiece. We might well have stopped right there, but having quoted a verse from Horace to illustrate a technical point he said that Horace was a great master of the theater and that his precepts will never become obsolete.

I answered, "You violate one of them, one only, and that in the manner of a great man."

"Which precept do I violate?"

"You don't write *contentus paucis lectoribus*." *

"If Horace had had to fight the octopus of superstition he would have written for everybody as I do."

"It seems to me you could spare yourself the trouble of fighting what you will never succeed in destroying."

"What I cannot finish others will, and I shall always have the glory of having begun the combat."

"Well and good, but suppose you succeeded in destroying superstition, what would you set up in its place?"

"I like that. When I free the human race from a ferocious beast which devours it, can you ask what new beast I shall bring as a substitute?"

"Superstition does not devour us, on the contrary it is quite necessary to our existence."

"Necessary to our existence! Horrible blasphemy, to which posterity shall do justice. I love the human race. I would see it like myself free and happy, and superstition cannot possibly coexist with liberty. In what way do you think superstition contributes to happiness?"

"Do you desire mass rule?"

"God forbid! There must be a sovereign."

"In which case superstition is necessary, or people would never obey a man called a monarch."

"Not a monarch. This name connotes despotism and slavery, which I hate."

"Then what do you want? If you want one man to govern alone you can but consider him a monarch."

"I want a chief chosen by a free people to rule them under a pact

---

* Content with few readers.

which shall bind them mutually and prevent him from ever becoming tyrannical."

"Addison shows that such a sovereign, or chief, can never be found. I am with Hobbes. Between the two evils, tyranny and anarchy, the less must be chosen. A people without superstition would be philosophic, and philosophers will not obey. The people can only be happy as long as they are crushed, treaded upon, and kept in chains."

"Frightful—and you are of the people! If you have read my writings you must have seen how I prove that superstition is the enemy of kings."

"I have read and reread you, especially when I am not of your opinion. Your dominant passion is the love of humanity. *Est ubi peccas.* This love blinds you. Love humanity, but love it as it is. It has not patience with the boons which you wish to confer upon it, and which would render it more unhappy and perverse. Leave it to the beast which devours it, this it holds dear. Nothing has ever given me such a hearty laugh as the picture of Don Quixote in utter perplexity trying to defend himself against the galley slaves whom in the greatness of his soul he has set free."

"I am sorry to see you have such a poor opinion of your equals. But, by the way, tell me, do you find yourselves free in Venice?"

"As much as one can be in an aristocratic oligarchy. The liberty we enjoy is not so complete as that in England, but we are satisfied."

"Even in the Piombi?"

"My detention was an act of despotism, but convinced that I had wantonly abused my liberty I sometimes thought the government justified in having me arrested without the ordinary formalities."

"Nevertheless you escaped."

"I used my right as they used theirs."

"Admirable! but this means that nobody in Venice can call himself free."

"It may be, but you must admit that to be free it is sufficient to believe you are so."

"I am not ready to admit that. You and I have different conceptions of liberty. The aristocracy, even the members of the government, are not free in your country, as, for example, they cannot even travel without permission."

"That is true, but this is a restriction which they have freely imposed upon themselves while keeping their sovereignty. Would you say that a citizen of Bern is not free because he is subject to sumptuary laws when he is his own legislator?"

"Very well. Let all the people make their own laws."

After this lively repartee he abruptly asked me where I had been before coming to Geneva.

"I come from Roche," I said, "I should feel that I had cheated myself if I had to leave Switzerland without having seen the celebrated Haller. My journeys are pilgrimages to render homage to my contemporaries, none of whom has made such an impression upon me as has M. de Voltaire."

"M. Haller must have pleased you."

"I passed three memorable days with him."

"I congratulate you. He is a man worthy of the greatest respect."

"I think as you do and am glad to hear you render him justice. I regret to say that I found him less favorably disposed toward yourself."

"Ah! it may be that we are both mistaken."

At this answer, whose merit was its quickness, all present burst out laughing and began to applaud.

Literature was not again mentioned and I was like a dumb person until M. de Voltaire retired. I then asked Mme. Denis if there was anything I could do for her in Rome, and went away well pleased with myself, for I was vain enough to think that on my last day in Geneva I had set this elusive casuist aright.

He left a bad taste in my mouth, which for ten years influenced me to cavil at everything that came from his immortal pen. I am sorry now, although in rereading my criticisms I find that I was often in the right. I ought to have distrusted my judgment, compounded as it was with prejudice, and reflected that if his ill humor on that third day had not made me hate him I should have found him sublime in all. I might then have kept silent, but an angry man always believes his rash statements justified. Posterity will place me among his snapping critics and the very humble reparation which I make today to this great man will perhaps not be read. If we meet in the realm of Pluto, freed of all the bitterness which is in our nature during our stay on this earth, we shall come to an understanding. He will accept my sincere apology and become my friend, and I shall be more than ever his sincere admirer.

I was busy half a night and almost all next day writing down my conversations with Voltaire. There was enough to fill a volume, and what is presented here is but the briefest summary.

Chapter XIV

FREDERICK THE GREAT

THE fifth day after my arrival in Berlin I presented myself to Milord Marshall, who, since the death of his brother, was called Milord Keith. I had last seen him in London on his return from Scotland after the restoration to him of the family estate which had been confiscated on his espousal of the Stuart cause. Frederick the Great had brought about this restitution. Milord Keith now lived in Berlin, resting on his laurels and enjoying peace. Ever dear to the king, he kept strictly out of politics. He was now eighty years old.

Simple in his manners, as he had always been, he said that he was pleased to see me again, then he asked me if I intended to stay long in Berlin. As I knew him to be partially acquainted with the ups and downs of my checkered career, I answered that I would willingly stay there should the king find me suitable employment, but when I asked Milord to extend to me his patronage for this purpose he said that in predisposing the king in my favor he would do me more harm than good.

"For," he added, "as his majesty prides himself on knowing men better than anybody else does, he likes to judge for himself. Thus it often happens that he discovers merits where nobody would have suspected them, and *vice versa.*"

He advised me to write to the king that I desired the honor of an interview.

"When you speak to him," added the venerable man, "you might say, as a matter of form, that you know me, and I have no doubt that he will then offer me the opportunity to speak of you. You may be sure that what I tell him will not be derogatory to you."

"But, Milord, am I to write to the king when I have never had anything to do with him? I have no idea how to proceed."

"I understand, but don't you wish to speak to him?"

"Surely."

"That settles it. Just tell him what you want him to do for you."

"Will the king answer?"

"Unquestionably. He answers everybody. He will inform you when and where it will please him to receive you. Follow my advice. His majesty is at present in Sans-Souci. I am curious to hear how your interview turns out. You can see from what I have told you that his majesty is not afraid of being imposed on."

As soon as I got home I went to my desk. I wrote to the king in the simplest and most respectful manner, asking him where and when I could present myself.

Next day I received a letter signed Frederick, acknowledging receipt of mine and saying that the king would be in the garden of Sans-Souci at four o'clock.

As can be imagined, I hastened to keep the appointment. I started at three o'clock, dressed in plain black. After entering the courtyard of the castle and not seeing anybody, not even a guard, I climbed a small staircase and was confronted by a door, which I opened. I found myself in a gallery of paintings. The custodian came to me and offered his assistance.

"I haven't come," I said, "to admire the masterpieces but to speak to the king, who wrote me that he would be in the garden."

"Right now he is at his after dinner flute concert on the mall. Did he set a time?"

"Yes, four o'clock, but he may have forgotten."

"The king never forgets. He will be there on the dot, and you would do well to wait for him in the garden."

I had been there a short time when I saw him appear, followed by his reader and a pretty spaniel. As soon as he saw me, he came toward me, and lifting his hat and calling me by name, he asked me in a thunderous tone what I wanted. Surprised at this reception, I stopped short, looking at him without answering.

"Well, why don't you speak? Didn't you write to me?"

"Yes, sire, but I have forgotten everything I wanted to say. I did not think that the majesty of a king would dazzle me. Milord Marshall ought to have cautioned me."

"He knows you, then? Let us walk. What do you want to speak to me about? What do you think of this garden?"

Asks me what I want to speak to him about, and in the same breath orders me to tell him what I think of his garden! To anyone else I would have replied that I was not qualified to judge, but as the king had been kind enough to take it for granted that I was a connoisseur I should have appeared to contradict him, and that is something which a king, even a philosopher, would never have forgiven. Therefore at the risk of giving him proof positive of my bad taste, I answered that I found the garden superb.

"But," said he, "the gardens of Versailles are much more beautiful."

"They are, sire, because of the fountains."

"I need fountains, I know, but I can't do a thing. I have spent more than three hundred thousand ecus to get some, but without success."

"Three hundred thousand ecus, sire? If your majesty had spent all that at one time the fountains would be here."

"Oho! I see you are a hydraulic expert."

Ought I to have told him that he was mistaken? I was afraid to displease him, and I bowed my head, meaning neither yes nor no.

Thank the Lord, the king was not interested in speaking about this science, or I should have got into difficulties, as I did not know its first principles.

Walking along and continually turning his head to the right and to the left, he asked me what were the land and sea forces of the republic of Venice in time of war. Thanks to God I found myself here on my own ground!

"Twenty frigates, sire, and a great quantity of small galleys."

"And land forces?"

"Seventy thousand men, sire, all subjects of the republic, one man from each village."

"That's not true. Do you think to amuse me by telling me fairy stories? But perhaps you are a financier. Tell me what you think of taxation."

That was my first interview with a king. Rapidly summing up the odd situation, taking into account his eccentricity, his abrupt way of launching curt questions, I saw that I should have to play my part in the style of the Italian comedians, who improvise their lines in constant fear of faltering and being greeted with hisses. Therefore, assuming the conceited air of the financier, even to the required pucker of the mouth, I replied to this proud king that I could speak of the theory of taxation.

"That's what I want," he said. "The practise is none of your business."

"There are three kinds of taxes, in relation to their effects; one is ruinous, the second, unfortunately, is necessary, and the third is always excellent."

"I like that. Go on."

"The ruinous tax is the imperial tax; the necessary is the military; and the excellent is the popular."

I had to mystify him. Not having reflected on the subject, I was thinking as the words came out, and nevertheless I must be careful to avoid absurdities.

"The imperial tax, sire, empties the purses of the subjects to fill up the chests of the sovereign."

"And this tax is always ruinous, you say?"

"Always, sire, as it impairs circulation, which is the life of commerce, that mainstay of the state."

"But a tax by which the armies benefit is always necessary?"

"Unhappily necessary. War is a great misfortune."

"Maybe. And the popular?"

"Is always excellent. The king takes from his subjects with one hand and pays them back with the other, giving them a course in public utility, founding necessary institutions, protecting science and the arts, doing everything to keep specie flowing into the social body; finally, the king adds to the general happiness by obeying rules dictated by his wisdom, to direct the use of this tax in the manner most profitable to the masses."

"There is some truth in all that. Without doubt you know Calsabigi?"

"I ought to know him, sire. Seven years ago, in Paris, we founded together the Genoese lottery."

"And in what class do you place this tax? for you will admit that it is one."

"Yes, sire, and that's not all it is. It is a tax of a good kind when the king uses the income from it for the public weal."

"But the king may lose."

"Once in fifty times."

"Is that mathematically established?"

"Certainly, sire, like all political calculations."

"They are often wrong."

"They are never so, sire, when God is neutral."

"Why drag God into it?"

"Very well, sire, destiny or chance."

"That's better. It may be that I agree with you about the mathematical probabilities, but I don't like your Genoese lottery. It looks to me like downright rascality. I want nothing to do with it, even if I could have the physical certainty of never losing."

"Your majesty thinks like a wise man. The ignorant people would not play unless deceived into over-confidence."

After this broken up conversation, which did honor to the high mind of the illustrious monach, he sputtered a little but did not find me unguarded. After we had arrived at a peristyle with double enclosure, he stopped in front of me, looked at me from head to foot; then after a short silence he remarked:

"Do you know that you are a good looking man?"

"Is it possible, sire, that your majesty can descend from the heights of scientific discussions to observe in me the least of the qualifications of one of your grenadiers?"

The king smiled shrewdly, but with gacious kindliness, and said, "As Marshall Keith knows you I shall speak to him about you."

Thereupon, lifting his hat as he did to everybody, he saluted me. I made a deep reverence and went away.

Three or four days later Milord Marshall imparted the agreeable news that I had pleased the king, and told me that his majesty would think of employing my services. I was curious to know how. Having nothing else to busy me, I decided to wait.

Among other sights of Potsdam I saw the king commanding in person the first battalion of grenadiers of his guard, made up of picked men selected for their courage as well as for their handsome appearance.

After having admired the beauty and elegance of the apartments of the castle, one could but marvel at the way the king lived. A poor room, a small bed hidden by a screen. No dressing gown, no slippers. The valet showed us an old cap which the king put on when he had a cold, and which he covered with his hat. It must have been very uncomfortable. A sofa drawn up back of a table on which were an inkstand and a litter of papers, pens and half burned copy books. Such was the office of his Prussian majesty.

The valet told us that these copy books contained the history of the last war, and that the accident which had burned them had so disgusted the king that he had given up the task. He must have resumed it later, as this work, which roused little interest, was published soon after his death.

Five or six weeks had passed since my singular interview with the king, when Milord Marshall announced to me that his majesty granted me a place as governor of a new corps of noble Pomeranian cadets, which had just been created. The number of cadets was fixed at fifteen, and there were to be five governors, three cadets to a governor. I was to receive a salary of six hundred ecus and take my meals with the cadets. The duty of the governors consisted in following or accompanying these pupils everywhere, even to the court, in lace dress. I had to decide without delay as the other four were already installed, and his majesty did not like to wait. I asked Lord Keith where the school was and then promised to answer the next day.

It took more self-possession than I had to keep from bursting out laughing at this extravagant proposition from a monarch so wise, but my surprise was really painful when I saw the dwelling of these fifteen noblemen of rich Pomerania. Three or four big, bare rooms, several smaller rooms, calcimined, each with a miserable little bed, a pine table and two chairs of the same wood; the young cadets, twelve or thirteen years old, unkempt, dressed in a fine uniform which contrasted glaringly with their rustic countenances. They were raising hob with their four governors, whom I mistook for their valets, and who looked at me with a sheepish air, not knowing that I was a prospective colleague.

At the moment when I was about to wish an eternal farewell to these miserable cubs, one of the governors looked out of the window and shouted, "Here comes the king on horseback."

I could not possibly avoid him. Moreover I was glad to see him again, especially in that place.

His majesty entered with his friend Icilius, examined everything, and saw me but did not say a word. I had on the brilliant cross of my order and was dressed in elegant taffeta. I had to bite my lips to prevent myself from bursting out laughing when I saw the great Frederick take umbrage at the sight of a night vase protruding from under a bedstead and still bearing traces of a certain kind of filth.

"Whose bed is that?" shouted the monarch.

"Mine, sire," said a trembling cadet.

"Very well, you are not responsible. Where is your governor?"

The unhappy governor presented himself and his majesty called him a churl and administered a scathing rebuke, at the conclusion of which he condescended to remind the governor that there were such things as servants and that cleanliness must be looked after.

This disgusting scene sufficed me. I crept away noiselessly and went to see Milord Marshall. I was all impatience to thank him for the good fortune which heaven had wished to bestow on me through his intermediacy. The kind old man laughed when I related in detail what I had just witnessed. He told me that I did well to scorn such a situation, but that I should nevertheless go and thank the king before leaving Berlin. I confessed my repugnance to presenting myself before a man whom I had found so difficult of approach, and Milord agreed to present to his majesty my excuses and my refusal.

Chapter XV

CATHERINE OF RUSSIA

I THOUGHT of leaving in the beginning of the autumn, but M. Panine and M. Alsuwieff kept telling me that I must not go away until I was able to say that I had spoken with the empress.

"I am sorry," I said, "but I have not found anybody who was willing to present me."

Panine told me to walk early in the summer garden, where her majesty went quite often, and where, encountering me as if by chance, she would probably speak to me. I told him that I hoped to meet her majesty on a day when he would be with her. He named a day and I went.

Strolling along alone, I contemplated the statues which bordered the promenade. They were of poor stone and execrable workmanship, and the names appended to them made them simply ludicrous. A statue in tears represented Democritus; a face distorted with laughter was supposed to be that of Heraclitus; an old man with a long beard was called Sappho, and an old woman with wasted breasts was labeled Avicenne. The rest were in the same style.

As I smilingly wondered what aberration could have inspired these absurdities, I saw the czarina advance preceded by Count Gregor Orloff and followed by two ladies. Count Panine was at her left. I stood respectfully aside to let her pass, but as soon as she was in range she asked me laughingly if the beauty of these statues had interested me. I answered, taking my cue from her, that they looked to me as if they had been erected to deceive fools or to amuse people who knew a little history.

"All that I can say," replied the empress, "is that they deceived my good aunt, who, moreover, did not care to go too deeply into these little deceits. I hope that nothing else you may have seen here has seemed as ridiculous as these statues."

I should have been lacking in veracity and courtesy if I had not taken the opportunity to point out that in Russia what was laughable was only a high light in the great picture of so much that was admirable. Then I entertained the renowned sovereign for more than an hour with my impressions of the wonders of St. Petersburg.

The speech led me into a digression about the king of Prussia. I praised the great man but criticized his unbearable habit of firing questions at one without giving one the time to answer. Smiling graciously, Catherine asked me for an account of my conversations with this monarch. I told her everything in the most advantageous way. She had the kindness to tell me that she had never seen me at the *Courtag*. The *Courtag* was a vocal and instrumental concert which she gave every Sunday at the palace after dinner. Everybody could come, and she walked about and spoke to those whom she desired to honor. I told her that I had been there only once, being so unfortunate as not to care for music. Turning around toward her dear Panine, she said with a smile that she knew somebody else who had the same misfortune. The czarina broke off to speak to M. Bezkoi, who came up just then, and as M. Panine withdrew, I quitted the presence, enchanted with the honor I had had.

This princess, of medium height, well shaped, and of majestic carriage, had the art of making herself beloved of all. The desire to know her constituted an introduction. Without being beautiful, she was certain of pleasing by her sweetness, her affability, and her wit, which she used with exquisite tact. There was not a bit of pretense about her, and her simplicity was the more admirable as

she could by rights entertain a very exalted opinion of herself.

A few days later Count Panine told me that the empress had asked him twice about me—a sure sign that I had pleased her. He advised me to watch out for occasions of meeting her. Liking me, she would have me come to her every time I saw her, and if I wished to be employed she would think about it.

Although I did not know myself what situation I could fill in this strange, disagreeable country, I was glad to hear that I had an easy access to the sovereign. Keeping that in mind, I went every day to walk in the garden.

I shall relate in detail the second interview I had with the empress.

Having seen me from a distance, she sent an officer to invite me to come and talk to her. They kept speaking of the bad weather which had prevented the holding of the carousel. She asked me if it were possible to give that kind of show in Venice. I told her of many similar spectacles which could not be presented outside of Venice, and which she would find amusing. While on the subject, I observed that the climate of my country was more agreeable than that of Russia, because there the beautiful days were the rule, while here they were the rare exception.

"For all that," I said, "the year is younger here than elsewhere."

"True," she said. "With you it is eleven days older."

"Would it not be an achievement worthy of your majesty to make the Russian year of the same age as ours by adopting the Gregorian calendar? All the Protestants have done so to their advantage, and England, adopting it fourteen years ago, has already gained several millions. Europe is astonished, madame, that the old style should hang on in a state where the sovereign is the visible chief of the church, and where the capital has an academy of sciences. They believe, madame, that the great Peter, who wanted the year to begin on the first of January, would also have abolished the old style, had he not believed it in his interest to conform to the ways of the English, who were commercially active in your vast empire."

"You know," she said kindly but somewhat slyly, "that Peter the Great was not a scientist."

"Madame, he was more than that. He was a genius of the first order. An unerring intuition took the place of science and made him pass the right judgment on every question concerning the welfare of his subjects. Native wisdom prevented him from making mistakes, and, aided by his mighty will, drove him straight to the heart of abuses which might have presented an obstacle to his great plans."

Her majesty seemed to have listened with pleasure, and was about to reply, when she saw that she was awaited by two ladies whom she had called to her. She said, "I shall answer you gladly another time." Then she turned toward the ladies.

The "other time" was eight or ten days later, when I had begun to think she did not care to speak to me, as she had seen me and had not had me called. She started by saying that what I had suggested be done for the greater glory of Russia was done.

"All the letters which we write to foreign countries, all the public acts which may be of interest to posterity, are from now on marked with two dates, one above the other, and everybody knows that the one which exceeds by eleven days is the date according to the new style."

"But I would dare observe to your majesty that at the end of the century the surplus days will be twelve."

"Not if we omit the leap year in 1800, as you will do. We shall thus check the progress of our error, and our epact will be the same as yours. Strange, is it not, that the epact is also eleven days? As to the celebration of Easter, let them talk. Your equinox is wrongly fixed at the 21st of March, ours at our 10th, and the arguments of our astronomers also hold good for you. You are mistaken just as we are. The equinox occurs often one, two, or even three days ahead of time. If we can ever be sure of the equinox, the law of the March moon has small importance. You know that you are not even in accordance with the Jews, who claim that their embolism is perfect. The celebration of Easter on the wrong day does not upset the public order in any way, and does not cause any change to the important laws which affect governmental action."

"What your majesty has just told me is full of wisdom and learning. You have filled me with admiration, but the Christmas holidays...."

"That is the only point on which Rome is right. You wanted to tell me, I presume, that we do not celebrate Christmas in the days of the winter solstice, as we ought. We know that, but it's a minor circumstance. Well, I would rather tolerate the trifling error of the Julian calendar than try, as Pope Gegory did, to proclaim that eleven days be dropped from the calendar after, say, the first of next month and the day immediately following be reckoned the twelfth. I should deprive two or three million poor Russians of their birthdays or saints' days, and they would say that by unheard of despotism I had shortened their lives. They would not complain aloud, as that is not the fashion here, but they would whisper into each other's ears that I am an atheist attacking the infallibility of the council of nicca. This naïveté in criticism, ridiculous as it really is, would not make me laugh at all. I have other matters for laughter which are much more agreeable."

The czarina could flatter herself that she had utterly confounded me. I have never for an instant doubted that she had studied up on the subject for that very purpose. M. Alsuwieff told me a few days later that the empress had most probably been reading a little tract, which he could name, and which said precisely all that she had told me.

Catherine the Great spoke very simply, and expressed her opinions with great clarity. Her balanced mind and even temper were reflected in her ever smiling face. Perhaps the smile came easily from much practise, but my statement must not be taken as a slur, as such complete facial control would be impossible unless exerted by a mental force superior to the ordinary workings of human nature. The behavior of the great Catherine, the very antithesis of that of the king of Prussia, showed her greater understanding. The outward kindness by which she encouraged people always gave her the advantage, while the studied gruffness of the soldier of Potsdam exasperated an interlocutor into a desire to get the better of him. When one examines the life of Frederick, one admires his courage, but observes at the same time that unaided by fortune he would have failed, while on the contrary Catherine had to rely very little on the blind goddess. She carried out certain enterprises which before she came to the throne had seemed stupendous to all Europe, and which she appeared to consider mere matter of routine.

Count Panine having told me that the Czarina would start within two or three days for her country house, I went to the garden for a last interview with her. I had been there but a few moments when the rain began to come down in torrents, and I was about to retire. At that moment the Czarina had me called and ushered into a room on the ground floor, where she was walking with Gregorovitch and a lady in waiting.

"I forgot," she said with an air of dignity, which, however, was all graciousness and kindliness, "to ask you if you believe that the corrected calendar is without mistakes."

"No, madame, as Gregory confessed. There is a trifling error which will produce no perceptible effect within nine or ten thousand years."

"So I understand. That being the case, I think Pope Gregory ought not to have confessed the miscalculation. A legislator should never show himself to be either fallible or hypercritical. A few days ago I had to laugh when I learned that if the basic error had not been corrected by the elimination of the leap year at the end of the century the world would have gained a year in the space of fifty thousand years. The equinox would have receded a day every one hundred and thirty years, so that Christmas would have come to be celebrated in summer. The great pontiff of the Roman church in wisely enforcing the change faced no such difficulty as I should confront if I were to attempt a similar measure. My people are too attached to old ways."

"I should have supposed that your majesty would find them obedient."

"I don't doubt that, but what an affliction for my clergy to find itself cheated out of the hundred or more saints' day festivals which would occur in the eleven days to be suppressed! You have only one saint for each day. We have a dozen. I must remind you, besides, that all old states are attached to their old laws. I am told that your republic begins the year in the month of March. This custom I consider praiseworthy rather than barbarous, for it is a relic of glorious antiquity. And it is much more sensible to begin the year on the first of March than on the first of January. But doesn't this create some confusion?"

"Not the slightest, madame. The two letters M. V. which we add to the date during January and February make a mistake impossible."

"Venice is likewise distinguished for a coat of arms which cannot be properly called a coat of ams, as it conforms to no known rules of heraldry. She is also distinguished for having portrayed her patron saint, the Evangelist, with a very pleasing countenance, and for addressing him in a fine Latin phrase which, I am told, contains a grammatical error, made respectable by age. But is it also true that you do not divide the twenty-four hours of the day?"

"Quite true, madame. We count the day as beginning at the beginning of the night."

"You see what force of habit will do! Your way of telling time is more convenient for you, and you do not care if it seems odd to the rest of the world. For myself, I think I should find it unhandy."

"Your majesty would know by looking at her watch how many hours the day would last. You would not need to listen for the cannon of the citadel which warns the public that the sun has passed the horizon."

"True, but for one advantage which you have in knowing the hour of sunset, we have two. We know that twelve o'clock is either noon or midnight."

The czarina spoke about the customs of the Venetians, of our propensity for games of chance, and asked me if the Genoese lottery had yet been established in Venice.

"They wanted," she said, "to persuade me to allow it in my states, and I would have consented, but only on condition that the stake should never be lower than a ruble, so I could keep the poor from playing."

I answered this wise observation by a deep bow.

Thus ended the last interview I had with the famous woman who was able to rule thirty-five years without ever making an essential mistake. The historians will always grant her high rank in the company of the great sovereigns, in spite of the rigid moralists who, with reason, will class her with courtesans.

Chapter XVI

NINA BERGONZI

WHEN I was getting ready to start for Barcelona, I saw at the bull ring a woman whose appearance was extremely imposing. I inquired of a chevalier of Alcantara at my side, who the woman was.

"That is the famous Nina."

"Why famous?"

"If you don't know her by reputation, her history would be too long to be told here."

Involuntarily staring at the woman, I saw two minutes later, an evil looking man, but rather well dressed, leave the imposing beauty, and approaching the chevalier, whisper something in his ear.

Turning towards me in the politest manner, the chevalier told me that the lady whose name I had asked desired to know mine.

Foolishly flattered by this curiosity, I answered the messenger, that the lady permitting, I would make it known to her personally after the spectacle.

"It appears, from your accent, that you are an Italian."

"I am a Venetian."

"She is too."

When the messenger had gone, the chevalier became less laconic and told me that Nina was a dancer, that the Count Ricla, Captain-general of the principality of Barcelona, where the bishop would not allow her to stay because of the scandal she created.

"The count is madly in love with her, and gives her fifty doubloons a day."

"But I hope that she does not spend them all."

"She cannot, but every day she commits some follies which cost her a great deal."

Quite curious to know a woman of this type, and far from fearing that this acquaintance could occasion some disagreeable happenings, I was impatient to see the end of the spectacle and speak to her.

As I went up to her, she received me with great ease of manner, and preparing to climb into a beautiful carriage drawn by six mules, she told me that if I would please her by going to lunch at her house the next day, she would be delighted. I promised and I did not fail her.

I found her in a very large house, about a hundred paces from the town. It was furnished richly and with considerable taste, and was surrounded by a large garden.

The first thing which struck me was a host of servants in dazzling livery, and a number of maid servants elegantly dressed, were going back and forth in all directions.

While I was advancing, I heard an imperious voice storming in the apartment into which I was about to be ushered.

The scolder was Nina, who railed at a man standing amazed before a heap of merchandise displayed on a large table.

"You must excuse my anger," she said, "against this foolish Spaniard who declares that these laces are beautiful."

As she wanted me to give her my opinion and I found them really beautiful but did not wish to contradict her on my first visit, I told her that I was not a competent critic.

"Madame," said the merchant, who was getting impatient, "if you do not care for the laces, you can leave them, but do you wish the cloth?"

"Yes, I shall keep them, and as to your laces, I want to convince you that it is not because I want to save some money that I do not like them...."

Saying these words this senseless woman took the scissors and cut them to pieces.

"It's a great shame," said the man, who had spoken to me the day before, "they will say that you are mad."

"Shut up, you ugly pimp!" she said, giving him a powerful slap.

The brute left, calling her a bitch, which only made her burst out laughing; then turning to the Spaniard she asked him how much she owed him.

The merchant did not have to be told twice and revenged himself by charging an additional price for the insults she offered him.

She signed the bill without looking at it and said:

"Go and find Don Diego Valencia, who will pay you at once."

The chocolate was brought and she commanded the man she had slapped to take chocolate with us at once.

"Don't be astonished," she said, "at the way I treat this object. He is a rascal of no importance whom Ricla has placed near me to spy on me, and I treat him as you have seen so that he can write Ricla all about it."

I thought I was dreaming, all that I saw and heard appeared to me so extraordinary. I had never imagined that there could exist a woman with such a character.

The wretch who had been slapped, was a Bolognese and a musician. His name was Molinari. He came and drank his chocolate without a word.

He having gone out after drinking, Nina passed a good hour with me, speaking about Spain, Italy, and Portugal, where she had married a dancer by the name of Bergonzi.

"I am the daughter," she said, "of the famous charlatan Pelandi whom you may have met in Venice."

After this confidence, in which she had manifested not the slightest reticence, she begged me to sup with her, supper being her favorite repast. I promised her to do so and I took a walk to be able to reflect at leisure on the character of this woman and on her great good fortune which she outraged.

Nina was an amazing beauty, but as I have never believed that beauty alone could suffice to make a man happy, I could not understand how a viceroy of Catalonia could be so deeply smitten as he was represented. Molinari, after what I had seen, I could only consider a wretch. I went to supper to enjoy the spectacle; for as beautiful as she was, she had not inspired me with any feeling.

It was at the beginning of October, but in Valencia there were twenty degrees Réamur in the shade. Nina walked up and down with her fool, both very lightly clad. Nina had only a shirt on and a thin skirt.

As soon as she saw me she came towards me and urged me to follow their example; but I declined for reasons which she had to be satisfied with, as the presence of that infamous blackguard shocked me to a supreme degree.

Up to the time of supper, Nina entertained me with a thousand lascivious stories of which she had been the heroine from the time she had begun her life as a libertine to her present age of twenty-two.

Had it not been for the presence of that revolting Argus, and without fail, although I had no feeling for her, all these stories would have had their natural effect, but it couldn't be done.

She invited me to supper the next day, saying that we should be tête-à-tête, as Molinari would be sick.

"He will have digested his wine and will be fit."

"I tell you, that he will be sick. Come again every evening."

"I am leaving the day after tomorrow."

"You shall not go away for a week, and we shall pass it together."
"That isn't possible."
"You shall not leave, I say, for that would be an insult and I would not permit it."

I went home, resolved to leave without paying any attention to her, and although at my age I was no novice, I went to bed, dumbfounded by the excesses of this megoera, for she had confessed what I knew, but what no woman ever tells anybody.

"I use him to satisfy my passion, as I am certain that he does not love me, and if I knew that he loved me, I would rather die than allow him anything, as I detest him."

The next day, at seven o'clock in the evening, I went to her house. She received me with an air of affected sadness, saying:

"Alas! We shall be alone at supper, as Molinari has the colic."

"You told me that he would be sick, have you poisoned him?"

"I am quite capable of it, but God forbid!"

"But you have given him something?"

"Nothing but what he loves; but we shall speak of that anon. Let us play: after that we shall sup and we shall laugh till tomorrow and tomorrow night we shall start over again."

"No, for I shall leave at seven o'clock."

"Oh! You shall not leave and your coachman will not quarrel, for he has been paid. Here is the receipt."

All this was said gaily, with a suspicion of amorous despotism which could not displease me. Not being in a hurry, I took the matter jestingly, calling her crackbrained, saying that I was not worth the gift she had presented me with.

"It's astonishing," I said, "being what you are and having such a household, you don't care to receive company."

"Everybody is afraid. They fear Ricla's love and jealousy, because the animal who suffers the colic writes him about everything I do. He swears he doesn't, but I know he lies. I am quite delighted that he should act thus and I am sorry that up to now he has had nothing important to communicate."

"He will write that I have supped tête-à-tête with you."

"All the better: are you afraid?"

"No, but it seems to me that you should tell me if I have anything to fear."

"You haven't, because I am the only one he can make responsible."

"But I should not like to be the cause of a quarrel which might injure you."

"On the contrary. The more I irritate him the better he will love me and the making up will cost him dearly."

"Then, you don't love him?"

"Yes, for the sake of ruining him, but he is so rich that I shall never succeed."

I saw before me a woman as beautiful as Venus, as corrupt as the angel of darkness, a horrible prostitute and born to punish anyone who could be so unhappy as to fall in love with her. I had known others of her kind, but none to equal her. I thought of taking advantage of this woman by making her contribute to my finances.

She asked for some cards, and she invited me to play what is called primiera. It's a game of chance, but so complicated that the most cautious is always sure to win.

In less than fifteen minutes I discovered that I could outplay her. Nevertheless she played in such good luck, that when we got up for supper, I was a loser by twenty pistoles, which I paid her at once. She took them promising me a return game. We supped well, and afterwards we committed all the follies which she would and that I could, for I was no longer at the age of miracles.

The next day I went to see her earlier. We started to play and she lost, as she did all the following days, so that I won from her two or three hundred doubloons which in my then state of finances was not a thing to be sneezed at.

The spy had recovered. The next day he supped with us and every day after that, but his presence did not bother me any longer. She had changed her tactics. She gave herself to me telling him to go and write to the count of Ricla what he pleased.

This count wrote her a letter, which she showed me, and in which this poor lover told her that she could return to Barcelona without fear, for the bishop had received orders from the count to consider her only as a theatrical woman who was in his diocese as a transient, and that she could then stay there all the winter in the certainty that they would leave her alone in Barcelona, if she behaved without scandal. She told me that during my stay in Barcelona I could only see her at night, after the count had left, which always occurred at ten o'clock. Moreover she assured me that I ran no risks. I would not have tarried in Barcelona if Nina had not told me that in case I needed money she would lend it to me.

She wanted me to start from Valencia a day ahead of her, and to wait for her at Tarragon, which I did and I passed, in this city full of ancient monuments, a most agreeable day. I prepared a delicious supper for Nina the way she liked it, and I was careful to have her room next to mine so as not to create any scandal.

She left in the morning and begged me not to start till evening, to travel nights and to arrive in Barcelona in the day, and to choose the hostelry of the Santa-Maria as my headquarters. She cautioned me to see her only after she had communicated with me.

* * * * *

In Barcelona, Casanova commits a grave imprudence: he wounds an emissary of the Count Ricla, and is locked up at the bottom of the tower for the space of forty-two days, which he employs in writing his "refutation of the Venetian Government by Amelot de la Houssaye." Then he receives the order to leave Barcelona in three days and Catalona in a week.

Chapter XVII

LIA OF TURIN

IN Turin I lodged in a private house, where the Abbe Gama awaited me. In spite of the good abbe's sermon on economy, I rented a very fine apartment occupying the whole first floor.

After having settled with the hostess everything in regard to the table I went out, and as I entered the café to read the public papers, the first person I saw was the Marquis Désarmois, whom I had known in Savoy.

We went for a walk in the beautiful boulevard which runs toward the citadel. I saw hosts of pretty girls. In Turin the sex has all the charms desired by love, but the police are most annoying. As the city is small and crowded, the spies are found everywhere. Thus it is possible to have some freedom only by using extreme precautions and having recourse to very clever procuresses, who must be well paid, for in the event of detection, they risk a barbarous punishment. Prostitutes and kept women, are not tolerated and the married women have all the liberty, but of course the police were too stupid to think of that.

Among the beauties which had attracted my eyes, only one captivated me. I asked Désarmois her name, for he knew them all.

"It is the famous Lia," he said, "the invincible Jewess, who has resisted the attacks of the most noted amateurs in Turin. Her father is a well-known horse dealer. It is easy to go to see her, but there is nothing doing."

The more difficult the enterprise was reputed, the more I felt incited to run the risk.

"Take me to see her," I said to Désarmois.

"Any time you say."

After we had dined, Désarmois conducted me to the gates of the Po, where Lia's father, the horse dealer, resided. I asked him if he had a good saddle horse. He called a boy, and gave him his orders. While he was speaking, his charming daughter entered.

She was dazzling. She was at the utmost not more than twenty years of age. Her waist was svelte as a nymph's. She had a superb mass of hair of the deepest black, a complexion of lilies and roses, wonderful eyes full of fire and wit, long heavy eyelids, and eyebrows so strongly arched that they seemed to declare war on all who should pretend to the conquest of so many charms. Everything about her showed education and a knowledge of the world.

Absorbed in the contemplation of this beautiful creature, I did not see the horse which was brought before me. Finally I examined it, posing as a connoisseur of horse flesh, and after having felt the knees and legs, pulled the ears and examined the mouth, I had someone mount it to show its paces. Then I said to the Jew that I would come back the next day with my riding boots on, to try it out. The horse was a spotted sorrel, and was worth forty Piedmont pistoles or about one hundred sequins.

"He is gentleness itself," said Lia, "and he is so fast that at an amble he can keep up with any other horse trotting."

"You have ridden him, mademoiselle?"

"Many times, monsieur, and if I were rich, I would never part with him."

"He too must dislike the thought of parting, as I am sure he enjoys carrying you. I shall not buy him until I have seen you ride him."

She blushed.

"You must please the gentleman," said her father. She consented, and I promised to return the next day at nine o'clock.

I was punctual, as may be imagined, and I found Lia dressed as a courier. What a figure! The form of a Callipigian Venus! I was already beneath her spell.

Two horses had been made ready. Lia swung onto hers with the ease and grace of a skillful rider. I mounted the other.

We were out a long time. The horse rode well, but what cared I for the horse? I had eyes and thoughts only for her. Before I left her I said:

"Beautiful Lia, I am going to buy the horse only to make you a present of him. If you do not accept I leave Turin today. I place no other condition on my gift than the pleasure of riding with you when I wish."

Seeing by her looks that she was listening favorably to my speech, I told her that I would stay six weeks in Turin, that I had fallen in love with her on the promenade and that the buying of the horse was only a pretext to find an occasion to let her know my feelings towards her. She answered in a very shy manner that the sentiment she had inspired in me flattered her infinitely, and that the generous present was not necessary to assure me her friendship.

"The condition which you impose is extremely agreeable to me, and I know my father will be pleased if I accept." Then she added: "The only favor I ask of you is to make the gift in my father's presence and to repeat that you will not buy unless I accept."

I saw myself on the good road more easily than I had expected, and did as she advised. Her father, who called himself Moise, found the bargain to his liking, complimented his daughter, received the forty pistoles, gave me a receipt, and asked me to honor him by breakfasting with them the next day. That was just what I wanted.

Next day Moise received me with the greatest consideration, and the beautiful Lia, dressed as a girl this time, told me that if I wanted to ride she would get ready at once.

"We shall ride another day, my charming Lia," I said. "Today I am glad to remain here and be entertained."

But the father, greedy like all of his race, told me that if I cared about driving he could sell me a pretty phaeton with two excellent horses.

"Show them to monsieur," said Lia, who may have been in league with her father.

Without answering, Moise went out to have the animals harnessed.

"I will look at them," I said to Lia, "but I shall not buy them, as I should not know what to do with them."

"Go for a drive with the lady you love."

"Yourself, of course, but perhaps you would not dare?"

"And why not, in the country near Turin?"

"Very well! Lia, I will look them over."

The father came back and we went downstairs. The carriage and the horses pleased me and I said so to Lia.

"Well!" said Moise, "I'll sell the rig for four hundred sequins now, but after Easter I can't let it go for less than five hundred."

Lia climbed in and I sat beside her. We drove about the open country for an hour, and when we returned I told Moise I would give him an answer the next day. He departed, and I went upstairs with the beautiful Lia.

"My dear," I said to her, when we were in the room, "this is costing me four hundred sequins, and tomorrow I shall fork over with pleasure, but on the same conditions as when I bought the horse,—and another, namely, that you grant me all the favors that might be expected of a long and requited love."

"You speak frankly. I will answer you the same way. I am an honest girl, and I do not sell myself."

"You must know, beautiful Lia, that all women, be they honest or not, sell themselves. When a man has the leisure, he buys with his attentions the woman his love desires; when he is in a hurry as I am, he uses gifts, and even gold."

"A man who would do that is a boor. He ought to permit the feelings to plead his cause, and be ready to serve his lady through a long and attentive courtship."

"Such would be the height of my ambition, Lia, but I am pressed for time."

Her father entered as I finished speaking. I went away, saying that I would not come the next day but the day after, and that then we should discuss the matter of the phaeton.

It was clear that Lia had taken me for a spendthrift who was fair game. She would have liked to have the phaeton, as she had had the horse. But I was no novice. I had made up my mind to sacrifice a hundred sequins on a chance; but my prodigality had to stop somewhere.

I decided to suspend my visits and leave the matter up to her and her father. I counted a great deal on the greed of the Jew, who being very fond of money must have been angry that his daughter did not find a way to make me buy the carriage, by giving or not giving herself to me, for that was probably quite indifferent to him. I was certain they would seek me out on their own initiative.

The next Saturday, I saw the beautiful Jewess on the promenade. We were near enough for me to approach her without seeming to go after her, especially as her looks said, "Come!"

"We don't see you any more," she said, "Come tomorrow early to breakfast with me, or I shall send you back the horse."

I promised to be at her house early and there was no doubt that I would keep the promise.

We breakfasted almost en tête-à-tête; for her aunt, as third party, was there only for form's sake. Afte breakfast, having decided to ride, Lia dressed in boy's costume in my presence but likewise in the presence of her aunt.

"'Will you kindly fix my frill?' she said.

That was like putting me on hot coals.

Nevertheless, in all this manœuvering I guessed a plot, and I decided to guard myself against it.

Her father came as we were mounting the horses.

"If you wish," he said, "to buy the horses and phaeton, I will take off twenty sequins."

"Your daughter," I answered, "will give you my answer on our return from the drive."

We started at a whirlwind pace, and Lia informed me that she had committed the imprudence of telling her father that she was in a position to make me buy the carriage, and if she did not wish me to quarrel with him, I would have the kindness to conclude the purchase.

"Make the bargain," she added, "and keep your gift until such time as you have convinced yourself that I love you."

"My dear Lia, you can make me obey, but you know on what condition."

"I promise you that we shall ride out alone when you desire, without descending anywhere. But I don't believe that you really care for me. Your infatuation is only a passing whim."

"To convince you to the contrary, I shall buy the phaeton, and keep it in a stable. And as to the horses, I shall have them cared for. But if within a week you do not make me happy, I shall sell the whole turnout."

"Come tomorrow."

"I will come, but I want a token of tenderness this morning."

"This morning? Impossible."

We entered the house, and I was astounded to hear her say to her father that the phaeton belonged to me, and that he must get it ready.

The Jew smiled. We went upstairs, the three of us, and Lia with an air of assurance said to me:

"Count the money."

"I haven't it on my person, but I'll give you a note."

"Here is some paper."

I did not hesitate to write to the banker Zappata to pay on sight three hundred and twenty sequins. The Jew went to get the money and Lia remained alone with me.

"In trusting me," she said, "you have made yourself worthy of my heart. My aunt is in the house, and as I cannot lock the door she might enter. But I promise you that tomorrow you shall be satisfied with me."

I said goodbye, and went away angry. Climbing into my phaeton I went home, and retaining the coachman I ordered him to find a stable at once.

I was embittered against Lia and did not intend to see her again.

I made the acquaintance of a very amiable chevalier, a military man, an amateur of letters and a great lover of horses. He introduced me to some pretty girls, whose company I nevertheless did not cultivate, for I should have had to waste my time in sentimentalities, and I wanted only solid pleasure, even if it cost me a great deal of money. The chevalier of Brezé was not my man, he was too virtuous for a libertine like myself. He bought the phaeton and the horse which I had promised to Lia, and I lost only thirty sequins.

A seigneur Baretti, who had known me at Aix-en-Savoie, took me to see Mazzoli, formerly a dancer, now the mistress of Chevalier Raiberti, a cold and very honest man, who was then in charge of the foreign bureau of his Allobrogian Majesty.

This woman, not at all pretty, was quite accommodating. She showed me some girls at her house, but not one appeared to me worthy to take the place of Lia, whom I thought I did not love any more, but I deceived myself.

I was bored and Désarmois, who always took his meals with me, did not like it. He advised me to get acquainted with a certain French woman, a well-known modiste in Turin.

She called herself Mme. R. She had in her service seven or eight young girls who worked in a room next to her shop. Désarmois believed if I went about it in the right way, I could appropriate one of them suitable to my taste. Having a well-filled purse, I did not believe the matter very difficult and I followed his counsel. I went to visit this woman, and I was very agreeablly surprised in finding Lia there, busy bargaining over a lot of things, but finding them too dear. She told me in a gentle, reproachful tone that she thought I had been ill.

"I was very busy," I said.

And then I felt all my fire returning.

"I shall have," I added, "the pleasure of seeing you tomorrow."

She invited me to a Jewish wedding, where I should find a numerous gathering and many pretty girls. I knew that this kind of ceremony was very entertaining, and I promised her to attend it. After bargaining a long time, and finding everything too dear, she went away. Mme. R. was replacing all the finery when I said:

"I will take all this on my account."

She smiled, and taking out my purse I counted her the money.

"Where do you lodge, monsieur?" she asked, "and at what time shall I send the packages around?"

"You could, madame, bring them over yourself, at nine o'clock, and breakfast with me."

"I could not leave this place a moment, monsieur."

Mme. R. in spite of her twenty-five years was still what we would call an appetizing morsel, and she had given me some inclination.

"I should like to have some black silk lace."

"Follow me, monsieur, I beg of you."

I was delighted to see in the room a crowd of young girls all attractive, very attentive to their task, and who hardly dared to lift their eyes to look at me. Madame opened some closets and showed me some magnificent silk laces. Absent-mindedly, as I was looking at the troupe of nymphs, I told her that I wanted them for two in the Venetian style. She knew what it was. At that time in Venice, they were all the rage. These silk laces cost me over one hundred sequins. Pointing at two of the young girls, Mme. R. told me that they would bring them the next day to my home with the goods which Lia had chosen, and which she had found too dear. They answered with a "Yes, mama." They got up, kissed their "mother's" hand, a ceremony which I found amusing, but which permitted me to examine them; I found them charming.

We reëntered the shop, and sitting down near the counter, I eulogized the beauty of these young persons, adding, which was not the truth, that I preferred her to her pupils.

She thanked me, and told me without more ado that she had a lover, and she announced him a moment later. It was the Count of Saint Gilles, decrepit and not at all fit for love making.

I thought that Mme. R. was jesting, but I heard the next day that she had told the truth. Everyone to his taste, and I suspected that this woman, still capable of a caprice, was more in love with the purse than with the person of her old man.

The next day the two soubrettes came to bring the merchandise. I offered them chocolate, but could not get them to accept it. The fancy took me to ask them to take Lia the things which she had picked out, and then to return and tell me how she had received my present. They waited until I had written a note, then went to do my biddings. I found it impossible to give them a single proof of my tenderness, as I had not dared close my door, and the mistress of the house and her ugly daughters were constantly going to and fro. But on their return, having awaited them on the staircase, I gave each one a sequin, and I told them that it would depend only on them to capture my heart. Lia had accepted my beautiful gift, and answered that she expected me.

In the afternoon, while walking aimlessly, I happened to pass in front of the modiste shop, and Mme. R. invited me to enter and bade me sit near her.

"Monsieur," she said, "I thank you very much for your generosity towards my girls. They came back delighted. Tell me frankly if you are really in love with the beautiful Jewess?"

"I am quite in love with her, but as I am not successful, I have made up my mind to be resigned to it."

"You have done wisely. Lia is a rascal, who thinks of nothing else but making dupes of those who are seduced by her charms."

"Is that not likewise the maxim of your charming pupils?"

"No, but they are only compliant when I allow it."

"Then I recommend myself to your kindness, for they would not even accept a cup of chocolate."

"That is the way they must behave. I see that you do not know Turin. Do you find yourself well lodged where you are?"

"How do you mean?"

"Have you perfect freedom?"

"I think so."

"Can you give supper to whom you please and do what you please in your apartment? I am sure it is not so."

"Up to now I have not had the opportunity to make the experiment; but I believe . . ."

"Don't fool yourself, because that is a house of police spies."

"Then you think that I could not give supper to two or three of your pupils?"

"I know very well, that I would not go there. The next day the whole town would know about it, and especially the police."

"And if I took lodgings somewhere else?"

"It would be everywhere the same, for Turin is a nest of spies; but I know a house where you could live as you please and where even my girls, with caution, could bring you whatever you bought at my place."

"Where is this house? I shall follow all your instructions."

"Don't confide in any Piedmontese," she said, "that is the most essential thing."

Then she told me about a well-furnished little house which was inhabited only by an old concierge and his wife.

"They will rent it to you by the month," she said, "if you pay in advance; they will not even ask your name."

The pretty little house was two hundred paces from the citadel, on a solitary street, having a door leading to the open country, and through which I could enter even with my carriage. I found everything as Mme. R. had described it to me. I paid without bargaining a month in advance, and the next day I settled there. Mme. R. admired my promptness.

I went to the Jewish marriage, and I enjoyed it immensely, for this ceremony had something at once symbolic and ridiculously grotesque but I resisted all the art which Lia employed to catch me in her nets. I rented from her father a closed carriage, which I placed, as well as the horses, in my little house. In this manner I found myself at liberty to go where I wished, from the front or the back, by day or by night, as I was quite in the city as well as in the country. I was forced to point out my lodging to the curious Gama, and I did not feel as if I ought to hide anything from Désarmois, for necessity rendered him thoroughly dependable.

However, my door, under my orders, was always closed to them as to everybody else, unless I gave precise instructions that I was expecting them. I had no reason to doubt the faithfulness of my two servants.

On Holy Thursday—early in the morning—they announced Moise and Lia. I did not expect their visit, but received them in great style. During the Holy Week the Jews dared not show themselves in the streets of Turin. I advised them, therefore, to stay the three days with me, and when I saw that the rascal offered me a ring for sale, I saw that I should not have much trouble in persuading them.

"I could not buy the ring," I said, "except at the hands of Lia."

He smiled, imagining without doubt that I would present her with the ring; but I had promised myself to cheat their hopes. I gave them a good dinner and supper, and in the evening they slept in a room not far from mine, in which there were two beds. I could have put them farther apart, and placed Lia in a room next to mine, which would have facilitated nocturnal excursion, but I had done too much for Lia to owe anything to a surprise or even to simple mystery. I wanted her to come to me of her own free will.

The next day Moise, seeing that I had not yet bought the ring, and having business which forced him to go out, asked me to let him have my carriage for the day, saying that he would return in the evening to fetch his daughter. I ordered the carriage to be got ready, and on his departure I bought the ring for six hundred sequins, but on my conditions.

I was in my own home, Lia could not deceive me.

Chapter XVIII

LIA, DAUGHTER OF MORDECAI

IT was in that city where I had begun to enjoy love hugely, and when I remembered that that had been almost thirty years before, I felt dazed; for in the life of a man, thirty years is a vast stretch of time, and nevertheless I still felt young, although I was on the threshhold of the fifties.

What a difference when I measured my physical and moral existence of that first period with that of my later. I could hardly recognize myself as the same man. As happy as I had been, so unhappy was I become.

I no longer had before me alluring prospects of fortune, and my imagination now could not paint the future in brilliant colors.

I admitted in spite of myself, that I had wasted my life. The score of years which I might have before me, presented a gloomy outlook wherein all was uncertain. I counted my forty-seven years and success seemed to fly from me at the enumeration.

That was sufficient to sadden me, for without the favors of the blind goddess, nobody in this world can be happy, at least not with the habits nature had created in me.

In my efforts to secure repatriation to my native city, from which I had been so long an exile I felt that I should be content to retrace my steps and undo all that I had done, up to then, good or bad. Everything conspired to make me feel that for me it was a question of rendering less disagreeable an inevitable descent terminating in death.

LIA, DAUGHTER OF MORDECAI

It is while descending that the man who has passed his life among pleasures of the world is obsessed with these dark reflections. In healthy youth there is no need of foresight. The present is the sole preoccupation. The horizon is always rosy, and happiness seems ever secure. Full of blissful illusions, one laughs at the philosopher who tells one that beyond that beguiling horizon are old age, misery, belated repentance, and finally death, the name of which alone suffices to inspire disgust and fear.

If such were my reflections twenty years ago, imagine to yourself, dear reader, what must be those which obsess me today, now that I am alone, despised, impotent and poor. These thoughts would kill me if I had not a means of distraction and of passing away the cruel time. My mind is as young as my heart; I don't know if I should say happily or unhappily, as neither is now in harmony with my physical forces. What good are desires if one has lost the means of satisfying them? I write to cheat my boredom, and I rejoice that I find solace in this occupation. If I prose away like a dotard, no matter. It is enough for me that I amuse myself.

When I entered the house, I found Mordecai sitting at the table surrounded by company, about eleven or twelve in number. Among them was his mother, ninety years old but in perfect health. I noticed another elderly Jew; the husband of Mordecai's eldest daughter. This daughter I did not think attractive, but the youngest won me at once. She was to marry a Jew from Pesaro whom she had never seen. I told her that never having seen her future husband, she could not be in love with him. She answered in a very serious manner that it was not at all necessary to be in love to marry. The old woman loudly praised the prudence of her grandchild; the girl's mother added that she had only fallen in love with her husband after the first child.

I shall call this pretty Jewess Lia, having reasons for not giving her right name.

During the meal sitting near her, I tried my best to tell her agreeable things so as to make her laugh; but it was all time wasted for she did not even take the trouble to look at me. I found an exquisite supper to which I did justice, and an excellent bed.

The next day my host came to tell me that I could give my dirty linen to the servant and that Lia would take care of it. I informed him that I had found the meatless supper excellent; not having the privilege of eating with or without meat every day I begged him not to forget the goose livers.

"You shall have them, but in our family Lia is the only one who eats them."

"Then it shall be Lia who will eat them with me, and tell her that I shall give her some very fine Cyprus wine."

I had none, but the same morning I asked the Venetian consul to get me some. This consul was a Venetian of the old stock. He had heard about me and manifested great pleasure in making my acquaintance. A real Pantaloon in the greater comedy, which is played without masks, he was gay, full of experience, and a gourmet fond of delicacies. He gave me in return for my money, old muscat wine of Cyprus, but he protested loudly when I told him that I lodged with Mordecai and informed him by what chance it had happened.

"He is rich," he said, "but he is a great usurer: and if you need money, he will treat you badly."

"I don't think I shall need any."

After having told him that I would not go away until the end of the month and until there was a good vessel sailing, I went to dinner and was quite satisfied.

The next day having given the wash to a servant I saw Lia enter. She came to ask me how I wanted the laces washed.

Lia with her eighteen years, showing herself unreservedly before me, without neckerchief, in a plain corset very much open, which offered to my view a magnificent bust,—she would have noticed the strong emotion it caused me, if she had looked at me.

Composing myself, I told her that I left the matter to her, that she should take care of my linen and that I would not have her think that I wanted things done cheaply.

"Then I shall take care of it myself, if you are not in a hurry."

"You are at liberty to make me stay at your house as long as it pleases you," I said.

But she seemed not to pay the slightest attention to my declaration.

"I am satisfied with everything," I told her, "except my chocolate, which I like well beaten and foaming."

"So as to satisfy you, I shall make it myself."

"In that case, amiable Lia, I shall ask a double portion and we shall take it together."

"I don't like it."

"I am mortified, but do you like goose livers?"

"Very much, and today I will eat some with you. My father told me I should."

"That will please me greatly."

"You are evidently afraid of being poisoned?"

"Far from fearing it, I wish we may die together."

The little imp affected not to understand and went away leaving me full of desire.

The fire which this beautiful Jewess had inspired in me, made me feel that I must hasten to find out about her or tell her father not to send her to my room any more. My Jewess from Turin had instructed me sufficiently in the love-making methods of women of that faith.

According to my way of thinking Lia was more beautiful than the other, and less difficult to approach, for the gay life in Ancona was not affected by conditions like those prevailing in Turin.

Thus does a rake reason, but his reason is not infallible.

They served me a dinner in the Jewish style, but it was excellent, and Lia having herself bought a superb goose liver, sat down in front of me with her beautiful bust covered by a muslin neckerchief.

The liver was exquisite. We wetted it with abundant libations of Scopolo, which Lia found even better than the liver.

When the liver was disposed of Lia got up to go out, but I protested as we were only in the middle of the dinner.

"I would remain," she said, "but I am afraid my father won't like it."

"Well. Call your master," I said to the servant who came in at that moment, "I want to speak to him."—"My dear Mordecai, the appetite of your daughter doubles mine, and you will oblige me by permitting her to eat with me every time we have goose livers."

"I do not find it to my interest that my daughter should double your appetite, but if you are willing to pay double, I'll make no objection to her keeping you company."

"That suits me wonderfully and I accept; and every day you shall have a *teston* more."

To show him my satisfaction I presented him with a bottle of Scopolo which Lia guaranteed was of the purest.

We dined together and seeing her made lively by the wine, which having diuretic qualities because of its tart taste, accomplishes marvelously what love desires, I told her that her eyes inflamed me and that she must allow me to kiss them.

"My duty forbids. No kisses, no familiarities," she said, "let us eat and drink together; my pleasure shall equal yours."

"You are cruel."

"I depend on my father, and I can do nothing."

"Shall I ask your father to allow you to be complaisant?"

"That would not be honest it seems to me, and my father might be offended and feel justified in not allowing me to see you any more."

"And if he said to you that you should not be too scrupulous about these bagatelles?"

"I should despise him and continue to do my duty."

Such a clear exposition made me judge that she would not be easy to capture, and that if I persisted I might start an intrigue the end of which I could not foresee and which was liable to cause regrets. I likewise refleced that I ran the risk of neglecting my chief business,* which did not allow me an extended stay in Ancona.

These considerations occupied me but a second. I said no more on the subject to Lia, and dessert having been served, I poured my beautiful Jewess some muscat of Cyprus, which she declared was the most delicious nectar she had ever tasted in her life.

To see her excited by the wine it seemed impossible that Venus should not exercise on her senses as much sway as Bacchus, but her head was strong, her blood took fire but her reason remained cold.

Nevertheless, encouraging her mirth, after the coffee I took hold of her hand to kiss it; she would not permit; but her refusal was expressed in a manner which could not displease me, for she said:

"Too much for honor and not enough for love."

This flash of wit pleased me, more so as it permitted me to judge that she was not a novice.

Postponing till the morrow the execution of my plan, I told her that I would sup with the Venetian consul, and that nothing should be prepared for me in the evening.

---

* To go to Trieste to visit influential personages who would facilitate his return to Venice.

The consul had told me that he did not dine but that every time I wished to sup with him I should give him great pleasure.

I returned at midnight. Everybody in the house was asleep, except the servant who waited for me and who was rewarded in a manner which made her wish that I would return as late every day.

Wishing to know the habits of Lia, I asked the servant about them, but she spoke only well of her mistress. According to her, Lia was always well-behaved, always industrious, the favorite of the whole family and deaf to lovers. Even if Lia had paid her, the servant could not have given her a better character. In the morning when Lia came to bring me the chocolate she sat on my bed saying that they had an excellent liver and that as she had not supped she would dine with good appetite.

"And why, my dear, have you not supped?"

"It may be because of your excellent Cyprus wine. My father is enthusiastic over it."

"He has found it to his taste? I am glad to hear it, we shall give him some more."

Lia was as the day before and her two half naked globes were my despair.

"Are you aware of the fact," I said to her, "that you have a superb bust?"

"But every young girl has a bust shaped like mine."

"You do not suspect that in seeing it I shall find extreme pleasure?"

"If that is so, I am delighted; for in letting you enjoy this pleasure, I have nothing to reproach myself. Moreover a girl does not cover her bust any more than her face, unless she is in formal company."

While she spoke to me, the little rogue was looking at a golden heart pierced by a diamond arrow which clasped the frills in my shirt.

"Do you like this little heart?" I asked her.

"Charming! Is it fine gold?"

"Certainly and that is what encourages me to offer it to you."

Saying this, I unhooked the pin, but thanking me, she told me gently, "that a girl who does not desire to give anything should not accept anything."

"Accept it and I swear that I shall never ask you the slightest favor."

"But I shall be your debtor; therefore I shall never accept anything."

I realized then that there was nothing to be had, or too little at too great a cost, but that I must make up my mind as to the course of my action I was to pursue. I spurned the idea of violence which might anger her or make her laugh at my expense. That would have degraded me or made me more enamored than ever to no good purpose. If she felt herself offended she would never come back again, and I should have no right to complain. Therefore I resolved to keep my greedy looks in check and to amuse her no longer with my amorous banter.

We dined quite valiantly and they served me some shell food which the Mosaic law forbids. While the servant was present, I invited Lia to share it with me, but she received my invitation with horror. As soon, however, as the servant had gone out, she took some and ate with surprising gusto, assuring me that it was the first time in her life that she had tasted it. This girl, I said to myself, this girl who breaks her law with such ease, who loves pleasure with such intensity and who does not hide from me the fullness of her enjoyment, this girl pretends to make me believe that she is insensible to the lure of love, and that she can control it by treating it as if it were a trifle! That is not possible! She does not love me but she takes pleasure in exciting my passion. She must have some resources to appease inclinations of her temperament which I judge to be very libertine.

I shall see, I said to myself, if this evening with the help of my excellent muscat, I can force her to do my will. But in the evening she excused herself for not eating and drinking by saying that it prevented her from sleeping.

The next day she brought me the chocolate, but her beautiful bust was covered by a white neckerchief. As usual she sat on my bed, and abandoning my resolution not to notice anything, I told her in a sad tone that she had covered her bust only because I had told her that I saw it with pleasure. She answered with an amiable nonchalance that she had not thought about it and that she had come with neckerchief because she had no time to put a corset on.

The hair dresser arrived, and Lia went out saying that she would return after dinner. I trembled with joy, thinking that I should have her, if not the same day, at the latest the next day, for the first step had been made; but I was still far from the goal.

Thus the days went on with no result.

I trembled seeing that I was really falling in love with Lia, and I said every day to the consul that I was in no hurry to start. I made paralogisms like a Celadon twenty years old. It seemed to me that Lia was the most virtuous of all girls, for, with fiery passions, an overpowering desire for pleasure, a mind ripe in reflections on the commerce of both sexes, she refused to complete her knowledge. I saw her as a model of virtue, a perfect example. She was all truth, without the slightest hypocrisy, without imposture; she satisfied only her desires through herself, denying herself the pleasures forbidden by the law, to which she wanted to be faithful, in spite of the fire which consumed her. It depended only on herself to be happy, and she resisted whole hours, tête-à-tête with a passionate man, adding fuel to the fire which devoured her, and being strong enough to permit nothing which could relieve her.

Oh! The virtuous Lia! She exposed herself every day to defeat and only prevented it by never taking the first step.

Neither to see nor to touch; that was her sole defense.

It will be seen what all this virtue created in my mind. At the end of nine or ten days, I became violent with Lia, not in action, however, but in eloquence.

She was humiliated, and confessed that I was right, and that there was nothing for her to say, and concluded that I should be wise to forbid her to present herself to me in the morning.

At dinner, as she requested, we took no chances.

I determined to beg her to come, but with covered breast, and without speaking of anything that pertained to love.

"Willingly," added the imp laughing, "but I shall not be the one to break the conditions."

Neither did I want to break them and three days later, being tired of suffering, I told the consul that I would start at the first opportunity. My resolution was all the more sincere that, as I thought I knew her secret, her gayety made me lose my appetite. I saw myself thus deprived of my minor happiness, without having secured the major one. The declaration to the consul, having so to speak bound me, I had gone to bed quietly. Nevertheless varying from my usual habits towards two o'clock in the morning I had to sacrifice to the cloacal nymph. I went out without a light, the house being familiar to me.

The temple was on the ground floor. Having descended in very light slippers I did not make any noise. Climbing the stairs again, on the first landing I saw through a chink a light in a small room which I knew to be unoccupied. I approached it without the slightest idea that Lia could be there at that hour. But judge my surprise when my gaze lighting on a bed, I perceived Lia stark naked, in company with a man naked as herself.

Finally humiliated and disgusted, I climbed noiselessly to my room, and peeped out of the window which overlooked the front door.

I had been watching some minutes when the happy lover appeared.

I went to bed, not only disillusioned, but indignant, humiliated.

Lia no longer seemed to me virtuous. I saw in her only a frenzied and hateful prostitute.

I went to sleep with the intention of driving her away from my room after having related to her the wanton scene I had witnessed.

The resolutions taken by a man in indignation or in a moment of spite, cannot survive a few hours sleep.

As soon as I saw Lia bringing my chocolate, with her cheerful and courteous air, I attuned my mood to hers, and told her calmly all that I had seen of her nocturnal exploits, during the last hour of her orgy. I ended by saying that I hoped she would offer me the next night as much to crown my love as to insure my secrecy.

She answered bravely that I could not hope from her any complaisance as she did not love me, and as far as the secret was concerned, she dared me to reveal it through a spirit of revenge.

"I am certain," she added, "that you are incapable of such an ill deed."

Saying these words, she turned her back on me and went out.

Reflecting on the singular character of this girl, I was forced to admit to myself that she was right.

I realized indeed that I should have committed a base action, but I was far from carrying it out, and I did not think about it any more. She had made her case completely when she said these few words:

"I do not love you."

It was unanswerable. She did not owe me a thing and I could not claim that she did. It seemed on the contrary that she was the one to complain, for what right did I have to spy on her? I had even less right to insult her by unveiling facts which I should never have known without an indiscreet curiosity which nothing could make licit. I could not accuse her of having deceived me, for what was I to her? She had disposed of herself, but did she not belong to herself? And I, as her preferred lover, should I have found her so reprehensible? All said, I had to keep quiet.

I dressed hastily and went to the Bourse, where I found a *péote* which sailed for Fiume the same day.

Fiume is on the other side of the gulf, opposite Ancona. From Fiume to Trieste it is only forty miles by land, about thirteen French miles, and I decided to take this way to my destination. I went down to the port, and having seen the *péote* and spoken to the skipper, I heard that the wind was fore and that next morning we should be in the canal.

I engaged the best berth and then I took my leave of the consul, paid Mordecai, and got my trunks ready.

Lia having heard from her father that I was going away the same day, told me that it was impossible to bring me my linen, my laces and silk stockings so soon, saying that she would have them all ready tomorrow.

"Your father," I said in the calmest manner, "could take them to the Venetian consul, who will be kind enough to forward them to me in Venice."

At dinner time the skipper came with a sailor to take my effects. I gave him my trunk which was ready, telling him that the other things would go on board with me at the time of sailing.

"Monsieur, I intend to sail an hour before sunset."

"I am ready."

When Mordecai heard that I was going to Fiume, he begged me to take charge of a small chest addressed to a friend, with a letter.

"I am happy to be able to render you this little service."

At dinner Lia sat at the table with me as if nothing had happened, speaking to me as usual, asking me if I found this or that to my taste, not in the least disconcerted by my monosyllabic answers, and my inability to look her in the eye.

I imagined that she wanted me to take her indifferent behavior for strength of mind, noble firmness, but it appeared to me only brazen effrontery.

In that moment I felt only hatred towards her, for she had deceived me while exciting me, and had offended me, by bluntly declaring that she did not love me. I despised her, for she seemed to want to convince me that I ought to esteem her for being shameless. Perhaps she thought I was grateful to her for having told her that she believed me incapable of revealing to her father what I had seen.

She did not see that her good opinion could not matter now.

While drinking Scopolo wine, she said that she still had some bottles left as well as of muscat wine.

"I present them to you," I replied, "they will serve to prepare you for your nocturnal debauches."

She answered smilingly, that I had enjoyed gratis a spectacle which assuredly was worth several gold pieces, and she was so satisfied with it that if I had not gone away so soon, she would gladly have furnished me with another one. This impudence made me feel like breaking her face with a bottle I had before me. In the way I took hold of the bottle she must have guessed my designs, and I might have committed a shameful crime, if I had not read in her countenance an expression of quiet courage.

I merely told her that she was the most shameless wench I had ever met, and I poured the wine into my glass most awkwardly out of the bottle I had caught up for quite another purpose.

After this scene, I rose and retired to the other room, not being able to stand it any longer; nevertheless, half an hour later, she came to share the coffee with me. This persistence seemed to me surprisingly insulting, but I calmed myself when I reflected that on her part this probably proceeded from a spirit of revenge. She had nevertheless revenged herself sufficiently in declaring that she did not love me, besides proving it.

"I want to help you pack," she said.

"And I," said I, coldly, "I beg you to leave me alone." And taking her by the arm, I led her out, closing the door on her.

We were both right. Lia had deceived, humiliated me; I had reason to hate her; I had discovered her to be hypocritical, sly, false and lecherous in a superlative degree; she was right in hating me, and I believe she would not have been sorry if I had committed a violence against her, so that I might bitterly expiate my discovery.

I have never found myself in a greater state of turbulence.

Towards evening, two sailors having come to take my other baggage, I thanked my hostess and in an indifferent manner told Lia to place my linen in a waterproof cloth, and to give it to her father, who had preceded me to the *péote* with the chest.

We started with a fair wind, and at that moment I believed that I should never find myself again face to face with Lia. It will be seen that fate decided otherwise. We had sailed about twenty miles with a good wind from behind, a cool breeze which made us glide over the water without any other movement than a sort of balancing motion up and down which is not disagreeable, when all at once a sudden calm seemed to have fixed us to the spot where we were. These sudden changes are not rare in the Adriatic, especially in this neighborhood.

This calm lasted a short time, then a strong northwestern wind having started agitating the waves, the sea became quite stormy, and our little *péote*, which was almost empty, began to pitch in the most cruel manner, making me quite sick.

Towards midnight, the wind, dead against us, became violent and we were in the greatest danger. The skipper told me that the only way to avoid turning over was to sail with the wind and return to Ancona, for we could not risk the attempt of making for any port.

In less than three hours, we were safely back in the harbor of Ancona, and the official having recognized us, kindly allowed us to land. While I was talking to the officer, thanking him for permitting me to recuperate in a good bed, the sailors took my baggage, without awaiting my orders, and carried it to Mordecai's house.

I was angry, for I wanted to avoid seeing Lia again, my intention being to go to the first hostelry.

At any rate it was done.

My Jew got up quite happy to see me again.

It was after three o'clock, I was quite sick, and as I wished to go to bed as soon as possible, I told him that I would get up late, that I would dine alone in bed, when I would call, and I made it especially clear that I wanted a light dinner and no goose liver.

I slept ten hours at a stretch, although I felt all broken up, but when I woke, feeling hungry, I rang the bell.

The servant who responded said that she would have the honor to wait on me, as Lia had been in bed since the day before with a violent headache.

I did not answer, thanking providence that in this manner I should be freed of the presence of that brazen hussy.

Having found the dinner too meager and feeling much better for having eaten, I told the cook to prepare a good supper.

The weather was terrible.

The Venetian consul, informed of my return and not having seen me in his home, guessed that the sea must have made me sick and came and visited me a couple of hours in my room. He assured me that the wretched weather would last a week at least.

This prediction disappointed me a great deal, not only because I could not avoid seeing Lia during that time, but also because I was short of money. Luckily, I had some valuables and that last matter worried me the least. Not having seen Lia at supper as I had feared, and believing that she was only feigning illness so as not to have to see me, I was relieved and felt less incensed against her. Nevertheless my surmises were quite mistaken. The next day she came as usual, asking for some chocolate to prepare my breakfast, but she had the usual calm cheerfulness which she knew so well how to affect.

"I shall take coffee, mademoiselle, and not wishing to eat any more goose liver I shall eat alone. Therefore you can tell your father that I shall only pay him seven paolis a day. And from now on I shall not drink any other but Orvietan wine."

"You still have four bottles of Scopolo and Cyprus wine."

"I never take back what I have given. They belong to you. Be kind enough to go away, and to come into my room as rarely as possible, for your ideas and your manners are of a kind to worry a Socrates, and I am not one. Moreover your presence revolts me. I am no longer fascinated by the sight of you, for I cannot help thinking that your beautiful body encloses the soul of a monster. I assure you that the sailors brought my baggage here without my consent, otherwise you would never have seen me again, and I am deathly afraid of being poisoned."

Lia went out without answering and I felt that after my uncomplimentary speech, she would be careful not to show herself again.

Experience taught me that girls of Lia's character were not rare. I had known them in Spa, Genoa, London and even in Venice, but this Israelite surpassed anything of the kind I had known up to that time. After his return from the synagogue Mordecai asked me gayly why I had humiliated his daughter, who swore that she had not done anything to complain of.

"I have not humiliated her, my dear Mardocheus, or at least that was not my intention, but as I had to eat simply, I told her that I did not want any more goose liver, and the reason is that I can eat alone and save three paolis a day."

"Lia is ready to pay them out of her own money, and she wants to dine with you to prove that you should not be afraid of being poisoned for she has told me that you fear as much."

"That's a joke which you must not take too seriously. I know quite well that I am staying at the house of an honest man. But your daughter is absurd by being too clever. I don't need to economize nor to make her pay the three paolis; to convince you of that, I shall pay six, but on condition that you shall dine with us. To offer to pay three paolis for me is an impertinence. In other words, my dear man, either I shall eat alone and pay you seven paolis a day, or pay thirteen to eat with the father and daughter. That is all I have to say."

Mordecai, like a good apostle, went away saying that he did not have the heart to let me eat alone.

At dinner, I addressed myself only to Mordecai, never looking at Lia nor laughing at the witty things she said for my benefit. I drank only Orvietan wine.

At the dessert, Lia having filled my glass with Scopolo wine, said that if I did not drink with her she would not drink either.

I answered, without looking at her, that if she was wise, she would never drink anything but water, and that I did not want to accept anything from her hands.

Mordecai, who loved wine, started to laugh, said that I was right and drank for three.

The weather being fair, I passed the rest of the day writing, and after supper, served by the domestic, I went to bed and to sleep. I was in my first sleep when I was awakened by a slight noise.

"Who is there?" said I.

I heard the voice of Lia saying in a low tone, "It is I. I do not come to worry you, but to have half an hour's talk with you and justify my behavior." Saying this she lay down beside me, but on the comforter.

This unexpected visit, so little in harmony with the character of this strange girl, pleased me, for having towards her only a feeling of revenge, I felt certain not to fall victim to all the wiles that her cunning would bring into play to gain a victory which she was seeking only in revenge for my coldness. Instead of forcing the issue, I told her gently that I realized that she was justified in her conduct, and that being in need of rest I begged her to go away.

"I shall not go away until you have heard me."

"Then speak, I am listening."

Then she began a speech which lasted a long hour and which I did not interrupt. It may have been artifice, or sentiment, or the power of an eloquence accompanied by a delicious voice, but her speech prevailed on me. After having confessed to the wrongs she had done me, she claimed that at my age and with my experience I must forgive everything to a girl eighteen years old, who, impelled by an ardent temperament and an irresistible excitement towards the pleasures of love, found herself unable to listen to the voice of reason.

According to her I must excuse everything on the score of this fatal weakness, for even if she became capable of wickedness, it was only because she had no control over herself.

"I swear to you that I love you," she said, "and I would have given you the most unmistakable proofs, if I had not had the misfortune to be in love with a young Christian, the one you have seen with me, who is only a rascal, a libertine, and who does not love me but whom I pay. In spite of my love and my burning passion I have never granted him what a girl can lose but once. I had not seen him for six months and you are responsible that I made him come that night, for you had put my body aflame with your love and your wines."

The conclusion of this apology was that I must bring peace to her heart by forgetting all and granting her my unreserved affection during the few days that I was to remain with her.

When she had finished speaking I did not permit myself the slightest objection. I made believe that I was convinced, saying that I pitied her for not being able to resist the impulses of her temperament, and ended by promising that she would see in my behavior no trace of resentment.

As this explanation was not the response the little knave desired, she continued to speak about sensual weakness and about the force of self-preservation which gives one strength to withstand the most powerful temptations, etc., etc. for she wanted to persuade me that she loved me and had been unyielding so as to excite my love and enforce my respect.

She wanted to convince me that it was her indomitable nature, not her inclination, which had steeled her. How many things I could have said to answer her arguments! I was going to say that it was rather her detestable nature, but I refrained. I wished to lead her on and, seeing what she was driving at, I awaited an attack, thinking to make her flounder in humiliation. Nevertheless the attack which to me appeared imminent did not take place. She made no movement with her hands, did not once approach her face near mine.

Finally tired, without doubt, of the struggle which for two hours she had carried on, she left apparently satisfied, wishing me a good sleep.

I must not forget to mention that before she left me I had to promise to let her make my chocolate as in the past.

Very early next day she came to get a stick of chocolate. She was in the most complete negligé; and was walking on tip toe as if afraid to wake me up, although if she had turned her eyes towards my bed she would have noticed that I was not asleep.

Seeing her false and cunning as ever I promised myself anew to defeat her ruses and to let her go all the way without helping her.

When she brought the chocolate, seeing two cups on the platter I said:

"Then it isn't true that you don't like chocolate."

"I feel myself obliged to free you from all fear of poisoning."

Something else I found very significant was that she was dressed up with bust covered, while half an hour before, she had come in a chemise, with her breasts exposed.

The more I saw her determined to tame me by the bait of her charms, the more was I strengthened in my resolution to humiliate her by indifference.

The alternative of my victory appeared to me to be only dishonor and shame, and that made me of ice.

In spite of my glacial air her wiles began when we were at table for, contrary to my orders, she served a magnificent goose liver, saying that it was for herself alone, and that if she was poisoned, she would die willingly. Mordecai, allured by the delicacy said that he also wanted to die and began to eat copiously. I could not help laughing as I said: "The three of us shall die," and I tasted it likewise.

"Your resolutions," said Lia, "are not very strong in the presence of the tempter."

This remark piqued me, and I answered that by saying too much she showed more art than prudence and that she would see that I had sufficient strength for any encounter.

She smiled a fine smile.

"Try," I said, "to make me drink Scopolo and muscat wine. I would certainly have drunk some if you had not reproached the weakness of my resolutions. I am convinced that they are invincible."

"The strong man," she said, "is without doubt the one who resists, but the amiable man is the one who knows how to yield sometimes."

"I admit that, but you must know likewise that the amiable girl is the one who never reproaches the weaknesses of which she is the object."

I called the servant and asked her to go to the Venetian consul and get some Scopolo and muscat wine. Lia, who could not restrain herself any longer, piqued me again by saying enthusiastically:

"I am glad to admit that you are the most amiable of men."

Mordecai, who did not understand the meaning of our words, was eating and drinking and laughing, and seemed quite satisfied.

In the afternoon I defied the dreadful weather by going to a café. There I thought about Lia and felt certain that the next night she would begin the struggle anew, and that, characteristically of her, the attack would be progressively stronger.

A few minutes after returning to my room, Lia knocked at the door, under the pretext that I had forgotten to give her the chocolate.

I opened the door and she begged me to leave it open, as she took the chocolate, and said:

"I have important things to tell you. It will be for the last time."

"You can tell me now what you want with me."

"No, because it will take too long. I can't come back until everybody is asleep. But you have nothing to fear, as you are master over yourself. You can quietly go to bed. I am no longer dangerous for you."

"No, assuredly, not dangerous at all, and to prove it to you, my door shall remain open."

Feeling more than ever determined to resist her wiles, I believed it better not to blow out the candles, for in putting them out, I feared to let her suspect that I was wavering. Moreover the light would render my victory more perfect and her humiliation more complete. I went to bed.

At eleven o'clock a slight noise announced the moment of the fray. I saw Lia enter with only chemise and a thin skirt on. She gently closed my door and locked it, and I capitulated.

After a moment of silence I said to her:

"Dear Lia, you force me to adore you; how could you desire that I should hate you? Is it possible that you have thrown yourself into my arms only to humiliate me, only to obtain a vain and futile victory? If that is your idea I forgive you, but you are mistaken, for passion, believe me, is a thousand times more delicious than the pleasure you might seek in revenge."

"No, my friend, I am here neither to triumph nor revenge myself, nor to obtain a shameful victory, I am here to give myself to you as much as I can; to make you my conqueror and master without reserve."

When on awakening I saw her with her after-the-wedding air of sweet and amorous satisfaction, the idea of my near departure saddened me. I told her about it and she begged me to postpone it as long as possible. I told her we would settle that the next night.

We dined voluptuously.

Mordecai, having become my host, tried to convince me that he was not avaricious.

I passed the afternoon with the consul and arranged for my departure on board a Neapolitan man-of-war, which was under quarantine and would go to Trieste afterwards. This arrangement forced me to pass another month in Ancona. I blessed the storm which had brought me back in spite of myself.

I gave the consul a golden box which I had received from the elector of Cologne, first removing the portrait which I wanted to keep. Three days later he gave me in return for it forty golden sequins, which was all I wanted.

My stay in that City cost me a great deal in my then financial state, but when I announced to Mordecai that I was remaining with him another month, he declared positively that he did not wish to be an expense to me, and I did not insist.

Then there remained nobody but Lia.

I have always believed, perhaps wrongly, that the Jew was not unaware that his daughter granted me her favors.

On this subject the Jews, in general, are not difficult, for knowing that the result will be an Israelite they think they get the better of a Christian by letting him do it.

I did not want Lia to repent of our union. What marks of gratitude, what proofs of tenderness, when I told her that I would remain with her another month! What blessings on the bad weather which had prevented me from going to Fiume!

I left this charming girl the little heart which had caused our first amorous talk and which might be worth ten sequins, but she refused any reward for the care she took of my linen during the six weeks. Besides she forced me to accept some beautiful Indian handkerchiefs.

I sailed from Ancona the fourteenth of November and on the fifteenth I found myself lodged at the Grand Auberge in Trieste.

www.ingramcontent.com/pod-product-compliance
Lightning Source LLC
Chambersburg PA
CBHW022106150426
43195CB00008B/294